Wesleyan Eucharistic Spirituality: Its Nature, Sources and Future

by Lorna Lock-Nah Khoo

The ATF Dissertation Series is a publication of ATF Press and covers the following subject areas: biblical studies, ethics and philosophical theology, church history and systematic theology.

Series Editors: Robert Gascoigne, Dorothy Lee, Katharine Massam and Gordon Watson.

ATF Press
Adelaide

T0126308

ATF Dissertation Series

1. *Living Truth and Truthful Living: Christian Faith and the Scalpel of Suspicion*, 2004, by Winifred Wing Han Lamb

Wesleyan Eucharistic Spirituality:

Its Nature, Sources and Future

by Lorna Lock-Nah Khoo

ATF Press
Adelaide

ISBN 1920691-31-6

First published 2005

Published by
ATF Press
An imprint of the Australasian Theological Forum
P O Box 504
Hindmarsh
SA 5007
ABN 68 314 074 034
www.atfpress.com

Cover design by Openbook Print, Adelaide, Australia

Contents

Foreword

Gordon Watson

This book has its roots in South East Asian Methodism but is fully aware of Methodism's role as a worldwide fellowship of churches placed in various cultural settings. It is written in clear concise English that makes the authors meaning plain; it is untrammeled by technical theological language.

The books purpose is not only to indicate the rich theological heritage of the Methodist tradition through the writings, hymns, and liturgical practises of John and Charles Wesley; but also to indicate the contemporary meaning and importance of the 'Wesleyan Eucharistic Spirituality' for the ecumenical church's worship and mission.

Dr Koo advances systematically in her treatment of the subject of 'Wesleyan Eucharistic Spirituality: Its Nature, Sources and Future'. Students will find the extensive bibliography and appendices a valuable source of information for further research. Here is not the voice of an uncritical admirer of the Wesley brothers but of one who appreciates the historical, theological and spiritual depth of their witness and contribution to the history and thought of the Western Christian tradition. There is appreciation of how the Wesleys' thought was grounded in the catholic tradition of the Fathers, the Reformers and the traditions of the contemporary English church in which they lived and worked.

One singly important aspect of Dr Koo's work is her insistence of relation of theology to the church's liturgy so that the logic of doxology, for example the unsurpassed biblical profundity of Wesley's eucharistic hymns, is as important for theological insight as for spiritual edification. This relationship between liturgy and dogma allows Wesley's theology to escape the often barren metaphysical speculation so often associated with eucharistic theology. But there is also understood the vital relationship between liturgy and dogma as not divorced from but integral with the church mission as the sanctifying power of the Holy Spirit is brought to bear on both the individual and the structures of civil life.

This book has a new vision of the importance of the Wesley brothers' eucharistic theology and experience to the contemporary church's search for relevance in post enlightenment culture that is evacuated of personal meaning and cosmic purpose. Thus it sheds light not only on an often neglected aspect of Wesleyan theology and practice but gives food for thought about the present situation of the church.

The Rev Dr Gordon Watson
Pentecost 2005

Dedication

Dedicated to our eschatological hope promised by the Lord Jesus Christ for:

- the late Revd Christopher Hulse Smith of St Albans, England
- the late Revd Raymond George of Bristol, England
- the late Professor John Deschner of Dallas, Texas, USA

and

- German Shepherds: Chippy, Black, Blackie, Walda, Duchess, Dogmatix, Doxologist (Doxy), Mischief
- Pomeranian: Rip
- Dachshunds: Ameer, Joy
- German Short-Haired Pointer: Patch
- Great Danes: Doggy, Waffles
- Golden Retriever: Chesed (Chessy)
- Guinea pigs: Guinea and Snowy

His creatures in my family's care who have departed from this life.

Acknowledgments

I wish to acknowledge the help given to me as I have researched and written this book: the Revd Dr Timothy A Macquiban, the late Revd Raymond George (from August 1995 till June 1998) and the Revd Dr Simon Chan (from February 1999). Without them, the thesis, which is now a book, would not have seen the light of day.

A word of thanks is also due to those who have been resource persons: my director of studies, Dr Brian Marshall, and friends who have been kind enough to advise me on sections of the emerging thesis: Prof Ted Campbell, Prof Richard Heitzenrater, Prof Geoffrey Wainwright, Prof Karen Westerfield-Tucker and the Revd Dr ST Kimbrough, Jr.

I am grateful for assistance and help of the following staff and institutions:

- The Revd Canon David Gillett, Principal and the Librarian of Trinity College Bristol
- The Revd Dr Neil Richardson, Principal and Ms Janet Henderson, Librarian of Wesley College Bristol
- Mr Jeffrey Spittal, Hon Librarian of the John Wesley's Chapel, Bristol
- Dr John Vickers and Mrs Penny Fowler of the Wesley and Methodist Studies Centre, Westminster College, Oxford
- Dr Pusey's Library, Oxford
- Duke Divinity School Library, North Carolina, USA
- Ms Wanda Smith of the Perkins School of Theology library, Southern Methodist University, Dallas, Texas, USA
- The Methodist Archives in Singapore
- Trinity Theological College (Singapore) library

Studying in a foreign land has its unique difficulties. Working on one's dissertation on a part-time basis (after two years of full-time study) while holding key pioneering responsibilities in the church (first in Bristol then in Singapore) was challenging. I am grateful especially for the support and prayers of the following people:

- from Birmingham: Ms Annie MacKinnon, the Revd John Bedford, Dr John and Mrs Janice Aston (all Baptists)

- from Bristol: Pastor Dave Mitchell and his Woodlands Christian Church members (an independent community church), the Revd Keith and Mrs Fran Page (Methodist), the Revd Ruth Bierbum, Mr Colin and Mrs Heather Locke (Anglicans), the Emmaus Community (different denominations)
- from Oxford: Drs Albert and Hiroko Ong, Dr Susie Lapwood (Anglicans), the Revd John and Mrs. Audrew Curnow, the Revd Brian Tebbut (Methodists); from Singapore: Dr Angelina Tan (Presbyterian), Ms Wee Lay Ching (Anglican), Mrs Lai Kheng Poussan (Assemblies of God), the Revd Dr Isaac Lim, Mr Ong Teong Hoon, Mrs Sally Chew, Ms Maria Ling, Rev Dr Daniel Koh (Methodists)
- over the Internet: Anglican Mrs Joyce Huggett (spiritual direction via Internet from Cyprus), the Revd Dennis Bolton (a Presbyterian minister from South Africa living in Canada)

I would also like to thank the following people who have contributed significantly to my faith journey and sacramental spirituality. Those who had a part in my faith journey were:

- family members–Mdm Loh Chooi Beng, my late mother, Ms Loh Chooi Cheng, my aunt, Prof Khoo Oon Teik, my conservative–evangelical uncle, Mrs Maisie Khoo my charismatically–orientated aunt;
- teachers–Ms Chai Ai Choo (Singapore), Prof Richey Hogg (USA), my theological father, the late Prof John Deschner of Dallas, Texas (USA)
- and spiritual friends–the Revd Malcolm Tan, OSL (Methodist, Singapore), Fr Francis Frost (Roman Catholic from Bossey/France), Ms Voon Choon Khing (Independent Church, Malaysia), Ms Wee Lay Ching (Anglican, Singapore), Mrs Lai Kheng Poussan (Assemblies of God, Singapore).

The late Revd Christopher Hulse Smith, my spiritual father, an English Methodist missionary to Singapore was the one who kindled in me a deep interest and commitment to the eucharist. Roman Catholics Fr Michael Arro, MEP, (Singapore) Sr Elizabeth Lim, RGS (Singapore) and Episcopalian Fr Ted Nelson (USA) further fuelled the interest with their own devotion to the sacrament.

Finance for my studies have been provided by partial scholarships from the Methodist Church Overseas Division (United Kingdom), The General Board of Global Ministries (United Methodist Church, USA), Lee Foundation (Singapore), Chen Su Lan Trust (Singapore), The

Methodist Church of Singapore. Friends have been gracious to me as well. To these and to the Trinity Annual Conference (TRAC) of the Methodist Church in Singapore which had appointed me for the 'No-Pay Study Leave Programme', I give my heartfelt thanks.

The unique opportunity to serve as Director of the Charles Wesley Heritage Centre in Bristol England from August 1997 to December 1998 not only assisted my financial situation but also allowed me to explore the practical implications of this thesis for global Methodism. For this very valuable experience, I thank the Warden of the New Room, the Revd Dr Canon John Newton, the Deputy Warden, the Revd Dennis Hearle and the General Board of Global Ministries.

Those who had their lives affected by my long absence from home made the most sacrifices.

I am most grateful for their patient waiting and love my father: Mr Khoo Oon Lock, and my furkids-corgis Tabitha the Twerp and Trax the Samseng. They provide the motivation to finish the study as soon as possible so that more quality time can be spent with them.

I have deliberately listed the denomination and location of some of the people acknowledged here. They include Methodists, Roman Catholics, Anglicans/Episcopalians, Baptists, Presbyterians, Assembly of God and Independents. They come from several continents. How each has contributed to the writing of this thesis is a miracle in itself. And therefore I thank God, the Father, Son and Holy Spirit for his wonderful, steadfast, enfolding and transforming love, experienced anew in the course of working on this thesis. May this book be a doxological offering acceptable to him.

Abbreviations

AM	*Arminian Magazine*
BCP	*Book of Common Prayer*
cf	refer to
Collection	*A Collection of Hymns for the Use of the people called Methodists*
CR	*Corpus Reformatorum*
CWJ	Charles Wesley's *Journal*
CWL	Charles Wesley's *Letters*
ENNT	*Explanatory Notes on the New Testament*
HLS	*Hymns on the Lord's Supper*
HP	*Hymns and Psalms*
JD	Journals and Diaries
JWJ	John Wesley's *Journal*
JWL	John Wesley's *Letters*
JWW	John Wesley's Writings
St	Saint
Sermons	John Wesley's *Sermons* (see Appendix B)
UMH	*United Methodist Hymnal*

Notes:

1. All quotations from the Bible are from the Revised Standard Version.

2. In order to reduce endnotes to a minimum, the Harvard System of noting references is used.

3. *The Hymns on the Lord's Supper* (*HLS*) by the Wesley brothers are referred to individually by their number and then by the verse (s) specified, eg *HLS* 71/1, 3.

4. Sermon references follow the numbering found on page 631, Volume III from *The Works of John Wesley* (*The Bicenntenial Edition of Wesley Works*). See Appendix B.

5. *Journal* references will be noted by dates rather than by page numbers of a specific edition eg *CWJ* 24/5/1738 (Charles Wesley's *Journal* 24 May 1738).

6. Letter references will be listed as either JWL or CWL or JWW with a number attached to it, eg JWL 3 or JWW 5. Details of that particular letter or article will be found in Appendix C.

7. References in the *Arminian Magazine* would be listed by year and by page, eg *AM* 1780: 263. Details of the reference will be found in Appendix D.

8. Selections from some primary sources will be *The Institutes of Christian Religion* by John Calvin will be referred to as *Institutes*, followed by the book, section and point eg *Institutes* 4: 17: 33.

9. Selections from the *Corpus Reformatorum* (1863–1900) will be referred to as *CR* followed by the chapter and section.

10. Some references are taken from the Internet, eg *The Apostolic Constitutions, Didache* and the *Theologia Germanica*. The location of the website will be given in the bibliography page.

11. The Journals and Diaries of John Wesley found in the *Bicenntenial Edition of Wesley's Works* vols 18–9, 23–24 cover the periods of 1735–1741 and 1782–1791. References to these will be listed as JD followed by the dates of the event, eg JD 17/10/1735 referred to in the *Manuscript Voyage Journal* and/or the *Georgia Diary 12. A Collection of Hymns for the Use of the People Called Methodists* is listed simply as *Collection* followed by the hymn and verse number, eg *Collection* 4/3.

12. Only the author's/writer's surname will be referred to in the chapters if the person's book or article can be found in the bibliography. The year of the publication will sometimes be given to assist the reader in locating the source.

Introduction

The Wesleyan revival of the eighteenth century was eucharistic as well as evangelical. We read that the early Methodists flocked to the celebration of holy communion in such numbers that the Anglican clergy were really overwhelmed by the multitude of communicants they had to deal with (Rattenbury 1948: 1–2). The Wesley brothers tried to form their followers' lives through many ways. Constant communion was one of them. Yet it was not simply a 'means of grace' as the rest. They lifted it above other means as 'the grand channel' of God's grace, where 'chiefly here (one's) soul is fed' (*HLS* 54/4).

What was it that the early Methodists found in the sacrament that led them to crowd the communion tables by the thousands? What was it that the Wesleys believed about the sacrament which set it apart from other 'means of grace'? If eucharistic spirituality is a hallmark of Wesleyan spirituality, what does Wesleyan eucharistic spirituality look like? What is the future of this spirituality in Methodism? These are some questions which this dissertation will address.

Much has been written about Wesleyan eucharistic theology and practice. Well-known books on Wesleyan eucharistic theology and practices include those by Earnest Rattenbury (1948), John Bowmer (1951) and Ole E Borgen (1986). Few writings on the spirituality of the Wesleys exist. Two most notable books are by Gordon S Wakefield (1966) and Robert G Tuttle (1989). There has been, to my knowledge, no comprehensive study done in Wesleyan eucharistic spirituality. This book will therefore be attempting something new.

> The term 'spirituality' has been used very freely and loosely in recent years. Spirituality has been defined as a response: It is seen as '. . . the conscious human response to God that is both personal and ecclesial'. In short, ' . . . life in the Spirit . . .' (Sheldrake 1992: 37) or ' . . . life of man facing his God, participating in the life of God; the

spirit of man listening for the Spirit of God . . .'
(Evdokimon 1966: 41).

It has also been defined as a view of life and a way of living: it is
described as the sum total of ' . . . attitudes, beliefs and practices
which animate people's lives and help them reach out towards
super sensible realities . . . ' (Wakefield 1983: 361) or ' . . . any
religious or theistic value that is concretised as an attitude or
spirit from which one's actions flow . . . ' (Aumann 1980: 17).
The spirituality for a person or community has been seen as

> . . . their life motivation, their disposition, what
> inspires their actions, their *utopia*, their causes,
> regardless of whether these are better or worse,
> good or evil, in accordance with our own or not.
> (Therefore) spirituality is an essential dimension
> of human life (Casaldaliga 1994: 4–5).

For the purpose of this dissertation, I have chosen a working
definition using some of the insights of the above definitions:

> Spirituality is an existential and experiential
> response to a 'call'. This response requires the
> involvement of the person's entire being: body,
> mind and spirit. The 'call' can be from the Divine
> (as in the case of theistic spirituality) or from
> within one's self, ie a conviction (as in non-
> theistic spirituality) and it is an invitation to
> move towards a goal of wholeness (however
> wholeness may be defined). The call and the goal
> will affect the whole of one's life. It will colour
> one's perception of the Divine, of self, of world, of
> time and will impact the formation of one's
> character.

Based on the above definition, five questions will be asked of
existing practices and beliefs of a group to surface the inherent
nature of their spirituality. The questions are: 'Who calls?',
'What is the nature of the movement, eg if it is a response, what

kind of a response is it?', 'How is its goal of wholeness understood?', 'How is formation done?' and 'How is perception affected by this?'

The first chapter of this book looks at the eucharistic practices of the Wesleys. The second chapter focuses on their eucharistic beliefs. Chapter three explores the sources of their beliefs and practices, highlighting areas where they have differed from their mentors and the significance of these developments. Chapter four asks five questions of Wesleyan eucharistic practices and beliefs and by doing so, there emerges what might be called Wesleyan eucharistic spirituality. Chapter five wrestles with the question of the future of eucharistic spirituality in Methodism.

Primary sources

What has been referred to as the 'Wesleyan corpus' in this book is drawn basically from the journals and letters of both John and Charles Wesley, the diaries, sermons and editorial works (including the *Explanatory Notes on the New Testament*) of John and the hymns of Charles (although most of the hymns were published under the names of both brothers).

Choice of style

Apart from England and North America, Asia and many other places around the world, many theological libraries do not have the luxury of owning several versions of basic Wesleyan (or other) 'primary texts' (eg the Wesleys' *Journals, Sermons*). One simply has to use whatever is available. In the light of the context where I live and work, and where I hope this book will make a contribution, I have deliberately chosen to list my references of such materials in a way that would make it easier for people to find them. The focus will not be on the specific page of a particular edition (which might not be available to the reader) but on the location according to the particular date in the journal or on the title of the specific sermon or writing.

1

Wesleyan Eucharistic Practices

1. Eucharistic observance

It had been said that the Wesleyan revival was not only evangelistic, it was also eucharistic (Sanders 1966:1). The number of Methodists who turned up for communion speaks for itself: Haworth 'near a thousand' (JWJ 22/5/1757), Leeds 700 to 800 (JWJ 2/5/1779), 1,700 (JWJ 5/8/1781), Manchester 1,100 to 1,200 (JWJ 1/4/1781), 1,300 to 1,400 (JWJ 18/5/1783); Maccles-field 1, 300 (JWJ 29/3/1782), Bristol 'nearly a thousand' (JWJ 2/10/1784), Birmingham 500 (JWJ 9/3/1786). There was a large number of communicants at West Street Chapel on the first few occasions in 1743. Services were about five to six hours long. When the two-thousand-strong United Societies in London had to go to West Street Chapel for communion on 29 May 1743, John Wesley divided them into three groups so that each group would not have more than 600 members going for the sacrament at the same time (JWW 1).

The vicar of Devlin wrote to his bishop in 1751, saying that on the previous Christmas, fifty faces that he had 'scarce seen before' appeared at the sacrament. One of these (Methodists) told him, 'it was a great trouble to the Society that they had not more frequent opportunities to receive the communion'. Some, he noted, had walked to communion on foot for about ten miles since that morning in very severe weather. The vicar added that in the several parishes in his vicinity, fully ninety per cent of those who attended the sacrament were Methodists' (Church 1948: 5). Gordon Wakefield wrote that at St Patrick's Cathedral, Dublin, special communion vessels had to be made to accommodate the number of Methodists (Dudley 1995: 143). It was not just the matter of lapsed communicants returning to receive at the table. John Wesley noted at a London service where they had such a large number of communicants ('as we have not had before, since the covenant-night '), 'fifty, perhaps a hundred of them, never communicated before' (*JWJ* 16/7/1786). Sometimes, the hunger of individual Methodists for the sacrament made them the catalysts for the reinstatement of eucharistic observance in their sphere of influence. While in the army, Methodist John Haime complained in the 'open camp' that they had no sacrament 'for a long season'. As the result, the Duke of Cumberland (his commanding officer) ordered that communion should be administered 'every Lord's Day to one regiment or the other' from then on (*AM* 1780: 263). Such 'enthusiasm' for reception of the sacrament was unusual in the churches during the time of the Wesleys. So was the desire to receive the sacrament regularly and frequently.

The Reformers—Martin Luther, John Calvin and Ulrich Zwingli—tried to encourage frequent communion. Luther (1483–1436) had called for daily celebrations in 1520. Calvin (1509–1564) had insisted that communion be observed once a week at least, for he believed that mere annual celebrations were an 'invention of the devil'. Zwingli (1484–1531) called for four communion services a year (Wainwright 1980: 327–8). It became apparent that it was not easy for the Reformers to change the practices their people had been used to for centuries, where celebrations were infrequent and where the laity would be observers rather than recipients at the table. Gregory Dix suggested one reason for the lapse of communion participation, especially among the laity before the Reformation. The laity, he observed, had somehow felt that communion, a sacred and special meal, was not intended for 'everybody'. Since 'everybody was now equally qualified in theory by everyone having received baptism, the only line of demarcation was between clergy and laity' (Dix 1945: 18f). The result was that they would watch while the clergy participated in the sacrament. Another reason (which was applicable to both clergy and laity) was that abstaining out of awe was understood to be equal to receiving with confidence and joy (Bynum 1991: 127). Hence by the fifteenth scentury, the daily communion were notable exceptions even in monasteries (Taft 1989: 423). Thus in spite of their good intentions to regularise communion, Luther, by 1523, had to be content with calling for the general practice of weekly communion. Calvin was restricted by the Magistrates of Geneva to having celebrations four times a year (Wainwright 1980:

327–8). In practice, even this practice was not carried out in subsequent years. According to Geoffrey Wainwright, the staple fare for Protestants became 'scriptures, prayers and psalmody' (Kimbrough 1995: v).

The Church of England Convocation met in 1604 and decided that in every parish church and chapel, communion was to be received at least three times a year including the Easter celebration (Cardwell 1884: 256). Students in colleges were to communicate four times a year (Cardwell 1884: 257). In most parishes, Archbishop Secker, the Bishop of Oxford, had to recommend that, between Pentecost and Christmas, there should be at least one celebration (Bowmer 1951: 7). In spite of these rulings, in practice the sacrament was not celebrated very often and where it was, few communicated. Hence John Wesley had cause to ask, 'does one tenth of those who acknowledge it is an institution of Christ duly attend the Lord's supper?' (JWW 2).

The reasons for such laxity in eucharistic observance were political, practical, theological and spiritual. After four purges in two hundred years as a result of religious persecution during the rule of Henry VIII, Mary, Elizabeth I and James I, with martyrs on every side, one can understand the anxiety about not appearing to have 'papist' or 'Jacobite' tendencies, which would be associated with a desire for more frequent communions. Maycock reported that Nicholas Ferrar (1592–1637), the founder of the 'little Gidding' religious community, was regarded by the Puritans as quasi-papist because he introduced the custom of having holy communion once a month (1938: 201, 239). In practice, the system of having several churches under one incumbent meant less quality time available for each congregation.

The emergence of deists, Arians and rationalists led to the downplaying of the mystical and supernatural (Bowmer 1951: 3–4). On the other side, those who reverenced the sacrament highly feared that familiarity would breed a certain lack of respect: that a more thorough preparation is necessary for one's participation in the sacrament. This was certainly the case with the Presbyterians and the high church group of the Church of England which came up with preparation manuals for worthy reception of communion (Clarke 1962: 12). They also advocated infrequent observance of the sacrament.

There were some exceptions: William Romaine at St Anne's Blackfriars, William Grimshaw of Haworth, were reported as having between 300 and 1,200 communicants (Bowmer 1951: 3). Eleven churches in London and Holy Trinity Church in Hull held weekly celebrations (Bowmer 1951: 6–7). There were some attempts at daily celebrations. John Wesley had communion daily for twelve days of Christmas, 1774 (*JWJ* 25/12/1774). Religious societies like the Society for the Promotion of Christian Knowledge (SPCK) often required their members to be regular communicants (Heitzenrater 1989: 38). On the whole, however, eucharistic observance was at a low point during the time of the Wesleys.

What we have seen thus far of the Wesleys and their followers in terms of eucharistic observance is significant. Where the reformers failed, the Wesleys succeeded in promoting frequent reception of the sacrament. What accounts for their success?

Firstly, it could be due to their high view of holy communion and their example which underlined their teaching. These would be known to all their people through their published writings. John and Charles Wesley grew up in an environment where the eucharist was highly respected and frequently celebrated. Samuel Wesley, their father, was a high churchman. Their mother, Susanna, was a non-juror. Samuel Wesley wrote a book entitled, *The Pious Communicant Rightly Prepared or a Discourse Concerning the Blessed Sacrament*. Samuel had communion once a month in his church (Bowmer 1951:19). For the benefit of a visitor, Samuel even offered to hold it weekly (Stevenson 1994: 141). After careful preparation by his mother, John was admitted to the table at the age of eight (Tyerman 1866: I: 18–19).

At Christ Church, Oxford, John was tutored by Dr George Wigan and Henry Sherman. They and Jonathan Colley, the Precentor, were high churchmen (Baker 1970: 13f). They introduced and instilled in him a deep respect for the traditions of the church and for the eucharist. After reading Thomas a Kempis's *Christian Pattern* while preparing for ordination, John wrote in his *Journal*, 'I set apart an hour or two a day for religious retirement. I communicate every week' (*JWJ* 24/5/1738). John's readings, especially writings of Jeremy Taylor and William Law, reinforced the importance of the eucharist for him. John was not content with the mere discipline of regular communicating. In his letter to his mother, he wrote: '. . . what shall I do, to make all these blessings (referring to the spiritual disciplines he was able to exercise) effectual, to gain from them that mind which was in Christ Jesus?'(JWL 1). While he was studying at Oxford, Charles started the practice of going for weekly communion and studying systematically with a few students. John was soon called in to help them in certain spiritual disciplines like self–examination and keeping of spiritual journals (Heitzenrater 1989: 65–72).

When John Clayton joined the Wesleys in their practices, he introduced them to the Manchester non-juror brand of theology and churchmanship. The Manchester non-jurors were a group of Anglicans who would not swear fealty to English sovereigns William and Mary because they had earlier given their allegiance to James II and his descendants. They also held high views of the sacraments and the patristic roots of the church.[1]

---

1.   The Manchester non-jurors were different from the majority of non-jurors. Called 'usagers' by people, they were referred by John Wesley as the 'essentialist non-jurors'. According to Ted Campbell, while most non-jurors would use the *BCP*, omitting the king's name, Bishop Archibald Campbell and Dr Thomas Deacon of this group would use only the more 'catholic' 1549 Prayer Book (1991: 28–30). The eucharist was for them the central act of Christian worship and they held to a rather strong position on sacrifice, believing that real permanent spiritual change was effected upon the elements during the eucharistic service (Overton 1903: 291–2). They would offer an *epiclesis* as well as an oblatory prayer in the eucharist (the latter was seen as the offering of the eucharistic elements to the Father as symbols of Christ's body and blood). The Manchester group practised the mixing of water and wine for the chalice and they also held prayers for the dead. Deacon published a new version of the *BCP* entitled: *A Compleat Collection of Devotions* (1734). In it was included some adaptations of liturgies and writings found in the *Apostolic Canons and Constitutions*. John Wesley was familiar with Deacon's book: there were several records of him reading

Friendship with Clayton, with non-juror leader Thomas Deacon and John Wesley's own readings of Justin Martyr's *Apology* and William Cave's *Primitive Christianity* (where there were descriptions of life and practices of the early church) influenced John to believe that the early church had daily communions which later became weekly ones. This practice of frequent communion, to Wesley, had apostolic origins. Accepting Vincent of Lerins' understanding that Christian doctrines and practices are to be judged by that which has been accepted 'everywhere, always and by all' (Campbell 1991: 30), he saw the practice as binding on all present churches. The Oxford Methodists continued their practice of weekly communions. Their social work and their sacramental observance made them stand out among the students and they were called several names including 'Bible bigots', 'Bible moths' (*Sermon* 107), 'Methodists', 'supererogation men' and 'sacramentarians' (JWL 2).

In 1739, John preached on the sacrament several times. The sermons include: *The Means of Grace, Stand ye in the Way, ask for*

---

it, especially during the first part of his voyage to America (JD 17, 18, 19, 20.21, 22, 23, 24, 25, 27, 28 October and 8 November 1735).

John himself sought to practise some of Deacon's ideas in America, which resulted in a host of complaints from his more down-to-earth parishioners. John was greatly influenced by Deacon's writings and those in the *Apostolic Canons and Constitutions* until he found out that they were not as ancient as he thought they were. An undated manuscript in Wesley's hand on a single leaf of paper from a notebook, along with his notes on the *Apostolic Canons and Constitutions,* contained these comments:

> I believe myself it a duty to observe, as far as I can without breaking communion with my own church: 1. to baptise by immersion 2. to use Water, oblation of elements (and) alms, invocation and *Prothesis* in the eucharist 3. to pray for the faithful departed 4. to pray standing on Sunday and in Pentecost 5. to observe Saturday, Sunday and Pentecost as Festivals 6. to abstain from blood and things strangled. I think it prudent (our church not considered): 1. to observe the stations 2. Lent, especially the Holy Week 3. to turn to the east at the Creed (Baker 1970: 40–41).

the old paths (*JWJ* 22/6/1739), *Believe* (*JWJ* 23/6/1739), *Why are ye subject to ordinances?* (*JWJ* 24/6/1739), *Cast not away your confidence which had great recompense of reward* (*JWJ* 24/6/1739), *All scripture is given by inspiration of God* (*JWJ* 25/6/1739), *Do this in remembrance of me* (*JWJ* 27/6/1739, 28/6/1739), *Who have believed, be careful to maintain good works* on Titus 3: 8 (*JWJ* 29/6/1739).

Throughout his life, John Wesley communicated very frequently. According to Bowmer, two years after Aldersgate, Wesley was celebrating on an average of once every four days, regularly on Sundays and whenever or wherever opportunity offered during the week. In 1740, he communicated forty out of fifty-two Sundays, had fifty-eight weekday celebrations in a space of one year. In the last nine years of his life, during January (when he was customarily in London), he received the sacrament every Sunday except possibly two (when he was ill and when he was barred from the table). In addition, he held celebrations on weekdays during visitations and in his own home. When weekday communions are added to regular Sunday ones, he would have communicated some fifteen times in one month, an average of once every other day. He once noted that he had been privileged to receive communion every day during the special days of the church eg the octave of Easter. Throughout his lifetime, John received on an average of once every four to five days (Bowmer 1951: 50–55).

John abstained from communicating while he was in Scotland. This was a notable departure from his usual practice. Bowmer observed that John had good friends among the Church of Scotland ministers and had opportunities to attend communion at Episcopal Churches there but there was no record of him doing so. Bowmer postulates that it could be that communion was infrequently celebrated there by both the Episcopal and Presbyterian churches or it could be that John Wesley was aware of political implications to himself and his followers should he be a communicant there. Jacobitism and Episcopacy were so closely identified that communicating as an Englishman could easily be seen as treason to his country. John Wesley could also have refrained from attending Presbyterian communions simply because he disliked their liturgy (Bowmer 1951: 125–127).

Communion sustained Charles throughout his life. The 'Holy Club' started with Charles and two or three young students committing themselves to weekly communion and a regimen of disciplined study (JWW 3). Records like this one abound in his *Journal:* 'I received much spiritual strength and comfort in the sacrament' (*CWJ* 18/12/1744). When he was sick in February 1738, both he and his sister Kezzy, who was nursing him, received communion daily. At his wedding, he had communion. He said of that occasion: 'I never had more of the divine presence at the Sacrament' (*CWJ* 8/4/1749). Bowmer has counted over one hundred similar references in Charles Wesley's *Journal* (1951: 189).

It must be admitted that, although daily eucharist was the Wesleyan ideal (*HLS* 166, 124/2), Charles seemed to have communicated less frequently than John. If Charles's *Journal* is to be the guide, one can say that in all the years recorded in the *Journal*, Charles had communion on an average of no less than twice a month (see Appendix A). This includes the times when he celebrated or assisted at the sacrament. In 1738, the year of his spiritual crisis, he had communion more than forty-six times (not counting the daily celebrations he had sometime in February that year). His last *Journal* entries of 1756, covering a period of barely two months, recorded his reception of communion five times (26/9, 3/10, 17/10, 31/10, 1/11). Although Charles's eucharistic observance might pale in comparison with John's, it is still very high in the light of the practice of the churches of his time. Was it his travel that prevented Charles from taking it more frequently? John traveled long distances too. Could Charles have been less disciplined than John in keeping a more accurate and detailed journal? It could well be. Was John observing with more rigor certain spiritual disciplines like weekly communion? This was not inconceivable, since Charles certainly was of a more easy-going nature than his highly disciplined brother. Whatever the reason for Charles's eucharistic observance record, he, like John, never flagged from preaching the necessity of observing the means of grace. For no less than six instances in 1756, Charles urged his hearers to go to the sacrament frequently (*CWJ* 4/10,

10/10, 21/10, 25/10, 26/10, 29/10). He also noted with triumphant joy that there had been an increase in communicants that year (*CWJ* 31/10) as well as in 1754 (*CWJ* 4/8/1754, 11/8/1754). It would be hard to imagine that Charles would be lagging in his communion observance himself while he preached strongly against the lack of observance to others.

Second, since the Wesley brothers put a lot of weight on eucharistic observance in their own lives, they actively sought to make communion available to their people. On board the *Simmonds*, sailing towards America as missionaries, the four Oxford Methodist clergymen—John Wesley, Charles Wesley, Benjamin Ingham and Charles Delamotte—celebrated communion for their fellow travellers (*JWJ* 17/10/1735, 18/12/1735, 21/12/1735). In America, John celebrated communion weekly on Sundays at 11 am and during great festivals and feast days at Savannah. Daily communion services were held during the Great and Holy Week, though not on Good Friday. The number of communicants varied from a dozen to two dozen. This number was good, considering a report that in John's predecessor's day there were 'on some Sundays, not ten persons in church and three at communion'. The report continued that John Wesley had forty every Sunday (Bowmer 1951: 32). Since their time at Oxford, both brothers had ministered to the prisoners, especially the condemned ones, giving them communion before their execution. Charles even went to give communion to the Kingswood colliers, possibly serving them the sacrament in the first eucharistic service of the Wesleys outside consecrated ground (*CWJ* 29/6/1740).

It is significant that the main precipitating reason for the Methodists becoming a separate entity from the Church of England was due to John's desire that communion be made available to the people of America. John noted that there 'for some hundred miles together, there is none either to baptise or to administer the Lord's supper' (*JWW* 3). It must be remembered that while baptism can be administered by lay persons in emergencies (de Ferrari 1967: 65), the Lord's supper cannot be. So John Wesley ordained people to serve in America. Charles had aptly discerned the ultimate outcome of John's ordinations. He said, 'Ordination is separation (from the Church of England)' (CWL 1).

Faced with centuries of inertia about reception of the sacrament, the Wesley brothers had to counter all the arguments people had against such regularity and frequency. Such arguments were deep-rooted. We note that even St Augustine had viewed communion with ambivalence. Familiarity, he felt, would breed contempt for it (Bynum 1991: 127). John Wesley's sermon, *The Duty of Constant Communion* (*Sermon* 101: which was published twice: in 1732 and in 1787), had three points against those who wanted to communicate less often. To those who were happy to do so three times a year or less, Wesley replied that the sacrament was instituted by Christ as a continual remembrance. As a command, it was to be obeyed constantly, not whenever we like. Otherwise, other commandments could be obeyed three times a year! To those who retort that the Church of England only required three times a year for communicating, Wesley pointed to a higher authority than his church—God himself. Christians are bound to obey God, even if the church did not command it. The *BCP* indicated that it was to be 'at least three times a year'. Hence the number was a bare minimum, not maximum. To the ones who felt that constant communion would erode the meaning, reverence and significance of the action, Wesley went to the root of the problem. Is it human boredom with old custom or fascination with new ones which provides the sacrament with its meaning, reverence and significance? True reverence is nurtured by obedience to his command to partake of the sacrament. Love, fear and faith in God would be deepened and the significance of the sacrament would then be made clearer. Wesley also retorted that God did not command us to observe the sacrament 'unless it abates your reverence!' John Wesley's scriptural argument against those who would refrain from regular communion because of 'awe' was convincing. It was more so when he identified the very human motivation behind the excuse, namely the fear of boredom with over-familiarity with the sacrament and the natural attraction to the novel and the new.

In 1788, when he revised the sermon on *Constant Communion* written at Oxford fifty-five years before, John stated that he had learnt to say more in fewer words but ended with: 'I thank God I have not yet seen cause to alter my sentiments in any point which is therein delivered' (*Sermon* 101).

We have seen that Charles Wesley also did his share of 'preaching up' the sacrament and urging the people to attend communion services. A sermon of his dated 1748 for example, was entitled *On a Weekly Sacrament* (Bowmer 1951: 227). The strong arguments which the Wesleys produced to convince their people regarding regular reception of the sacrament was the third reason for their success in bringing about a eucharistic revival.

Fourth, the Wesleys' *Rules of the Band Societies* required the members to be, among other things, at church and 'at the Lord's Table every week' (JWW 4). Those who did not comply were expelled (An Old Methodist, 1869: 83). Those who were to be accepted as helpers were asked, 'Do you constantly attend church and sacrament?' (JWW 5) John advised his elders (his ordained ministers) in America to 'administer the supper of the Lord on every Lord's Day' (JWL 3). American liturgist White commented that the *Sunday Service* which John Wesley had revised for the American Methodists presumed that there would be weekly communions. The long exhortations and warnings about the proper reception of the sacrament which were in the 1662 *BCP* were left out. There was no need to give notice of an upcoming celebration of communion if the celebrations were weekly. There was also no need to warn people to prepare themselves, if they were already prepared by frequent confessions and sharings in their small groups (White 1991: 21). One significant breakthrough took place when the Wesleys required of (not just suggested to) their members to observe constant communion. Their members—mostly lay people —were firmly introduced to a eucharistic discipline which had been, over the years, practised only by some clergy or those in religious orders in the Church of England. The feeling that this spirituality was for the more 'pious' or those in 'full-time' service thus disappeared.

Fifth, testimonies of experiences with the Lord at the Table told by Methodist leaders and members played a part in popularising communion among their people. Albin reported that Wesleys' preachers were in the practice of carrying packets filled with letters from individuals describing their religious experiences, including those stories about spiritual experiences during communion. On certain days called 'letter days', the preachers would read out these testimonies to their people, encouraging them with stories of God's faithfulness (1985: 277).

The *Hymns on the Lord's Supper* published in 1745 was sold in all the Methodist preaching houses and went through nine editions during the lifetime of the Wesleys (Kimbrough 1995: iii). The sixth point is that the Wesleyan eucharistic revival owed no little debt to the liturgical, spiritual and devotional value of this book. More will be said about this book later.

Even as we note the effectiveness of these methods used by the Wesleys to encourage eucharistic fervour—namely, leading by example, making the sacrament available, countering arguments against constant communion, utilising their small group structure and discipline (Bands, Societies), fostering eucharistic interest and devotion through the sharing of certain testimonies and the introduction of Charles' *HLS*—we cannot but still wonder: Were these enough to account for the eucharistic revival? Was there a *stronger* reason for the Methodists' enthusiastic embracing of the eucharist? If there was, what was it? We will look for some answers in chapter 2.

While the attendance for communion at the major centres of Methodist work—Bristol, London and Manchester—were very high (Bowmer 1951: 216) and there was also a report from as far away as Harbour-grace Newfoundland that their monthly communion drew two hundred communicants which was 'more than all the other Missionaries in the land have' (*AM* 1785: 491), there was no general administration of the sacrament in many of the English provincial chapels during the time of the Wesleys (Bowmer 1951: 216). It was difficult to find ordained priests to celebrate at these places. Thus the success of the Wesleys in bringing about the eucharistic revival was short-lived. We shall see in chapter 5 the decline in eucharistic observance, the precipitating factors of the decline and the seeds planted by the Wesleys which await a revival.

2. Eucharistic rationale

The mystics of the passive school (with Quietists like Molinos), whose writings John Wesley read at one stage of his life, and the Moravians in England led by Philip Molther would have the Wesley brothers abandon the sacrament in favour of 'stillness' —quietly waiting upon God to act (*JWJ* 31/12/1739, JWL 4). The mystics of the 'quietist' tradition seemed to hold this position:

1. To one who seeks after the mystical experience—he must have love as his only end. He must choose such means as lead most to love while remaining flexible towards these means . . . for they will be beneficial for a season. But lest he become tied to these means, as the end is attained, the means cease.

2. For the 'attainer' (perfect finder): pure love possesses all virtue in essence. Even good works are worked essentially, not accidentally. Sensible devotion in prayer is a hindrance to perfection; the attainer needs no public prayer since he prays without ceasing; scripture is not needed by one who converses face to face with God. Communion is not needed, neither is fasting. He renounces reason and understanding, preferring obscure or general knowledge over the particular (Tuttle 1969: 164–5).

The Moravians of England insisted that there are no degrees of faith and that one must have sure faith before one partakes of the sacrament. Sacraments and prayer, according to this group, should be discarded in favour of 'waiting on God in silence'. To participate in the sacrament or the other means of grace before sure faith, to them, is considered worse than useless (Sugden1983: 167). Thus they clashed with the Wesleys' strong insistence on keeping the sacraments. One outcome of this disagreement was the breaking away of the Methodists from the Fetter Lane Society where many had already been swayed by Molther's teachings (*JWJ* 20/7/1740, JWW 3). Charles Wesley encountered, in addition to the Moravians in England, some subversive preachers in 1756 who hindered Methodists from attending communion services in parish churches by either not advising their people to go, or not going there themselves (*CWJ* 25/10/1756). Some even kept the meetings going until it was too late for the members to attend the communion services in the nearby parish church (*CWJ* 3/10/1756). Such neglect of the sacrament, whatever the reason, was unacceptable to the Wesleys. John and Charles responded in sermon and song against such teachings and practices, giving four reasons why one should take the sacrament.

Firstly, it is a matter of obedience. It is significant that Wesley entitled his sermon *The Duty of Constant Communion*. It is firstly a 'duty', ie it is not a matter of advantages or benefits. To all the excuses made by people who were reluctant to come to the Table, John Wesley hammered home one point over and over again: the practice of constant communion is a matter of obedience to the express command of the Lord (*Sermon* 101). While the Wesleys believed that there would be spiritual benefits received at the sacrament, they chided those who complained that despite constant communicating, they had not received the benefit they expected. Whether benefits have been or have not been felt, the command to receive communion constantly has to be kept. Benefits will come sooner or later, though 'perhaps insensibly' (*Sermon* 101). Graphically, the *HLS* illustrated this: 'Obedient to thy gracious Word, We break the Hallow'd Bread' (*HLS* 30/2 cf. *HLS* 1/5, 54/3,118/4), 'If Jesus bids me lick the Dust I bow at his Command' (*HLS* 86/7). The brothers saw through what these people were actually doing in the name of faith or benign neglect—their actions were a blatant denial of Christ's command and that amounted to gross disobedience:

> In vain the subtle tempter tries
> Thy dying precept to repeal,
> To hide the letter from our eyes,
> And break the testamental seal,
> Refine the solid truth away,

And make us free—to disobey.
(*HLS* 90/2 cf 62/10)

Would not taking the eucharist (or using any of the 'means
of grace') not be engaging in works-righteousness? Are we not
to just 'wait' passively for the Lord to act sovereignly in our
lives? These two concerns of the passive mystics and English
Moravians were addressed by John Wesley: God has
commanded us to take the means of grace which he has
ordained. We are called to obey. When we focus on God and
not on the means, we are not trusting in the means but in the
God who will fulfil his promises through the means. To their
fear of disobeying God if they used the means of grace, Wesley
clarified that using the means is not the same as the keeping of
Jewish ordinances frowned upon by St Paul (Colossians 2: 20).
Even the scriptural references about 'waiting' for God to act (eg
2 Chronicles 20: 2, Isaiah 26: 8) also required action on the part
of the people, not passivity (*Sermon* 16).

Second, while answering the faith question of the quietists
and the English Moravians, John taught that there are degrees
of faith and that God has chosen certain methods to create and
continue that faith (however little), and that is through the
'means of grace'. This is another reason why constant
communion is essential. The sacrament as 'means of grace' is
not a 'dead external Sign' (*HLS* 55/1). The sign 'transmits the
Signified, the Grace is by the Means applied' (*HLS* 71/1). One
encounters Christ at the Table and receives the benefits of his
passion: 'chiefly here my Soul is fed . . .' (*HLS* 54/4) sang
Charles. The benefits derived from communion—the forgiveness of our sins and the refreshing of our souls—are so crucial
to a Christian's life and sanctification. We should receive what
God wants to give us. John Wesley advised Mr Knox, a seeker:
'lose no opportunity of receiving . . . the Lord's Supper' (JWL 5
cf *Sermon* 84). In *The Nature of Enthusiasm* (*Sermon* 37) preached
in 1749, John Wesley described one form of enthusiasm as
imagining that one can obtain grace without using the means to
it which God has provided. In the *Sermon on the Mount Discourse
13* (*Sermon* 33) of 1753, he asserted that one who is wise will
base one's hope of salvation on God's own means of obtaining

it. Communion, John taught, is one of the essential 'works of piety' (*Sermon* 43). So strongly would John feel about the necessity of the sacrament that he rebuked his brother Charles: 'Why do you omit giving the Sacrament at Kingswood? What is reading prayers at Bristol in comparison to this?' (JWL 6).

The third reason the Wesleys gave for constant communion was that they, like Zwingli, believed that the communicant's position at sacrament is a demonstration of the believer's allegiance to Christ. In fact, Charles Wesley's favourite word for holy communion in his *Journals* is 'sacrament '. The root idea of the Latin word *sacramentum* is 'an oath of allegiance' of a soldier. Indeed, the Wesleys taught that one renews one's baptismal vows at the Table (*Sermon* 101). The vows of commitment to the Lord are made before human witnesses: 'True followers of the Lamb . . . and to all mankind declare . . .' (Bowmer 1951:175). It is made also before God and his angel hosts:

> Father, Son and Holy Ghost,
> Present with thy Angel Host,
> While I at Thine Altar bow,
> Witness to the Solemn Vow!
> . . .
> Register the oath in heaven.
> (Baker 1962: 182)

Communion invites active commitment. John therefore disapproved strongly the practice of non-communicating attendance.

> It has been the custom ever since the Tabernacle was built, to have galleries full of spectators while the Lord's Supper was administered. This I judged highly improper and therefore ordered none to be admitted but those who desired to communicate (JWJ 1/4/1759).

He quoted the practice of the early church regarding the seriousness of this offence:

> If any believer join in prayers of the faithful and
> go away without receiving the Lord's Supper, let
> him be excommunicated, as bringing confusion to
> the Church of God (*Sermon* 101).

The fourth reason for the Wesleys' insistence on constant eucharistic participation was because it was the practice of the early church. The ideal was for daily communion: 'in the ancient Church, everyone who was baptised communicated daily' (*JWJ* 17/6/1740). Even after the experience of assurance at Aldersgate, John Wesley still insisted:

> Let every one therefore, who has either any desire
> to please God, or any love of his own soul, obey
> God, and consult the good of his own soul, by
> communicating every time he can; Like the first
> Christians, with whom the Christian Sacrifice was
> a constant part of the Lord's Day service. And for
> several centuries, they received it almost every
> day; four times a week always, and every Saint's
> Day besides . . . (*Sermon* 101).

He pointed to the comments on Matthew 6: 11 in *ENNT* that the early Fathers interpreted 'give us this day our daily bread' in a 'sacramental sense . . .' Ted Campbell saw the motive behind John Wesley's interest in following the practices of Christian antiquity. He observed that John was trying to apply the 'methods' or practices of the early church to the church of his time in the hope that the church of his day could regain the early church's spiritual stature (Campbell 1991: 107–8). A telling sign therefore of the spiritual health of Christians would be to see how faithful they are to constant reception of communion. John indicated that 'daily bread' ' . . . was daily received in the beginning by the whole Church of Christ and highly esteemed till the love of many waxed cold . . . ' (*Sermon* 26).

In *Sermon* 80, *On friendship with the world*, John observed that when believers are 'falling away' from the Lord, the signs are the lessening 'of exactness' in private prayer, family duty, fasting, public service attendance and in the partaking of the Lord's supper. Charles puts it in verse:

> Why is the faithful seed decreased,
> The life of God extinct and dead?
> The daily sacrifice is ceas'd,
> And charity to heaven is fled.
>
> Sad mutual causes of decay,
> Slackness and vice together move;
> Grown cold, we cast the means away,
> And quench'd our latest spark of love.
> (*HLS* 166/11–12)

The cry of the Wesleys, then, was 'Restore the daily sacrifice!' (*HLS* 166/16).

While most of the time the Wesleys had to battle with those who downplayed the importance of the sacrament, they had to deal also with those who had such an exalted view of communion that they would not partake of it. We have referred to that group earlier as the ones who were afraid that the frequency of reception might take away the respect due to the sacrament. John's reply, as we have seen, was to point them away from their fears of irreverence and from their very natural attraction to the rare, the new and the novel things. He pointed them again to the question of obedience. Spiritual reverence comes out of a faith response to either the love or fear of God. Such reverence will not be lessened by frequent communion (*Sermon* 101).

Finally, the Wesleys had to deal with those who, on the other end of the spectrum, had excessive trust in the feelings they experienced at the sacrament. Rattenbury observed that there was a difference between the evangelicals of the nineteenth century and the Wesleys regarding communion (1948: 6). To the Wesleys, communion was not only a duty but a joy (*HLS* 30/5). This is again underlined by scholars studying the *HLS*, sung by Methodists during their lengthy communions (sometimes up to five hours because of the crowd) (*JWJ* 29/5/1743). Scholars comparing the *HLS* with those of the Tractarian and evangelical writers have noted that the most distinctive feature of the Wesleyan eucharistic hymns is the mood of joy (Dearing 1966: 24).

The Wesleys were very aware that there is a danger in relying on positive feelings alone. Charles, for instance, recorded several entries in his *Journal* about the times when reception of the sacrament gave him no comfort (*CWJ* 1/5/1738, 19/5/1738, 1/6/1738, 2/6/1738, 3/6/1738, 16/9/1739, 3/2/1751). After ministering to nearly 40 colliers, Charles confessed,

> I always find strength for the work of the ministry, but when my work is over, my strength, both bodily and spiritually, leaves me. I can pray for others, not for myself. God by me strengthens the weak hands, and confirms the feeble knees; yet am I myself as a man in whom is no strength. I am wary and faint in my mind, longing to be discharged (*CWJ* 16/9/1739).

Yet, even when there was no feeling, the Wesleys called for a holding on to the 'ancient paths' (*HLS* 90/5 cf 86/1–4). There were reports that some Methodists were feeling 'the blood of Christ running upon their arms, going down their throats, poured like water upon their breasts and heart'. Some had dreams of that. John Wesley told them that they had overheated imaginations and expelled them from the Society (*JWJ* 6/9/1742 cf JWL 7). Feelings was not the main criterion. To those who might be tempted to trust in the sacrament excessively, especially because of good feelings they receive, the Wesleys replied:

> With joy we feel its sacred power
> But neither stars nor means adore . . .
> (*HLS* 62/8).

The means are 'earthen vessels' which cannot bear 'that heavenly life in Christ conceal'd' (*HLS* 101/2). John's position was: use the means but do not put one's trust in the means but in Christ who provided the means (*Sermon* 1).

> We know that there is no inherent power in . . .
> the bread and wine received in the Lord's
> Supper; but it is God alone who is the Giver of
> every good gift, the Author of all grace; that the
> whole power is of Him, whereby, through any
> of these, there is any blessing conveyed to our
> souls.
>
> . . . Remember also to use all means, as
> means; as ordained not for their own sake, but
> in order to the renewal of your soul in
> righteousness and true holiness. If, therefore,
> they actually tend to this, well; but if not, they
> are dung and dross . . . (*Sermon* 16).

So for the Wesleys, communion is to be observed constantly
not because of the 'good feelings' one receives (or the lack of
these) nor for any 'magical' effects one associates with it, but
because it was the Lord's command and it is a real means of
grace. It is the place where the believer renews commitment
vows to the Lord, and as it was a practice of the primitive
church in its more 'holy' days, restoring the practice in the
present church might restore the church's spiritual health. This
rather objective rationale for constant communion with its
authority and example taken from Scripture and tradition,
called forth from the believer a response based on an act of will
and trust. Perhaps it was not enough to sustain the eucharistic
observance of the Wesleys' followers?

We have to concede, after noting the Wesleys' reasons in
pressing for frequent and regular communions, that their
eucharistic rationale is not dissimilar to those held by some of
the reformers nor those held by the early church. Yet where the
reformers failed (in bringing about a eucharistic revival), the
Wesleys succeeded to a significant degree during a certain
period of time. We have to return to the question asked in the
last section: Could the motivation which spurred the Wesleys
and their people be deeper than their eucharistic rationale
presented? We will look for some answers in the next chapter.

3. Eucharistic place and presidency

Where was communion to be celebrated? This question would contribute to the Methodist movement's shift from being a revival within the Church of England to a separate entity from the established church. The usual practice for the Wesleys was to have it in Anglican churches. This was certainly the case from 1741 till 1743. Understandably, some were held in homes of the sick or in prisons, as the need arose (*CWJ* 25/8/1737, 9/7/1738). In Charles's *Journals*, one notes that some Methodists were being 'repelled' from Anglican communion tables as early as 1740 (*CWJ* 20/7/1740, 27/2/1740). Even before this happened, the Wesleys were already making the most of their eucharistic celebrations with the sick allowed by canon law. There is a possibility that Charles did have some communion in homes where no mention is made of any sick person being present (eg 20/11/1738 at Bray's; 24/11/1738 at Mrs Townsend's; 30/11/1738 at Mr Gambold's). The first Methodist communion service to be held outside Anglican church buildings (and outside homes) was in 1740 when Charles gave the sacrament to about 80 colliers at Kingswood (*CWJ* 29/6/1740).

As early as 1741, Methodists started using unconsecrated buildings of their own, eg Kingswood school, for communion services (*CWJ* 12/4/1741). In 1743, consecrated chapels of the Huguenots were purchased for Methodist communion services, eg the West Street Chapel in London (JWW 1). City Road Chapel London was the first of those which was built by the Methodists with sacramental worship in mind (Baker 1970: 213 cf JWW 3). The gradual physical distance which separated the Methodists from their Anglican churches (and hence, their Anglican roots), fuelled by the fact that they had by then their own ordained leadership, contributed in some way to the emergence of the Methodists as a separate denomination in later years after the death of the Wesleys.

More difficult than the question of where communion could be celebrated was the question: Who can preside at communion? Born to a high church father, with upbringing and associations to match (eg his links with the Manchester non–jurors who were 'higher' than most in churchmanship).

John, a self–proclaimed 'bigot' of the Church of England (JWL 8) would answer: only a priest can celebrate communion, but not any priest. The priest must be one who has been ordained by a bishop with apostolic succession recognised by the Church of England. Wesley wrote:

> We believe it should not be right for us to administer either Baptism or the Lord's Supper unless we had a commission so to do from those bishops whom we apprehend to be in a succession from the apostles (JWL 9).

August Spangenberg, a Moravian John Wesley met in America, complained that John would not accept Calvinist and Lutheran pastors because they did not have the kind of apostolic succession he recognised (Baker 1970: 42–43). In Wesley's eyes, however, the succession of the Moravians and Roman Catholics were valid and they had legitimate ministers.[2]

Wesley placed a lot of weight on practices of the early pre-constantinian church, more so if he thought they were universally observed then. He thought they had apostolic origins and to depart from them was to break church unity (Campbell 1991: 30 which his great reverence for the 'communion of saints' would not allow (Todd 1958: 171–3). Apostolic succession and the priestly celebration of the eucharist were among these.

A priest in Wesley's understanding is different from a layperson in two ways: Firstly, ordination has conveyed an 'indelible character' (JWW 6) upon the person. This 'indelible character' received during the laying on of hands by the bishop with the words, 'Receive the Holy Ghost, for the office and work of a Priest in the Church of God . . .' meant the receipt of

---

2.   While John Wesley affirmed his acceptance of Roman Catholic claims to apostolic succession (JWL 30/12/1745) his appreciation of the Moravian episcopal elections and practices in his early ministry (cf *J W J* 28/2/1736) did not prevent him from baptising Mr Tackner, who had already been baptised by the Moravians. The British Parliament recognised the Moravian *'Unitras Fratum'* *'as'* an ancient Protestant Episcopal Church' only in 1749 (Cross 1974: 1512).

special spiritual authority to perform the assigned priestly functions, eg celebrate the sacraments (JWW 6, JWL 10). Second, the priesthood, while instituted by God, is commissioned by the church as a regular ministry to offer the Christian sacrifice. The 'honour to administer the sacraments is peculiar to the Priests of God,' says Wesley when he reaffirmed that his unordained preachers did not administer the sacraments (JWW 7). As the church, joined with Christ's eternal sacrifice, offers herself in the sacrament, there is needed a duly ordered minister to offer the sacrifice in the name of all. Since there is an 'outward' and real sacrifice, there has to be an 'outward' and real priesthood. In a letter to Mr Hall, John Wesley wrote that he believed that there is an outward priesthood, and consequently an outward sacrifice, ordained and offered by the Bishop of Rome, and his successors or dependents, in the Church of England, as Vicars and Vicegerents of Christ . . .

> We believe there is, and always was, in every Christian Church, (whether dependent on the Bishop of Rome or not), an outward priesthood, ordained by Jesus Christ, and an outward sacrifice offered therein, by men authorized to act as ambassadors of Christ, and stewards of the mysteries of God (JWL 30/12/1745 cf. Rattenbury 1948: 76, 77).

The priestly office of the minister is that of a representative of the priesthood of all believers or of the corporate Body of Christ. The priest performs the sacramental function on behalf of the church. Hence, as Rattenbury observed 'Wesleyan belief in the sacrifice and the priesthood made it impossible for them to sanction lay administration' (1948: 89). Rattenbury qualified the nature of the sacrifice:

> I find no evidence that the Wesleys regarded their priesthood as an office which qualified them to offer sacrifice for other people: they offered the sacrifice of the whole Church, or shall I say more precisely the Church its

> oblation through their instrumentality. They
> did not offer sacrifice, in any sense, for other's
> salvation: there is not the slightest hint of
> propitiatory sacrifices (1948: 133).

On 20 January 1746, John Wesley's reading of Lord Peter King's 'account of the Primitive Church' and later, Bishop Edward Stillingfleet's *Irenicon*, convinced him that bishops and presbyters are essentially of one order (*JWJ* 20/1/1746, JWL 12). He was also convinced that neither Christ nor the apostles left any specific form of church government to be perpetuated. Episcopacy is scriptural and is hence lawful (JWL 11). It is however, not absolutely necessary, ie it is for the *bene esse* not of the *esse* of the church. It must be noted that this made no difference in his beliefs regarding the priesthood nor of the Christian sacrifice (Rattenbury 1948: 76). It affected only his understanding of who can ordain and who can be recognised as a legitimate minister. There is evidence that he started to recognise ministerial orders of non-episcopal churches (JWL 13).

John Wesley continued to believe that bishops usually performed ordinations in the ancient church but presbyters could ordain in case of necessity. He also believed in succession—though this was more open to presbyterial involvement—while Charles was exclusively episcopal. Hence he had no qualms about ordaining his preachers himself, assisted by other presbyters. Although the word 'priest' was changed into 'elder' in the *Sunday Service* which he edited for use in America, Wesley never retracted from his understanding of sacrifice or sacrificing minister (Rattenbury 1948: 13).

The shortage of ordained Anglican clergy to celebrate the sacrament for the Methodists meant that outside the key Methodist centres like London and Bristol, it was increasingly difficult for them to receive communion regularly. Firmly committed to the centrality of the sacrament in their spirituality and loath to do without regular reception, Methodists began to push the Wesleys for the ordination of their preachers. They were also unhappy about having to receive communion from priests whose lives and theology were sometimes questionable. While John Wesley understood their objections, acknowledging that the 'unworthiness of the Minister or the unworthiness of some of the Communicants . . . greatly lesson the comfort of receiving' (*AM* 1780: 103), he insisted that the validity of the ordinance does not depend on the goodness of the minister: 'the holy God does bless the ministry of unholy men because God is not limited by their unholiness' (*Sermon* 104). Charles Wesley, in his poem *Wicked Priest* proclaimed:

> Whate'er the messenger he sends,
> He gives the efficacious grace:
> The word and sacrament depends
> On Christ for its assur'd success . . .
> (quoted in Baker 1962: 213).

Unfortunately, this failed to convince many of their followers. It might be significant to note that when John Wesley re-edited the *39 Articles of Religion* for the American Methodists, he removed *Article* Number 16 on 'the Unworthiness of Ministers which hinders not the efficacy of the Sacraments'. Could it be that he too began to share their beliefs, or was it his recognition of the strong feelings of his people on the matter that brought about the deletion? We do not know. Perhaps he too shared a concern that at least, on a subjective level, the character of the minister does affect the response of the people. By the time of his re-editing, he had already ordained Methodists to serve there. The removal of the clause could have been his way of insisting that those whom he sent should live worthy lives as ministers of the word and sacrament.

In spite of the preachers' clamour for authorisation to celebrate communion, John Wesley never wavered in seeing the priestly ministry as the 'ordinary' gift/office of the Spirit and lay preachers as 'extraordinary' messengers (*Sermon* 115). To John, the Old Testament offices of 'priest' and 'prophet' are distinct. His preachers were the 'prophets'. The *Minutes of Several Conversations* (JWW 5) had this on its record:

> Question: In what view may we and our helpers
> be considered?

> Answer: Perhaps as extraordinary messen-
> gers—to provoke the regular ministers to
> jealousy—to supply their lack of service towards
> those who are perishing for lack of knowledge.

Hence he would not give them permission to celebrate communion if they were not ordained.

The situation worsened, with the closing of parish communions by unsympathetic priests to the growing number of Methodists (eg *JWJ* 25/2/1747). Even some Independent Churches were barring the Methodists from receiving communion (*AM* 1789: 470, 472). Desperate pleas for ordained ministers were heard from Methodist preachers serving in America. John explored several possibilities for the ordination of his preachers. One of these plans was proposed by Joseph Benson in 1775 and developed by John Fletcher. It had to do with purging the unsuitable preachers and getting Anglican bishops to ordain the more qualified ones. Fletcher proposed the organisation of the Methodists thus as a 'daughter church of our holy mother'. Unfortunately, the plans were rejected by John Wesley (Heitzenrater 1995: 256). Other plans included the purported enlisting the assistance of an Orthodox bishop —which John Wesley denied (JWW 8). Wesley also sought the cooperation of the English bishops (JWL 14). Every door was shut. Finally in 1784 at 4 am, in a private house on Bristol's Dighton Street, John ordained Richard Whatcoat and Thomas Vasey as deacons, with Anglican priests, Thomas Coke and James Creighton assisting. The next day, he ordained Coke to be Superintendent of the Methodist Churches in America. Coke was instructed to ordain Francis Asbury, a layman in America, and to set him apart to be a Joint Superintendent together with him. Whatcoat and Vasey were ordained elders on the same day and their ministry would be in America (*JWJ* 1/9/1784, JWW 3, JWL 14).

Charles was shocked when he was told about the ordinations by a Bristol layman. He dissolved his partnership with his brother, though not his friendship (*CWJ* 1). On 1 August 1785, John ordained John Pawson, Thomas Hanby and Joseph Taylor for Scotland (*JWJ* 1/8/1785). They were told explicitly to lay aside gown and bands when they crossed the border into England, ceasing to administer the sacraments (JWW 3). Wesley felt that the ordinations were justified because both North America and Scotland were outside the immediate jurisdiction of the Church of England. Later, in 1789, John ordained Alexander Mather, Henry Moore and Thomas Rankin for work in England. While he was alive, no preacher, even those ordained by him, administered the sacraments in England (Bowmer 1951: 79).

We noted earlier that Wesley was pushed to ordain his preachers when he saw America as having 'hundreds of miles . . . there is none either to baptise or to administer the Lord's Supper' (JWW 3, JWL 14). If the ordinations, as Charles saw it, constituted separation from the Church of England, it was not just John's high view of the sacraments (seeing them as something essential to the life of a Christian) but his insistence that only ordained elders could celebrate the sacrament, that made him take the step that would, in time, sever his movement from his beloved church.

What seems to surface in this study of the questions of place and presidency are five interesting features of Wesleyan eucharistic practice. Firstly, despite the lay orientation of the Methodist revival with lay leadership at almost every level of its work, the sacramental leadership was strictly clerical. Yet in spite of the insistence of the Wesleys on this, Methodist lay participation and enthusiasm for the sacrament contrasted sharply with the passive and (for the most part), non-communicating participation of the laity at the sacrament from the medieval period of church history. The Methodist laity recognised that the sacrament was for them, not just for the clergy. Perhaps the Wesleys' teaching on Christian perfection had a part to play here. If holiness is not an option for only one section of the church, namely the clergy, then the laity, called to holiness, are entitled to the very means of grace which will assist them in the sanctification process, the holy communion.

Secondly, while the needs of the work the Wesleys were engaged in played a major role in bringing forth Wesleyan eucharistic practices, the brothers were not mere pragmatics. The needs did not determine their agenda, nor was the most pragmatic choice the one finally taken. Some decisions were made with ambivalence and with prayer for signs of divine approval. For example, when Charles found that the Kingwood Methodist band members were refused communion at the Temple Church, he administered the sacrament to them in their school instead. His *Journal* records:

> I had prayed God to show me some token if this was His will concerning us: and indeed, my prayer was answered; for such a sacrament was I ever present at before. We received the sure pledges of our Saviour's dying love, and were most of us filled with all peace and joy in believing (*CWJ* 12/4/1741).

The decision to ordain in an irregular way (despite John Wesley's appeal to primitive Alexandrian Church practice in which presbyters elected their own bishops and consecrated him themselves through the laying on of their hands) rather than let the lay preachers administer the sacrament is another case in point. What that specific situation conveys is that the Wesleys were responsive to the changing needs of their people and were not afraid to risk new ways of meeting those needs, but they would do this only *after* theological, not just practical ramifications have been considered. John's views about the consecration of churches was such that he was theologically open to meeting outside consecrated buildings. He saw consecration of church buildings as an indifferent matter at best, a superstition at its worst (JWW 9). His views about ordination were more severe and that would not be compromised.

Thirdly, it was so important to the Wesleys that their people could receive the sacrament that they were willing to pay a very high price for making the sacrament available. The price for both the brothers was risking ecclesiastical censure for departing from their usual church practice of having the sacrament only in an Anglican or a consecrated church building. The price for John Wesley was the separation of the Methodists from his beloved Church of England as the long-term result of his ordinations.

Finally we see in this section the rather relaxed approach the Wesleys had regarding the specific place of eucharistic celebration, but we observe at the same time that the Wesleys were very particular about who could preside at the Table. The insistence on clerical celebration of the sacrament based on the belief that a real outward sacrifice takes place at the eucharist and that a properly ordained priest must preside at it raises for us a question: why is this emphasis on priesthood and sacrifice so important for them? We will explore this question in chapter 2.

4. Eucharistic requirements

Who can come for communion? In the Church of England of the Wesleys' day, any baptised person could (Waterland 1737: 536–7). Difficulties of travel, the size of dioceses, market days, farming conditions and lack of good artificial light for churches meant that not very many people received confirmation at the hands of a bishop in those days (Sykes 1962:145). Hence while having being confirmed was 'highly expedient' (Waterland 1737: 538), it was not the main criterion for reception of the sacrament. Yet many spiritual leaders at that time had several requirements for reception of the eucharist other than the main criterion of baptism. Daniel Waterland (1683–1740), a Cambridge–educated Anglican theologian, who was actively engaged in the theological controversies of his time, namely those on the divinity of Christ, the Trinity, deism and the eucharist (Cross 1974: 1462), listed competent knowledge, sound faith, true repentance consisting in restitution, readiness to forgive, peaceableness and charity for the poor (Waterland 1737: 536–558).

The Moralists[3] were Anglicans represented by people like William Law and Jeremy Taylor (whose writings influenced the Wesley brothers in their younger years). Concerned with

---

3. Theological shifts took place after the English Civil War where Anglicanism became more moralistic (Allison 1966: ix–xi I). Selleck (1983: 23) described the advocates of this trend as those from the 'holy living school'.

the need for conscious and serious discipleship, they sought to combat the prevalent atmosphere of antinomianism by producing several manuals or treatises for people to use in preparation for their reception of the sacrament. The Moralists' strong belief in human autonomy and responsibility sometimes led them to stress the believer's part in the preparation for reception to the point of almost giving the impression that God's acceptance might be dependent on human effort (Allison 1966: 88–9). Taylor in *Worthy Communicant* called for pre-Communion preparation which would require the communicant to break out of the habit and domination of sin so as not to 'pollute the sacrifice of Christ' (Selleck 1983: 21–22).

The Manchester non-juror leader Thomas Deacon who exercised some influence on the Wesleys' earlier theology and spirituality named faith, the giving of alms and strict self–examination as the required preparation for communion (1716: 301–303). Like the Moralists, the non–jurors produced several well-known 'preparation manuals': Thomas Ken (1637–1711) with his *A Manual of Prayers for the Use of Scholars of Winchester College* (1679) which featured meditations on the eucharist and prayers for different parts of the service and John Johnson with his *The Unbloody Sacrifice* (1714). Bowmer reported that John Wesley sailed to America with 500 copies of Johnson's book and probably imposed some teachings of the book on his congregation in Georgia (1951: 30).

The Moralists and the non-jurors were not the only ones producing preparation manuals. Other well-known writings of this genre around that time include Brian Duppa's *Holy Rules and Helps to Devotion both in Prayer and Practice*, the anonymous *A Week's Preparation towards a Worthy Receiving of the Lord's Supper*, Bishop John Gauden's *The Whole Duty of a Communicant: being rules and directions for a worthy receiving of the most holy sacrament of the Lord's Supper*, Simon Patrick's *Christian Sacrifice* (Part IV). The father of the Wesley brothers, Samuel Wesley Senior, also wrote a manual entitled, *A Pious Communicant Rightly Prepared*.

The Moravians, whom the Wesleys associated with rather closely during the years just before and after John's Aldersgate experience, interviewed individually all those who wanted to come for communion to assess their spiritual state before admitting them to the sacrament (*JWJ* 12/8/1738).

> Our (Moravian) constant enquiries were, 'is Christ formed in you? Have you a new heart? Is your soul renewed in the image of God? Is the whole body of sin destroyed in you? Are you fully assured beyond all doubt or fear, that you are a child of God? In what manner, and at what moment, did you receive that full assurance?' If a man could not answer all these questions, we judged he had no true faith. Nor would we permit any to receive the Lord's Supper among us till he could (*JWW* 10).

Spangenberg and the Moravians required absolute faith as the criterion for reception. They would not give the sacrament to those who had doubt or fear, for that was understood to be incompatible with having absolute faith (*JWJ* 7/11/1739). After the Aldersgate experience where John felt the assurance of his salvation, he went to visit the Moravians at Marienborn. To his pain, the Moravians refused him communion because they deemed him a *homo perturbatus*, a zealous English churchman whose head had ascendency over his heart. His companion during that trip, Benjamin Ingham, was given the sacrament (Heitzenrater 1984: II: 68).

The concern for worthiness in communion reception was shared by the Puritans. Before the bread and wine were served to the seated congregation, the Puritans would first conduct an examination of their communicants (Stevenson 1994: 167). The feelings of fear and anxiety of people regarding the need for worthy reception of the sacrament was very real during the time of the Wesleys. In the *Arminian Magazine*, we read account after account of the early Methodists struggling with these feelings:

> About a month before Christmas I had a strong desire to receive the Sacrament; yet I trembled at

the thought, *lest I should eat and drink my own damnation . . .*

When the time came, I was *overwhelmed with dread, and went trembling to the altar . . .* (*AM* 1788: 516. Italics mine).

When I approached the table of the Lord, it appeared so awful to me that I was like to fall down, and *as if I was going to the judgement seat of Christ* (*AM* 1790: 11. Italics mine).

I joined the Society; but *for a long while durst not venture to go to the Lord's Table.*

One Sunday I was determined to go; but when I approached, *my heart failed me, and I went back without receiving but, though the distress of my mind, my legs were scarce able to support me; and, being filled with fear, guilt and shame, I trembled exceedingly:* however at last, as a poor, weary, heavy–laden sinner, who had nothing to plead, but 'God be merciful to me for Christ's sake', I ventured to eat of that bread, and drink of that cup (*AM* 1779: 571–3. Italics mine cf. *AM* 1779: 301–2).

(after determining to go for Communion) . . . but for weeks before, whenever I thought upon it, *I was filled with horror.* As the time drew nearer, my temptations were stronger; and all I had done in sinning against God, from the time I first received the sacrament to the present day, was brought home to my mind, with such aggravations, that I thought I had *trampled upon the blood of the cross, and crucified the Son of God afresh, and that now, for me there remained no more sacrifice for sin.*

(When he was receiving communion, a little wine was spilt accidentally) I thought I should have dropped to the ground. How I got to my feet, I know not; but the *distress I now felt was inexpressible* ... (*AM* 1779: 186–7. Italics mine)

In a sense the great concern about being a 'worthy' communicant during the time of the Wesleys was not surprising if we consider the history of eucharistic practice in preceding centuries. During the Middle Ages, theologians were even asking about the proper dispositions necessary for viewing the Host (McCue 1989: 432).

In a culture where great stress was put on proper preparation and worthy reception of the sacrament, there were only a few voices which were raised in deep concern about possible negative effects of these efforts. John Tillotson (1630-97) was against the over-emphasis on worthy reception of the eucharist and the production of preparation manuals. He feared that these might discourage the sinner from coming to the Table (1728: I: 229–230). Waterland shared his concern as well (Waterland 1737: 565; cf 1738: 105). Non-juror Robert Nelson sounded the same note in his *A Companion to Festivals and Fasts* (1704). He advised that great care must be taken, when a man is habitually prepared, that 'he does not impose on himself so much actual preparation as shall make him lose an opportunity of receiving the sacrament, when he has not had time to go through with that method he has prescribed to himself' (Nelson 1704: 464). Non-juror Deacon reminded people that communion is first a response to the work of Christ rather than 'our' work for him (1734: 301–303).

Thus far, we see that requirements listed by the church leaders in time of the Wesleys had to do with three concerns: adequate faith (however defined), adequate knowledge and more importantly, worthiness (discovered through intense self-examination; with evidence of repentance seen in holy living, good relationships with one's neighbour and good works). Where did the Wesleys stand on eucharistic requirements?

In his earlier years, it seemed that John Wesley had three criteria: 'valid' baptism, adequate and intensive preparation (to ensure that there would be knowledge, faith and worthiness) and evidence of compliance to the rubrics of the Church of England. As we mentioned earlier, confirmation was not seen as necessary for the sacrament. John Wesley would admit only people who were baptised by ministers who had been ordained by bishops with apostolic succession. This ruled out the Dissenters, the Calvinists and the Lutherans. John Wesley baptised Thomas and Phoebe Hird, who had been Quakers, and two of their children while they were travelling on the *Simmonds* to America (*JWJ* 16/11/1735). There is a record of Thomas and Mark Hird (the twenty-one-year-old son) receiving communion later (*JWJ* 10/6/1736), although the whole family could have been admitted to communion as early as Christmas (cf *JWJ* 21/12/1735). Even after his Aldersgate experience, John continued baptising Dissenters and was summoned before Dr Edmund Gibson, Bishop of London, partly to answer questions about that (*JWJ* 12/5/1742). Charles obviously followed John's practices, for he too was summoned by the Bishop of London over the same issues, albeit much earlier (*CWJ* 21/10/1738). John Wesley remembered with regret years later that he had turned away a pious Lutheran minister from the Table while he was in America (*Sermon* 132). Although he recognised the baptism of Moravians, John's attitude toward them was ambivalent; while he seemed to recognise the validity of their sacraments, he baptised Ambrosius Tackner, a Moravian who had received what Wesley called 'lay baptism'. The next day, Tackner was given communion (JD18/10/1735, 19/10/1735)

John also required evidence of preparation for communion. His own experience had been that worthy communicating 'with faith and humility and thankfulness' brings about the forgiveness of sins (JWL 15). While in Georgia, John took great pains to prepare new communicants for the sacrament, conducting classes for even one person (Bowmer 1951: 32, 33). It is possible that John Wesley also insisted on intensive preparation using the discipline observed by the Manchester non-jurors. His parishioners in America accused him of restricting the benefits of the Lord's supper to a small number of persons and refusing it to everyone who would not conform to his

> set of penances, confessions, motifications and constant attendance at early and late hours of prayer very inconsistent with the labour and

employment of the colony . . . refusing to administer the Holy Communion to well disposed and well living persons, unless they should submit to confessions and penances (Baker 1970: 45).

John also required the keeping to the rubrics of the *BCP* regarding the sacrament. The communicant was required to inform the celebrant of his or her intention to communicate before the communion service. When Sophia Hopkey in Georgia failed to inform him of her intention to communicate, he repelled her from the Table. In this particular situation, Wesley's pastoral act of discipline was complicated by the fact that he had been in love with Hopkey and she had just chosen to marry someone else. Her uncle brought a charge against him as a result of that and John had to leave his post in America to avoid the court case (Heitzenrater 1984: II: 49–61).

Charles Wesley, however, probably had a less rigid nature than his brother: he had experienced grace without the usual preparation:

> Last Saturday . . . I . . . found myself utterly adverse to prayer, and spent half an hour in vain striving to recollect my dissipated thoughts. Upon this I gave out, and passed the whole night in the utmost trouble and discomposure of mind. I rose in the morning two hours later than usual, in utter despair of receiving the Sacrament that day, or of recovering myself in less than two or three. In this condition I went immediately to church. On my way a thought came across me that it might be less sin to receive even without the least immediate preparation (for the whole week till Saturday evening I had spent to my satisfaction) than to turn my back upon the Sacrament. I accordingly resolved if I found myself anything affected with the prayers, to stay and communicate. I did find myself affected and stayed. I not only received the Sacrament at that

time with greater warmth than usual, but
afterwards found my resolutions of pursuing
considerably strengthened. This wasn't all: on
Sunday night I received a great blessing from
God and have continued since in a better frame of
mind than I have yet know' (CWL 2).

In a letter to her son Samuel, Susanna Wesley affirmed his
desire to 'again receive the Holy Sacrament' but chided him
regarding his concern for his own worthiness: 'you complain
that you are unable and inconstant in the ways of virtue: alas!
what Christian is not so too?' (*AM* 1788: 36) Since elder brother
Samuel exercised a strong influence on Charles while the latter
was under his care in school, could this wisdom from their
mother not have been passed on to Charles through Samuel?

In his later years John Wesley taught that there were three
requirements which were necessary for the reception of
communion. The first was the acknowledgment of one's need.
On 7 June 1740, John wrote in his *Journal* that 'no fitness is
required at the time of communicating but a sense of our own
state of utter sinfulness and helplessness' (*JWJ* 7/6/1740).
Secondly, there must be the willingness to change one's life.

All the preparation that is absolutely necessary
is contained in those words: 'repent you truly
of your sins past; have faith in Christ our
Saviour, amend your lives, and be in charity
with all men; so shall ye be meet partakers of
these holy mysteries' (*Sermon* 101).

Only let a man first 'examine himself'
whether he understand the nature and design
of this holy institution and whether he really
desire to be himself made conformable to the
death of Christ, and so, nothing doubting, 'let
him eat of that bread and drink of that cup'
(*Sermon* 120).

The third requirement was the desire to receive all that God
wants to give:

> Inasmuch as we come to his table, not to give
> him anything, but to receive whatsoever he
> sees best for us, there is no previous
> preparation indispensably necessary, but a
> desire to receive whatsoever he pleases to give
> (JWL 16).

Adequacy of faith is not the issue (although some basic understanding and faith is required), but an openness to receive from God, relying on the merits of Christ. John Wesley reminded his people that the disciples were unconverted when the eucharist was instituted and when they first received it on the night Jesus was betrayed (*JWJ* 27/6/1740). Charles pleaded for 'faith or faith's increase' (*HLS* 76/3) at the sacrament.

Prayer, self-examination would be good but they are not 'indispensably necessary' (JWL 10, JWL 16). The Wesleys did not require fasting before communion. John wrote, 'Prepare yourself by prayer, if you have time; if you have not, however, come . . .' (*Sermon* 101). Like some of the earlier voices of Ken and Tillotson, the Wesleys were concerned that too much emphasis on preparation resulted in people neglecting the very sacrament which could be a means of healing to them.

The Wesleys were not uninterested in preparing their people for the sacrament. Even when they differed from many of their contemporaries regarding the importance of preparation, they gave the Methodists a book which contained meditations in prose and poetry about the eucharist. It contained John's edited version of Daniel Brevint's treatise *The Christian Sacrament and Sacrifice* as its preface and Charles's 166 *HLS* which were mainly inspired by the Brevint text.[4] Wesleyan eucharistic theology owed much to Brevint's book.

Brevint (1616–1695) was born to a Huguenot family in Jersey and he inherited the French Reformation tradition which had laid claim on the island. He studied at the

---

4. Wainwright in his preface to the facsimile of the *HLS* (reproduced by the Charles Wesley Society) indicated that there were several hymns which owed little to Brevint (Kimbrough 1995: 9). The Wesleys, for the most part, followed Brevint's theology of the sacrament.

Protestant University at Saumur and then went to Oxford where he received his Masters' degree and a fellowship. Exiled to France during the Commonwealth, he met John Cosin and was ordained an Anglican priest, having been a French Reformed pastor. His friendship with King Charles II earned him three positions: the rectorship of Brancepeth, the prebendaryship of the Cathedral and deanery of Lincoln (Stevenson 1994: 98–107). Brevint wrote many books in his lifetime, most of which had anti-Roman Catholic themes. During his exile period in Paris, he wrote *The Christian Sacrament and Sacrifice*. Although this book was against the Roman Catholic understanding of the mass and sought to put forward a more ancient and scriptural teaching on the sacrifice, it was more devotional in tone than apologetic. Each section, filled with scriptural references, lengthy typologies and theological reflections, was concluded with personal, moving prayers. Brevint presented the eucharist as a commemorative memorial, a real means of grace, a trustworthy pledge and a once-and-for-all sacrifice of Christ, calling forth the sacrifice of our lives and goods in response to his work. What emerged from Brevint's book was the powerful sense of the eucharist as a real encounter with the Christ of the cross.

A comparison of the Wesleys' edited version of the Brevint text and the original text itself shows how intentional the Wesleys were in being different from their eucharistic mentor and others about the question of eucharistic requirements. Brevint described communicants as 'worthy' (Brevint 1673: 13). He also implied that Christ would not die for Pilate and the Jews alone (Brevint 1673: 14). He warned about unworthy participation in communion (Brevint 1673: 42, 64–67). John Wesley, editing Brevint, removed the words 'worthy' from Brevint's description (Wesley 1745: 7) and left out Brevint's reference to Pilate and the Jews (Wesley 1745: 7). He dropped Brevint's long warnings about unworthy reception (Wesley 1745: 13,19). Those who should not come for communion, according to Wesley, are the intentionally 'wicked and impenitent' (Wesley 1745: 13) who take the elements 'wickedly and irreverently' (1673: 50); Brevint has it as 'the impious' (1673: 42). Where Brevint writes (1673: 58) that those who are admitted to the dinner of the Lamb 'must not' doubt of being admitted, Wesley writes, 'need not' (Wesley 1745: 17). What we see here is an intentional 'softening' of Brevint's emphasis on worthy reception and a warmer welcome to those who have a desire to receive.

Thus we see that in spite of the strong culture and tradition of using preparation manuals and teaching the need for adequate preparation for the sacrament, the Wesleys gradually came to encourage their people to set aside their fears of judgment and, with joyful expectation, receive all that the Lord wants to give them at the Table, just as they are. With their position on the eucharistic requirements in sharp contrast with most of the leaders of their day, the Wesleys had to address three issues which their people were concerned about. The first issue is the question of taking the sacrament 'unworthily'. On the one hand, proper spiritual preparation can help one enjoy the gifts of God given at the Table (Gerrish 1993: 172). On the other, proper preparation can be seen primarily as a safeguard against one partaking of the sacrament 'unworthily' and thus bringing judgment upon oneself. The motivation would thus be more from fear than from a sense of joyful expectation. Theologians differed on whether the unprepared—be they unbelievers, unrepentant ones or the underprepared Christian —receive Christ at the sacrament. Calvin would say that although Christ's presence is not dependent on the faith or worthiness of the communicant, the efficacy of the sacrament cannot be received by them (*Institutes* 4: 17,33, cf 2: 1406–7; *CR* 9: 89): 'That Christ is received without faith is no less monstrous than that a seed should germinate in a fire' (*CR* 9: 27). Taylor, sharing Calvin's view, puts it very bluntly: 'The Blessed Sacrament before him that hath no faith is like messes of meat set upon the graves of the dead . . . the dead have no portion in them' (1667: 143). The 29th *Article of Religion* in the *BCP* stated that the ' wicked receive not Christ . . .' All the writers were agreed that even if the unworthy communicant receives nothing efficacious at the Table, the person also receives condemnation upon himself (cf. 1 Corinthians 11: 27–30). It is interesting to note that John Wesley left out the 29th *Article of Religion* in his edition for the new church in America.

The Wesleys encountered the fear of the people when they tried to encourage constant communion: 'What if we are not worthy to receive the sacrament?', 'We cannot live up to the life of holiness communicating requires', 'We do not have time to prepare ourselves adequately to receive . . .' John addressed some of their concerns in his *The Duty of Constant Communion* by pointing to God's grace which is not dependent on our worthiness. If we wait until we are worthy, we can never come at all! Why refuse his grace here when we do not refuse his grace in other instances? God commands us to receive the sacrament constantly. Can we use worthiness as an excuse to disobey his commands? He reminded them of their baptismal commitment which predates the commitment required at communion. The promise to commit had already been made at baptism. Communion is not adding something new to that. It is the same promise (*Sermon* 101). Indeed the oft-quoted concern about 'eating and drinking unworthily' has to do with taking the sacrament 'in a rude and disorderly way' by being drunk or by ignoring the needs of others who are hungry. It has nothing to do with coming to the Table with the acknowledgment of one's unworthiness. There is also no warrant in Scripture for one who feels unworthy because 'he has lately fallen into sin' to impose the penance of 'fasting from reception of the sacrament' on himself. No other preparation is absolutely necessary except the desire to receive the sacrament, the willingness to trust in the God who invites one to the Table and the openness to change one's life. As Charles wrote: 'We only can accept the grace' (*HLS* 128/2).

The second issue the Wesleys encountered in stating their requirement for the sacrament was: how much faith is needed before a person can come? The Moravians, as we have seen, had required absolute faith, defined as the absence of doubt or fear, as the criterion for reception. John Wesley saw that there were two categories of people: the convinced unbeliever or heathen and the seeker or the spiritually receptive unbeliever who has some degree, albeit a small degree, of faith. John would admit the latter group to the Table, inviting them to rely on the merits of Christ in their hearts (cf *Sermon* 16). The faith they need will be given at communion. He said,

> I believe it right for him who knows he has not
> faith (that is conquering faith) . . . to communicate
> . . . because I believe (these) are means of grace to
> unbelievers (*JWJ* 31/12/39).

The third issue had to do with perceived 'scriptural warrant'
for the need of preparation. When detractors of the Wesleys
pointed to the parable of the wedding garment (Matthew 22:
11) as proof that preparation is absolutely necessary for
reception of the sacrament, John Wesley replied that in the
passage from Matthew 22: 11, the wedding garment referred to
was holiness (*Sermon* 120 cf. *JWJ* 14/10/1789). This holiness was
required but the passage was not talking about holiness as a
prerequisite for receiving the sacrament:

> . . . It cannot: For the commemoration of his
> (Christ's) death was not then ordained. It relates
> wholly to the proceedings of our Lord when he
> comes in the clouds of heaven to judge the quick
> and the dead (*Sermon* 120).

It must be appreciated at this point that the Wesleys were
ministering not to a normal sedate and 'respectable' congregation but to a great number of people on the fringe of or
outside ordinary church life. The miners of Kingswood had a
reputation of being a wild and ignorant group of people (*JWJ*
27/11/1739, *JWJ* 20/7/1760, JWL 18, JWW 1); many of Wesley's
preachers were illiterate, having come from 'low trades' such as
'tailoring and the like' (*Sermon* 104). Many of the prisoners were
in a state of poverty. All these people were quite unlikely to
have the appropriate knowledge/understanding or adequate
faith that the preparation manuals required. Issues of morality
and ethics were possibly stronger daily challenges for them in
their subcultures than for those in the mainstream of society.
Those who laboured in the mines, for example, would not have
sufficient time or energy to engage in in-depth spiritual
introspection and examination. The news of the free grace of
God which welcomes them to the Table 'just as they were'
could thus be easily misunderstood, abused and taken

advantage of. Yet the Wesleys took the risk of preaching it. We can only imagine how unusual and liberating the news of free grace (even for the worst of sinners) is for people who are already alienated by societal and class condemnation and burdened by the judgment of one's conscience.

The Wesleyan revival affected not only adults but children too. John Wesley recorded that Mr James Hindmarsh, one of the Masters at Kingswood school, once reported (*JWJ* 26/9/1770) that ten of the children at Kingswood gathered round about him, asked him earnestly what they must do to be saved. He spent some time answering their question and tried to explain to them the nature of the Lord's supper as well. They prayed and, when bedtime came, the children withdrew to their rooms. Instead of sleeping the children spent the night wrestling in prayer. A maid was sent to persuade them to return to sleep. Instead of persuading them, she was persuaded by them to seek the salvation of her soul as well. Wesley recorded that they soon received assurance of salvation and it was not long before eight of the children and three maids were given their first communion.

There seemed to be no uniform practice as to when children were admitted to communion in the Church of England at the time of the Wesleys. Taylor in his book *The Worthy Communicant* indicated that 'infants, fools and madmen' could receive communion (it was ' lawful') but that was unnecessary since they cannot sin nor fall from grace (1667: 135–6, 147f, 156f). This opinion was quite similar to that of Luther's (1972: 162). Deacon, however, argued that children should be admitted to communion because they were included in all the Old Testament 'sacraments' like the passover, the eating of the manna and drinking of the water from the rock and in participation in the corporate fasts and feasts. As heathen feasts which include children defile them spiritually, the Christian sacrament sanctifies them. Although children are unable to discriminate or discern Christ's body, show forth his death or participate in self-examination fully, yet such limitations did not prevent the Church from baptising them. As Christ blessed them at baptism, He can make communion a means of grace for them too. They would need to be put under church discipline after communicating and practice of excommunication is as applicable to them as it is for adults (1716: 341–379). Not surprisingly, Deacon included an office in his service book of 1734 (*The Compleat Collection of Devotions*) for administration of the sacrament to infants. John Wesley himself was admitted at the age of 8 by his father (Tyerman 1866: 18–19). Moravians permitted children to communicate if they could give evidence of their faith. Their leaders would examine the children first in private, then in public. If the children were deemed ready, there would be an exhortation before the children were confirmed through the laying on of hands. Communion was then given to the children (JWW 11). It must be said that such openness to children was not unquestioned by people of that time. There were even those who found instructing young children about communion a questionable practice. John Wesley received a letter from a Miss MB on 4 March 1777 asking:

> Is it not useless, if not absurd, to teach children of six or seven years old, the answers to the question on the sacrament of the Lord's supper? Alas! what can they comprehend of that sublime mystery? How crude must be their conceptions (if they have any) of those deep and strong expressions! Ought I then against my judgement to teach it them, because their parents expect me so to do? (*AM* 1788: 103).

Yet when nine-year-old Elizabeth Bushell from Wilton was refused communion at her parish church, John Wesley placed the child on his knee and questioned her. Satisfied with her replies, he administered the sacrament to her (Bowmer 1951: 121). This was not a surprise because children of the first Methodists were often admitted as members of the Society at an early age. Albin in his research on the background of early Methodists suggested that the youngest admitted was seven years old (1985: 278). If those in the Society were required to observe constant communion, children were not exempt from the rule. There was evidence that Charles Wesley also administered the sacrament to children (*CWJ* 6/8/1749). At Kingswood School (which was set up for the sons of Methodist preachers), John Wesley held a communion where the children were allowed to receive. He later wrote:

> I suppose such a visitation of children has not been known in England these hundred years (*JWJ* 12/9/1773).

> It pleased God once more to pour out His Spirit on the family at Kingswood. Many of the children were much affected. I talked particularly with some, who desired to partake of the Lord's Supper. They did so the next morning. Afterwards, I spent a little time with all the children, and easily observed an uncommon awe resting upon them all (*JWJ* 2/10/1784).

We see that the practice of the Wesleys and of their leaders would be to prepare the children through some instruction, then examine the children individually for evidence of understanding and experience of the love of God. Communion would be given to them after that (JWW 1). What we see here is similar to the Wesleys' requirements for adults: some basic understanding and knowledge of the sacrament, some basic faith and the expressed need/desire to receive all that God wants to give them.

The Wesleys believed in free grace but they certainly did not believe in cheap grace. Hence there was a need for spiritual accountability for the sake of serious discipleship, especially with regard to participation in the sacrament. In their *HLS*, they warned people about taking the 'mystery' lightly (*HLS* 56). The virtue in the sacraments 'did not proceed from the mere elements but from the blessing of God in consequence of His promise to such only as rightly partake of them and are qualified for it' (JWW 12). Hence those damned for taking the sacrament unworthily (and it was clear that the Wesleys believed in divine judgment on unrepentant communicants) are not damned by some inherent power in the sacrament but by their participation in a thanksgiving for the grace they are just then actually refusing. 'Excommunication' of a kind was practised in the Methodist Societies as a form of discipline on those who were habitually unrepentant. In a letter to Mr John Benson, John Wesley instructed that those who have not 'constantly met their Classes', who did not 'solemnly promise to deal with stolen goods no more' should not be given tickets (JWL 32). The tickets referred to are the 'class tickets'. Class tickets were issued to Society members who had already been examined by their leaders in the area of morals and spiritual state. In Scotland, metal tokens were used in place of tickets. With the tickets or tokens, members could be admitted to Methodist communions (JWJ 1/4/1759). Visitors could request admission 'notes' from Wesley or his assistants before the service. These gave them permission to partake. According to Bennet's *Minutes,* such 'admission notes' were in use since 1747 (Bowmer 1963: 112).

Does the use of admission tickets and tokens to members indicate the introduction of a more rigid ruling regarding admission to the eucharist and thus a change in the Wesleys' more open eucharistic hospitality policy? No. Membership in the Methodist Societies, Classes and Bands indicated that the person was not only seeking 'to flee from the wrath to come' but was committed to seeking a life of holiness. The three eucharistic requirements of the Wesleys: acknowledgment of personal spiritual need, desire for the means of grace and willingness to change one's life, are met in the membership criteria. Hence all members could receive the admission ticket or token. The only extra dimension added was to ensure that the person *continues* to acknowledge need, *continues* to desire the means and *continues* to be open to change his or her life. Where the person failed to do that, the person would not be given admission to the Table. There was no place for a past-orientated commitment to the three requirements. The Wesleys pushed their members into having ongoing openness and commitment to the Lord. Did this mean that the Wesleys were now no different from those around them who required intensive preparation? No. The Methodists had their 'habitual' preparation in their Societies, Classes and Bands. This preparation was for daily holiness in heart and life. The 'preparation schools' called for intensive and focused preparation for the sacrament. The Methodists stressed more the grace of God. The concern is whether the potential communicant had the willingness and openness of spirit to receive that grace. This had nothing to do with the high requirements of knowledge, faith and worthiness laid upon people by the preparation manuals.

John Wesley certainly expected parish priests to discipline their flock with the practice of excommunication, commending those who actually dared to do so to powerful parishioners:

> Nay, who dares repel one of the greatest men in his parish form the Lord's table; even though he be a drunkard or a common swearer; yea, though he openly deny the Lord that bought him? Mr Stonehouse did this once. But what was the event? The gentleman brought an action against him for the terror of all such insolent fellows in succeeding times (JWW 2).

Two actions of John Wesley, however, could raise questions as to whether he had second thoughts about the practice of excommunication. When he abridged Fleury's *Moeurs des Chretiens*,[5] he omitted chapters covering the relics of the martyrs and confessors, eucharistic mysteries, ascetic orders and excommunication. He also omitted *Article* 33 of the *Articles of Religion* which was about excommunication when he abridged them for the Methodists in America. Was this an indication that John did not believe in excommunication? In the case of Fleury, John could have been reacting to possible Roman Catholic connotations in those passages he omitted. In the case of the *Articles of Religion*, Wesley's concern could have been more pastoral. The *Article* was entitled *of excommunicate Persons, how they are to be avoided* and that title in some ways

---

5.   Claude Fleury, a Roman Catholic, wrote *Moeurs des Chretiens* in 1682. The book described the life of the Christian community from the first to the seventh century, with special attention to the areas of discipline and ritual. The English translation of the book, *An Historical Account of the Manners and Behaviour of Christians,* was published in 1698. While John Wesley was in Georgia, he studied Fleury's work and abridged it, limiting it to the first three centuries (Campbell 1991: 35).

militated against the more generous spirit of the Wesleys' preaching of grace for all. Aware that the people in America were already living with the lack of ready spiritual resources which the English Methodists could take for granted, eg having opportunities for parish communions (however infrequent) and established Methodist societies, John was perhaps keener on encouraging them to come for the sacrament than to discourage them further with a threat of punishment. Certainly in his other writings we have mentioned, John Wesley seemed to approve the practice of excommunication.

One discipline John Wesley sought to impose on his people was a sense of reverence for the sacrament. This was not a 'requirement' for reception of communion but it was an attitude Wesley sought to inculcate in his people. When one reads John Wesley's accounts of eucharistic services, one notes his approval for 'serious' congregations (*JWJ* 6/8/1768, 26/10/ 1784, 10/9/1786) along with the factors which brought his disapproval: people moving around unnecessarily, coughing or spitting (*JWJ* 3/4/1756), caught up with their own wandering thoughts and imaginations during the service (*Sermon* 14). John believed that one's attitude should be humble as one approaches the sacrament (*Sermon* 2) and after reception, one should leave reverentially, not 'bowing, courtesying and talking to each other just as if they were going from a play' (*JWJ* 27/3/1752) or talking in 'the most trifling manner' (*JWJ* 23/4/1758). Even priests are to be mindful of giving glory to God at the sacrament. John remembered a 'dreadful inscription' placed just over the communion table which warned of curses on the priests should they not glorify God (*JWJ* 13/8/1759). He recorded with approval the celebration led by a bishop as that done with 'admirable solemnity' (*JWJ* 1/6/1775). Let it be said that reverence, seriousness and solemnity does not mean the absence of joy. Mentioned earlier was the fact that Methodist eucharistic services were joyous occasions. We note that the reverence and seriousness John looked for had to do with the inner disposition of respect for God and the sacrament rather than a depressed demeanour or the maintenance of a starchily formal mood. It is possible for reverence, seriousness, solemnity and joy to be present at the sacramental gathering at the same time.

Perhaps one of the most controversial questions today regarding Wesleyan eucharistic requirements has to do with John Wesley's use of the phrase 'converting ordinance' for communion. Interestingly, Wesley referred to the phrase twice (*JWJ* 27/6/1740, JWL 16), pointing to the sermon *The Duty of Constant Communion* (also known by the Scripture passage it was based on: *Do this in remembrance of me*) as the place where he had first mentioned the concept. However, careful reading of the printed sermon failed to locate the actual phrase. This does not necessarily mean that Wesley had not referred to it in his preaching. He had been known to preach extemporaneously before (*JWJ* 17/10/1735, 28/1/1776).

In any case, some Methodists saw Wesley's words 'converting ordinance' as a proof that Wesley practised a totally 'open' communion where anyone, even the unbaptised and the unconverted, could come to receive the elements. Davies is of the opinion that the older John Wesley no longer limited the sacrament to only baptised and episcopally confirmed people. Where there is evidence of real faith and intention to live a holy life, communion would be given (1961: 207–8). Lawson commented that 'the modern Methodist usage of a communion open to all who sincerely desire to take it is in accord with the spirit of Wesley's rule' (1994: 108). Certainly there is much in Wesley's sermons which warrant this view. The sermon preached on 21 April 1777 (*Sermon* 132) had Wesley's recalling of his practice of barring Dissenters and Lutherans from communion and not accepting lay baptism in his earlier years. It ended with 'full of these sentiments of zeal for the church, for which I bless God, He has now delivered me'. Did this imply that he now accepted Dissenter and Lutherans even lay baptism? Added to this sermon is John's refusal to see baptism as automatically guaranteeing new birth:

> Say not then in your heart, 'I was once baptised
> and therefore I am a child of God'. How many are
> baptised gluttons and drunkards, baptised liars,
> commons swearers etc. To say then that ye cannot
> be born again, that there is no new birth but in

baptism, is to seal you all under damnation,
consign you to hell, without help, without hope,
Lean no more on the staff of that broken reed,
that ye were born again in baptism (*Sermon* 18).

In the *Means of Grace* (*Sermon* 16), he had preached that
anyone can come to the Table as long as they are willing to
receive what God wants to give. The openness of the Table to
anyone seemed unmistakable.

Others have criticised this position as a misinterpretation of
the Wesleyan teaching. Wainwright insisted that 'there is no
active support in Wesley for the sloppy and sentimental
practice of parts of late Methodism in regularly welcoming the
unbaptised to the Lord's Table' (1987: 85). White agreed with
his position (1983: 129) as did Staples (1991: 263–4).

Bowmer in an article for the Wesley Historical Society
pointed to the context of Wesley's teaching found in his *Means
of Grace* sermon. Bowmer argued that the context of the sermon
was not referring to the admission of 'outsiders' to the
sacrament but that Wesley was struggling to get 'insiders', ie
members of the Society, to attend:

> Wesley's premise was 'The Lord's Supper is a
> converting ordinance' but his conclusion was
> not 'therefore everyone may come' but
> 'therefore members ought not to stay away,
> even if they had not received the full assurance
> of faith' (1963: 109–113).

He also argued that Wesley, while defending himself against
the charge of encouraging his people to partake without due
preparation, had indicated that he was referring to the
conditions of membership in the Methodist societies when he
said:

> . . . the habitual preparation which I had in
> terms declared to be indispensably necessary
> was 'a willingness to know and do the whole
> will of God 'and 'earnest desires of universal
> holiness' (JWL 17).

It must be said that the latter group of people do have a point. With regards to baptism, it would be difficult (though not impossible) to imagine the Wesleys going against the history of church tradition by admitting the unbaptised to the Table. The records of the early church would certainly place baptism as the most primary requirement for the sacrament. The *Didache* stated, 'let none eat or drink of your eucharist but such as have been baptised into the Name of the Lord, for of a truth the Lord hath said concerning this, give not that which is holy unto dogs' (chapter 9: 5). Hooker saw communion as linked to baptism in the way that communion continues the life that has begun in baptism: 'no dead thing is capable of nourishment. That which groweth must necessarily first live' (1940: 67). Waterland saw confirmation as highly expedient but baptism as strictly necessary (1737: 538). Taylor wrote that no unbaptised person can come to the holy communion (1667: 145). John in his early ministry required baptism before he administered communion to the person (*Sermon* 132). Baptism as a prerequisite for communion did not appear to be an issue of contention during the time of the Wesleys since most of the early Methodists were already baptised. Albin found in his study that of those whose church affiliation was recorded, 63.4% of the early Methodists had Church of England roots. Non–conformists accounted for 10%, Roman Catholics for 2.8%, Quakers 1.6% (Albin 1985: 276). Other than the Quakers, it would be natural to expect that all the Wesleys' followers were already baptised. Did the Wesleys insist that the Quakers be baptised before joining the Societies where they had to take the sacrament constantly? There was no evidence of that but we do have at least a record of four Quakers plus seven more who were 'educated among the Quakers' baptised by John Wesley between the years 1747 to 1756 (*JWJ* 1/5/1747, 6/4/1748, 30/4/1750, 2/8/1752, 16/10/1756).

Bowmer's textual study does underline the importance of knowing the context to which Wesley was addressing a sermon. If the 'converting ordinance' reference was meant to be only for 'insiders' (those in the Society) who were possibly baptised and in the 'seeker' category I mentioned earlier, then the table is not as 'open' as it had been made out to be by some present Methodists.

Although I believe a case cannot be made that the Wesleys were for opening the table to anyone regardless of the person's baptismal state, level of basic knowledge and faith regarding the sacrament, I would like to argue that if Wesley's reference to 'converting ordinance' means that preventing and justifying faith are given at the sacrament, there remains a possibility that the sacrament has the potential to inject life where there had been none there before (ie this could describe a pre-baptism or a pre-conversion stage). Could John Wesley have inadvertently laid a foundation which could be built upon by their followers in a different generation and culture facing a new missiological challenge? More of this will be explored in chapter 5.

How did Wesley come to see and emphasise the converting role of the sacrament? Was it his 'heart warming experience' which changed him? Or more possibly, an experience of encountering Christ at the Table himself? While seeking saving faith, he did decide to pray and use all other means of grace (*Sermon* 16). He did preach that the sacraments are not 'dry breasts', for God will deliver what he has promised (*Sermon* 104). Perhaps this shift in his thinking came from his own experience. One wonders if he reflected on that negative experience of being barred from the Moravian communion which he attended in Germany (Benham 1856: 40). In the light of what he had experienced as the gracious, seeking love of God, could he have wondered if Christ would have given him the faith he so badly sought at that time had he been able to communicate? It could very well come out of his encounters with those close to him who had such an experience: Charles (eg *CWJ* 24/5/1738 and 25/5/1738), his mother and, certainly, many of his followers. On 20 September 1739, for instance, he notes in his *Journal* that a woman who felt that she was without 'living faith' took holy communion. John noted in his *Journal* that she found that faith at the table (*JWJ* 20/9/1739).

Rack thought the 'converting ordinance' clause of Wesley was 'one new and highly unusual notion . . . to eucharistic doctrine'. He believed that Wesley used it to assure those who had been frightened off the sacrament by the intensive preparation schools of their time. Rack wrote of this 'converting ordinance' idea:

> This is so unusual and has so little precedent. The eucharist has then been seen as a sacrament of sanctification—a confirming ordinance. He (Wesley) only added a converting function to it after his conversion. There was little encouragement for such a notion in tradition. Luther and Calvin admitted that the eucharist might sometimes, exceptionally act to bring remission of sins or 'ingrafting into Christ'. High Church Anglicans stuck to the 'confirming' function, though it is interesting that Waterland admitted that the eucharist might convey all aspects of Christ's work, including cleansing from sin; and Wesley may well have read this. In his 1733 *Sermon on Constant Communion*, he says that it conveys 'forgiveness of our past sins' (1989: 405).

Careful reading, however, of *Article* 25 of the Anglican Church (*Of the Sacraments*), does support Wesley's view that communion is a 'converting' as well as a 'confirming' sacrament. The words used in the *Article* correspond to Wesley's words: 'Communion *quickens* as well as strengthens' (italics mine). The teaching was not new as Rack supposed, but perhaps it was not so clearly spelt out or emphasised during Wesley's time. It was present in embryonic form. Rack also suggested that the Puritans and the Moravians had no such teaching about 'converting ordinance', although among the Independents there were a few exceptions. People like William Prynne, John Humphreys and Jonathan Edward's father-in-law, Solomon Stoddard in New England, opened communion to the unconverted in hopes of converting them, meeting with some success in local revivals (Rack 1989: 405). Selleck agreed with Rack that Wesleys 'converting ordinance' idea was a departure from Anglican and reformation divinity and called it Wesleys' 'lasting offering to sacramental theology'. He indicated that Wesley could have borrowed and developed Stoddard's idea of 'converting ordinance'. Stoddard had merely seen the sacrament as a converting ordinance because it preached the word, ie the sacrament was a visible word. Wesley saw it as more than that, for the sacrament is of itself a real means of grace (Selleck 1983: 135–6).

The study of Wesleyan eucharistic practices leaves us with three questions. Earlier in this chapter we noted that the Wesleys, like the reformers and Anglican divines before them, called for very regular and frequent celebrations of the eucharist. We looked at the Wesleys' teaching regarding the rationale for communion and found that they did not differ very much from those held by the reformers or from their contemporaries. However, where the others failed, the Wesleys succeeded in starting a eucharistic revival, at least for a period of time. Even the efforts put in by the Wesleys to encourage eucharistic participation do not seem to adequately explain the reason for their success and for their followers' enthusiasm for the sacrament. The question arose: Was there a reason other than the Wesleys' effective efforts which motivated their people to respond in this way?

We saw the Wesleys' openness to use different places for their eucharistic celebrations. We saw how open they were to using lay leadership in their societies. However, this openness stopped short of allowing lay people as presidents of the eucharist. John Wesley's strong belief that a real outward sacrifice takes place at the eucharist and a properly ordained priest must preside at it and Charles's intense interest (which we shall see in the next chapter) in the concept of eucharistic sacrifice leaves us with another question: why were they so concerned about priesthood and sacrifice?

Finally, we noted that against the background of a culture living with preparation manuals and concern for adequate knowledge, sufficient faith and evidenced worthiness for eucharistic reception, the Wesleys were amazingly open in their eucharistic requirement. We therefore ask: why were the Wesleys so different from their contemporaries in their eucharistic requirements? For some answers to these three questions, we turn to the Wesleys' eucharistic theology.

2
Wesleyan Eucharistic Theology

Within the writings of the Wesleys on eucharistic theology and practices, we find three main emphases: a focus on the theme of the encounter with the presence of Christ, a stress on divine initiative and grace, and the role of the eucharist as a therapeutic sacrament.

1. Encounter with the presence of Christ

1.1 The dynamic encounter
The Wesleys believed that the eucharist is firstly, an encounter. This encounter can be experienced. It not only touches the five senses, it can radically affect the lives of those who have experienced it.

Zwingli[1] saw communion as an act of memory, remembering Christ and his death. The remembrance facilitates the contemplation of faith, illustrating and confirming the word that has been proclaimed. When the Wesleys edited Brevint's *The Christian Sacrament and Sacrifice*, they described in even less sympathetic terms; the Zwinglian position. They called it: 'a bare Memorial only' (Wesley 1745:13), replacing Brevint's milder description of it as 'a Representation made of outward shew without substance' (Brevint 1673: 44). They then followed

---

1. Zwingli believed that the main contribution of the eucharist was in stimulating faith in a Christian, encouraging the person to live the Christian life. Focusing on the subjective work of God in the eucharist (as opposed to the objective word of God), his 'memorialistic' position displayed a desire to protect the sovereignty of God, the freedom of the Spirit and the basis of the Christian status as faith in Christ (hence, there can be no other alternative meeting place). The elements merely remind us of Christ's work through his body, which is the sole source of salvation (Cocksworth 1993: 22–23).

Brevint, stating their position in marked contrast to the Zwinglian view:

> I want and seek my Saviour Himself, and I haste
> to his Sacrament for the same Purpose, that SS
> Peter and John hasted to his Sepulcher; because I
> hope to find Him there . . . (Wesley 1745: 13)

Communion to the Wesleys was not a 'dead external sign' (*HLS* 55/1). Even Archbishop Cranmer's receptionist understanding that communion creates the faith that helps to get the real job of communing with Christ done fell short of the Wesleyan eucharistic faith.[2] The focus of the eucharist for the Wesleys was not on the faith (nor of the worthiness) of the recipient. It is on the reality of a dynamic encounter with the presence of Christ.

Rattenbury aptly described the *HLS* as 'a Protestant Crucifix', a verbal one at that, made of 'carved words' (Rattenbury 1948: 16). The Wesleys invited their followers to be 'transported' (*HLS* 94/1) to see Christ's 'tremendous agony' (*HLS* 6/1), sufferings and death (*HLS* 8/2; 1/1; 3/2–3; 11/1; 20/1–4; 100/1) at the Table. In very visual and graphic language, the Wesleys presented the crucifixion and called upon believers to use all their senses not only in remembering it (*HLS* 77/2, 3; 39/1; 3/3; 4/3) but in experiencing it. The readers or singers of the *HLS* are invited in the sacrament to see (*HLS* 132/2; 140/2), touch (*HLS* 39/1; 131/2–3), hear (*HLS* 4/3–4; 7/3), feel (*HLS* 73/4) and taste (*HLS* 53/2; 158/3; 33/2). They are thus led 'sensibly' to believe (*HLS* 30/4).

Indeed the early Methodists experienced the reality of the encounter. Something happened during communion (cf *CWJ* 9/9/1741, 8/5/1744, 17/9/1748). There were visions: Mrs Planche claimed that she had 'marvelous views' of the Lord's sufferings and death for her during the sacrament (*AM* 1791: 420). Margaret Austin wrote, 'I saw Christ lay with his open side and I thought I could see his heart bleeding for me' (Rack

---

2.   Cranmer's position has as its focus the recipient rather than the elements. Faith of the recipient is the main ingredient. The sacrament has no intrinsic value if faith is absent (Cocksworth 1993: 29).

1997: 9–10).[3] Some of these were apparently seen in faith-inspired imagination rather than in a trance–like state (cf Elizabeth Down's testimony in Rack 1997: 9–10). Charles recorded:

> . . . in the prayer of consecration I saw, *by the eye of faith*, or rather, had a glimpse of, Christ's broken mangled body, as taken down from the cross. Still I could not observe the prayer, but only repeat with tears, 'o love, love!' At the same time, I felt great peace and joy; and assurance of feeling more, when it is best (*CWJ* 25/5/1737. Italics mine).

There were auditory experiences. Charles recorded:

> Yesterday, Miss Betsy plainly informed me, that, after her last receiving the sacrament, she had heard a voice, 'go thy way, thy sins are forgiven thee' and was filled thereby with joy unspeakable (*CWJ* 9/6/1738).

John Wesley reported this of the meeting at Macclesfield:

> We administered the sacrament to about thirteen hundred persons. While we were administering, I heard a low, soft, solemn sound, just like that of an Aeolian harp. It continued five or six minutes, and so affected many, that they could not refrain from tears. It then gradually died away (*JWJ* 29/3/1782).

Physical healings were known to take place at the table. A feverish and pregnant woman suffering a violent cough who

---

3.   Visions were not limited to communion times. It took place during class meetings as well (*AM* 1779: 301–2). Henry Rack acknowledged that 'a sense of the supernatural' is a 'marked feature' in some of the printed lives of the early Methodists (Rack 1997: 9).

was dying received the sacrament. Charles recorded that 'at the hour of receiving' she began to recover and was out of danger within a few days (*CWJ* 21/2/1735). The *Hymns* made reference to the healing power of the sacrament (*HLS* 58/1; 20/3; 25/3). There was expectation of deliverance from the powers of evil as well:

> Write our protection in Thy blood,
> And bid the hellish fiend pass by.
> (*HLS* 41/2)

The often sensory and definitely significant experiences did not leave the communicants unaffected. The Wesleys noted that many were 'wounded and many healed' at the Lord's supper (*JWJ* 20/7/1777). Intense temptation and inner struggles which for some always took place before communion were resolved at the sacrament (*AM* 1779: 301–2 cf *JWJ* 6/3/1760: Elizabeth Longmore's testimony). There were other effects of the service on individuals: The *HLS* proclaimed that one's past, present and future are touched by the sacramental encounters.

Negatives of one's past are dealt with at the Table. Communion brought to some a strong conviction of sin. Richard Jeffs, who was determined to renounce the Methodists and join the Quakers, ventured to receive communion. John Wesley noted: '. . . he had no sooner received, than he dropped down, and cried with a loud voice, "I have sinned; I have sinned against God" (*JWJ* 4/11/1744). The Wesleys promised that when we grieve over our sins (*HLS* 6/1–2, 120/2), we receive pardon, grace, assurance (*HLS* 28/3; 38/3; 164/1–3; 1/4). Our pain and suffering are handed over to Christ, and 'harboured in his breast' (*HLS* 93/4); we find the power of sin subdued (*HLS* 160/3 cf 33/4; 37/2). Testimonies affirmed the hymnic claims. There were many accounts of those who were freed from the burden of sin. John Wesley reported his mother's experience:

> (About) two or three weeks ago, while my son
> Hall was pronouncing those words, in delivering
> the cup to me, 'The blood of our Lord Jesus
> Christ, which was given for thee'; the words

struck through my heart, and I knew God for
Christ's sake had forgiven me all my sins (*JWJ*
3/9/1739).

There were those who felt the assurance of God's
acceptance. Thomas Tennant, one of the Methodist preachers,
reported: '(I was) . . . enabled to believe that Christ died for *me*,
and was filled with peace in the Holy Ghost' (*AM* 1779: 471–3).
Ruth Hall claimed: 'I then found an uncommon degree of
Assurance, that I should see eternal life . . .' (*AM* 1781: 663–4).
Howell Harris was drawn to the sacrament when he was dead
in sin, and received forgiveness there; afterwards the love of
God was 'shed abroad in his heart by the Holy Ghost, then
given him' (*CWJ* 6/5/1740).

The present is affected too. Charles described one of the
present fruits of the encounter as having one's eyes opened
(*CWJ* 14/5/1740). Conversions took place at the eucharist.
Wesley appealed to his followers' experiences when he wrote to
the Revd Mr Church. He said:

> For many now present know, the very beginning
> of your conversion to God (perhaps in some the
> first deep conviction) was wrought at the Lord's
> supper (*JWJ* 27/6/1740).

At Avon and Malmsbury, he noted that one 'was still full of
her first love, which she had received at the Lord's Table' (*JWJ*
2/6/1740). A study of the lives of 555 early British Methodists
(recorded in the *Arminian Magazine* and other early sources) by
Albin reported that 4.5 % of these people were converted while
preparing for or receiving communion. This is quite a
significant percentage considering that in most of the cases
studied, conversions took place when the individual was alone
(42.8%) rather than when the person was in a public preaching
service (27.7%)(Runyon 1985: 275).

Other present graces include the gifts of strength, comfort,
love, peace (*CWJ* 20/10/1736; 5/6/1738; 6/6/1738; 11/2/1739;
28/9/1740, 20/4/1746; 7/8/1748) nourishing us (*HLS* 4/2,

9/1–2, 30/6), cheering our hearts (*HLS* 30/5), meeting our every need as it seems best to him (*HLS* 76/4).

Not only did the Wesleys teach that one's past and present are affected by the encounter at the Table, they taught that one's future is marked by it as well. The 'tokens of His favour' we receive (*HLS* 162/1) serve as 'pledges' (*HLS* 53/2, 100/2–3, 107/1) and 'earnest' (*HLS* 103/1–2, 158/2) of that glory/ rest/bliss that is to come. 'Sealed and stamped' (*HLS* 30/3) as his, with his love put in our souls (*HLS* 31/3, cf *HLS* 166/4 'impregnated with life Divine'), we can live a life of holiness (*HLS* 31/2) now, as Christ lives in us (*HLS* 164/7; *HLS* 30/6, 30/8). There is a new hunger for God: what Charles called the 'drawing of the Father or preventing grace' (*CWJ* 6/4/1740, cf. *HLS* 28/1; 94/2; 113/1) which safeguards one from falling into sin. This rekindles a deep desire for the restoration of the *imago Dei* within oneself (*HLS* 32/2) and a growing love of God and neighbour (*CWJ* 1/8/1736).

Again, Methodist testimonies bear witness to this teaching of the Wesleys:

> I found my heart drawn out in desire after God . . . I now loved to read the Bible, and to pray to God, according to the faint light I had (*AM* 1779: 241).

This was echoed by two others

> . . . and for some weeks after, the things of eternity were the very delight of my soul. O! how precious was the word of God? How did I love private prayer? To converse about the ways of God, was my meat and my drink, by night and by day. Thus I went on for several months, drawn by love, and allured by the goodness of God my Saviour (*AM* 1779: 183).

> After this I walked in the loving fear of the Lord, and in the comforts of the Holy Ghost. I found great sweetness in the word; yea, and in all the other means of grace . . . (*AM* 1779: 471–3).

One's view of life and the world was changed. Thomas Olivers saw that all of his life was tied in with the sacrament:

> In eating and drinking, I took care to do it to the glory of God; to this end I received my daily food, nearly in the same manner as I did the body and blood of Christ (*AM* 1779: 87).

Communion was seen as a time for fresh re-commitment to God. Thomas Rankin wrote that 'I . . . fully resolved to dedicate myself to God. In order thereto, I purposed to partake of the Lord's Supper . . .' (*AM* 1779: 183). Margaret Baxter recognised the reception of holy communion as a point of the renewing of her baptismal covenant (*AM* 1984: 196).

Specific changes in lifestyle made by Methodists at the table ranged from the seeking of solitude:

> I broke off from all my companions, and retired to read on the Lord's day; sometimes into my chamber, at other times into the field; but very frequently into the church-yard, near which my father lived. I have spent, among the graves, two or three hours at a time, sometimes reading, and sometimes praying, until my mind seemed transported in tasting the powers of the world to come (*AM* 1790: 11 cf. *AM* 1779: 301–2).

to discovering a call to active service:

> Meantime I found an earnest desire to live to the glory of God, together with much love to precious souls. And hence I found a desire of preaching . . . (*AM* 1779: 471–3).

The encounter with Christ in the eucharist was not seen simply as an experience which is individualistic in orientation. Charles reported on several occasions that the eucharist brought upon the communicants 'the spirit of prayer' and 'the spirit of intercession' (*CWJ* 24/2/1745, *CWJ* 27/4/1746, *CWJ* 23/6/1745) and on one occasion 'strong intercession for departed friends' (*CWJ* 10/3/1745). Once Charles recorded that at the table, they received 'the Spirit of prayer for my dear desolate mother, the Church of England' (CWL 3).

Communion services and such prayers were often accompanied by tears and cries, affecting even the celebrant:

> I began the sacrament with fervent prayer and many tears which almost hindered my reading the service. I broke out into prayer again and again . . . (CJW 24/7/1748 cf *CWJ* 4/1/1745; 13/1/1745).

The eucharist as taught and experienced by the Wesleys was *not* a refuge for those who wanted to avoid emotional involvement. We find such accounts over and over again in the *Journals* and in the *Arminian Magazine*:

> The whole congregation were in tears, or in triumph; crying after God, or rejoicing in His favour. The cloud rested upon us the whole time of communicating (*CWJ* 5/7/1747).

Charles wrote of one of the Methodist Society's celebration of the sacrament, 'we all found, more or less, the power of His resurrection' (*CWJ* 14/4/1745). There is no surprise therefore that despite the Wesleys' great success in their preaching ministry, John could write: 'I found much of the power of God in preaching, but *far more* at the Lord's table' (*JWJ* 13/11/1763. Italics mine). Holy communion to the Wesleys was a dynamic encounter which could be experienced and which changed lives.

1.2 The presence of Christ
Communion is more importantly an encounter with a person, the living Christ. It is significant that John Wesley's favourite description for holy communion was 'the Lord's Supper'. The phrase appeared more than 200 times in the Jackson edition of his *Journal*. 'The Lord's Table' was Charles Wesley's second

favourite term for communion in his *Journal,* appearing on no less than seven occasions. John used it more than fifty-eight times. The emphasis of the brothers is doubtless on the One whose supper or table it is. John Wesley's second favourite term for the sacrament is 'communion'. It appeared about seventy-five times in Jackson's edition of his *Journal.* The relational intimacy of the word in terms of divine–human interaction is significant.

We read in contrast Zwingli's focus. Zwingli's orientation was drawn towards the human participants of the communion. His early writings indicate an interest in the role of communion in strengthening the faith of weak believers and assuring them of the forgiveness of their sins (Stephens 1986: 180, 192). His later writings stressed the place of communion as the location where believers publicly make a stand of loyalty to God. Communion was the oath or pledge of allegiance (Stephens 1986: 181). This concentration on the human and subjective aspect of the sacrament was due to his concern that the sovereignty of God and the freedom of the Spirit would be compromised or curtailed by talk of Christ's actual presence being bound in some way to the sacrament. Yet by down-playing the more God-ward and objective understandings of communion, he succeeded only in producing a rational and cerebral theology which allowed very little place for dynamic divine intervention.

Both Luther and Calvin would agree with the Wesleys on the reality of the encounter. All four saw communion as a sacrament, a means of grace. They believed in the presence of Christ at the eucharist. Yet the Wesleys differed from Luther and Calvin on the nature of that presence. Luther sought to emphasise that the Christ who comes to us in the eucharist is the same one who came in the incarnation: Christ's body in the sacrament is the same as the one he had on earth. Luther argued using the concepts of *communicatio idiomatum* (communion of properties) and ubiquity (omnipresence) (Stookey 1993: 53). John Wesley, commenting on Matthew 26: 26, 28, dismissed the argument: '. . . it is grossly absurd to suppose that Christ speaks of what he then held in his hands as his real, natural body . . . ' (*ENNT*). The Wesleys rejected the Lutheran idea of ubiquity.

We need not now go up to heaven,
To bring the long-sought Saviour down;
Thou art to all already given,
Thou dost even now thy banquet crown:
To every faithful soul appear,
And show Thy real presence here!
(*HLS* 116/5)

Borgen observed:

(John) Wesley rejects the Lutheran views of
consubstantiation and ubiquity, which require a
communicating of the properties of the divine
nature to the human. Christ is only omnipresent
according to his divine nature; therefore, in order
to communicate the benefits of his human life and
death to us, these must be, as it were, at the
disposal of Christ's omnipresent God (1986: 65).

Calvin possibly sensed that Luther's argument had the
danger of confusing the two natures of Christ. Trying to
safeguard the integrity of the person of Christ, Calvin taught
that the body of Christ is in heaven and it retains all its human
properties (*Institutes* 4: 17: 26 cf *Sermon* on 1 Corinthians 10:
15–18, *CR* 49: 667). The attributes of divinity cannot destroy its
true fleshy nature (*Institutes* 4: 17: 24). What believers receive at
communion is the whole Christ (*totus Christus*). Calvin was
careful to affirm that 'the sacraments direct our faith to the
whole, not to a part of Christ' (*Institutes* 3: 11: 9) and that not
only His Spirit and divine nature are mediated to us but also his
whole humanity which was centred in his earthly body. Union
with Christ is union with the whole Christ (Wallace 1953: 200).
Yet Calvin speaks often of the presence in terms of *'virtus'* or
power of Christ given to believers (Gerrish 1993: 178 footnote
70). This sometimes gives the impression that he is talking
about a quasi-physical matter linked to Christ (Gerrish 1993:
177) rather than the person of Christ himself.

Calvin also had reasons for not wanting to talk about the
localisation of the presence: he was aware of the abuses of
transubstantiation and he held a very strong view of the

transcendence of God. He thus insisted that there is no descent of the body of Christ, no 'transfusion of substance' (*CR* 9: 70, *CR* 9: 521. Commentary on 1 Corinthians 11: 24, *CR* 49: 487, cf *CR* 16: 430). Using the spatial language of his time, Calvin taught that the whole Christ (*totus Christus*) is received by the believer at communion through the Spirit of Christ, who lifts the believer up to heaven to partake of his life:[4]

> Christ, then, is absent from us in respect of His body, but dwelling in us by His Spirit, He raises us to heaven to Himself, transfusing into us the vivifying vigour of His flesh just as the rays of the sun invigorate us by His vital warmth (*CR* 9: 33).

> The bond of connection is therefore the Spirit of Christ, who unites us to Him and is a kind of channel by which everything which Christ has and is, is derived to us (*Institutes* 4: 17: 12).

Mindful of the same concerns as Calvin, the Wesleys were able, without resorting to Calvin's solutions, to affirm the integrity of Christ (without giving the impression of separating the natures, as Luther did) and avoid the danger of locating his presence in a way which downplayed divine transcendence. They did it in two ways: by the use of Trinitarian images and terms and by the utilising of time-transcending rather than spatial language. Unlike Calvin, they were also able to avoid the impression that the encounter was with a power or some quasi-physical matter by the use of personal pronouns and focusing on the person of Christ. Brevint's *Treatise*, attached to the

---

4.   There have been times when Calvin would speak of Christ's 'descent ' to earth (*CR* 16: 677) but Wallace commented that he does that only after 'he has made it clear that Christ remains entire in heaven . . . and that the descent is always a "spiritual and heavenly one"' (Wallace 1953: 208). Sometimes Calvin speaks of the descent of Christ as a mode by which he raises us up to himself (*Institutes* 4: 17: 16).

Wesleyan eucharistic hymns which contain very moving, personal prayers to the Christ, sets the tone for the *HLS*.

To the Wesleys, the presence we encounter at the eucharist is that of Christ. It is the same Christ as he who walked in Palestine but yet it is a Christ seen from post–resurrection perspective, ie seen through eyes of those who share the historic Christian faith. The boundaries of time are suspended as our human past is seen in the light of the relationship between the Father and the Son. Gallaway described this relationship as that which 'extends Christology in one way, emphasizing the cosmic significance of Jesus' life and ministry, identifying his work with the origin and goal of creation'. The relationship between the Son and the Spirit 'extends Christology in another direction, by recognising that the work of Jesus is not simply concerned with the past but with the future of creation as well' (1988: 2–3). The total Christ is thus presented. The question of 'Which body of Christ is it?' which so concerned Luther fades to insignificance.

Staples noted that the Wesleys stress the presence of Christ more in terms of his divinity (1991: 227). There could be some truth in Staples' observation, if we look at the references to Christ which have been traditionally reserved for the Father, eg 'the Ancient of Days '(*HLS* 156/1), the 'author of Life Divine' (*HLS* 40/1), the 'God of angels' (*HLS* 21/6). Christ is presented as the Old Testament God who saves his people, the 'Rod of Moses' (*HLS* 27/2), the 'Rock of Israel' (*HLS* 27/1). Christ's divine nature is implied very strongly in terms like 'the God of angels dies' (*HLS* 21/6), 'expiring God' (*HLS* 6/1), 'Jehovah dies' (*HLS* 21/4). Perhaps this was the Wesleys' reaction against the threat of Arian theology present during their time. There is, however, no confusion of the relationship between the Son and the Father. As the Son who is one with the Father, Christ reveals the Father by being the 'Beam of the Eternal Beam' (*HLS* 164/7) who shows forth the heart of the Divine, 'the Great Invisible' (*HLS* 116/3), whose nature is love (*HLS* 30/3–4, 29/4), the 'eternal Lover' (*HLS* 162/3) who suffers and dies for us (*HLS* 1/2, 21/2, 9/5, 12/1). It is interesting to see that John Wesley, when he edited Brevint's book, often omitted the 'Jesus', preferring to address him as 'Christ' (Wesley 1745: 6, 21; Brevint 1673: 12, 72).

Central to the Wesleyan eucharistic hymns is the theme of the God–man as sacrifice. More of this will be mentioned later but we note here that Christ's humanity is acknowledged clearly here. He is called 'the Second Adam' (*HLS* 32/2), who is the Saviour (*HLS* 116/5). He saves by being the paschal/spotless Lamb (*HLS* 4/1, 35/1, 116/1, 117/1, 2/3 cf 166/1). He is described as the 'Traveller with garments dipped in blood' (*HLS* 17/1), the 'Martyr' (*HLS* 2/4), the 'Victim Divine' (*HLS* 116/1) 'the Great High Priest' (*HLS* 129/1 cf the new Melchizedek and Aaron *HLS* 46/2), 'the Victim' (*HLS* 5/1, 131/1), 'the Wheat that is cut down' (*HLS* 2/1), the 'Redeemer of mankind' (*HLS* 12/2), 'Author of salvation' (*HLS* 28/1), 'the World's Atonement' (*HLS* 163/5).

Kishkovsky lamented that there was a 'certain absence of the resurrection' in the Wesleyan eucharistic hymns. He stated that there was only one direct reference with 'some indirect allusions' to the event, so the cross and crucifixion appeared seemingly 'in and of itself as the point of entry to joy, salvation and life . . .' (1995: 81). While I would agree with his observation that the Wesleys have that tendency to focus on the cross, the number of occasions at which the resurrection was referred or alluded to in the Wesleyan eucharistic hymns appeared more substantial than his remarks seem to indicate. The allusions were about his 'rising' (*HLS* 4/4; 19) and he was given certain titles, eg 'Triumphant Head/Lamb'(*HLS* 128/3; 21/9), 'Strong Trium-phant Traveller' (*HLS* 17/1), 'Lord of Life' (*HLS* 34/1). The resurrection story from John's gospel finds a place in *HLS* 29/1 and 55/2–3. Christ is seen as the firstborn or 'Elder Brother' (*HLS* 132/3) of humankind. In both Brevint's and John Wesley's edition of his text, the resurrection is mentioned at least once (Brevint 1673: 81, Wesley 1745: 24).

Christ's cosmic significance in his role now as Intercessor (*HLS* 140/2; 117/2) in heaven (*HLS* 118/1) for us is clearly addressed in his title as the 'Advocate' (*HLS* 163/6) who pleads our cause before the Father with his bleeding hands, his body 'torn and rent' (*HLS* 118/2–3), offering Himself perpetually to the Father (*HLS* 117/1) even *now* as eucharist is being celebrated. He pleads for pardon for us (*HLS* 120/4) whose names are graven on his hands, whose lives are set among the precious stones on 'his loving breast' (*HLS* 117/2, using the image of Aaron's ephod). His wounds are effective intercessors for us:

> Five bleeding wounds He bears,
> Received on Calvary;
> They pour effectual prayers,
> They strongly speak for me:
> Forgive him, O forgive! they cry,
> Nor let that ransomed sinner die!
> (*Collection* 194/3 cf. verses 1–2)

The time-transcending Christ, presented against a trinitarian background, breaks out of theological time–bound categories applied to the eucharist. The meal is not simply a past-orientated memorialistic gathering. It is not just a present space-located action-be it understood as transubstantiation or Calvin's 'upward lifting' of communicants to heaven. The question of the permanence of the consecration which would tie the presence of Christ to the elements becomes less of an issue in this light. The dynamism of the experience can scarcely be contained and frozen in time. The Wesleys therefore rejected the Roman Catholic and the non-juror inclination to see the consecration as permanent (cf *HLS* 63/2). There could be no reservation of the sacrament for them. In John Wesley's editing of Cave's work for the *Christian Library*, it is significant that he omitted passages in Cave which indicated the early church's practice of reserving the sacrament and that reserved consecrated elements were carried about by the early Christians (Campbell 1991: 96).

While the Wesleys proved to be true sons of the reformation and of the Anglican Church of their parents, they moved beyond Cranmer's receptionist position. They did not state that the efficacy of the sacrament depended totally upon the inner state of the communicant. As we have seen in chapter 1, while some basic faith is called for, the sacrament can bestow faith where adequate faith is lacking. The influence of the non-juror friends discerned in the Wesleys' inclusion of an *epiclesis* on the elements in their eucharistic hymn collection (cf *HLS* 72) affirmed that there was some form of objective consecration.

Bowmer also believed that the Wesleys were not pure receptionist in their theology, in that they did not deny absolutely a presence apart from the believer (1951: 176), but he felt that the Wesleys did not give a very satisfactory account of the relationship between the real presence and the elements. I wonder if he was a bit unfair in stating the latter. The position of Lancelot Andrewes, in his Christmas Day sermon of 1618, could be a close description of the Wesleyan view:

> Christ in sacrament is not altogether unlike Christ in the manger. Eucharistic elements are both outward symbols but 'yet in them find we Christ'. The sacrament consists of a heavenly and an earthly part, the *res sacramenti* and the *signum sacramenti*, the *signum* and the *signatum*, which are united together without either being 'evacuate or turned into the other' as are the two natures of Christ. Christ in the eucharist is truly present and to be adored *(res sacramenti)*, but we are not to adore the sacrament. The elements are the vehicle of the Spirit, the proper carriages to convey it (quoted in Dugmore 1942: 41).

Similarly, Waterland's illustration citing St Bernard, comparing the sacraments with instruments of investiture and describing the elements as a deed of conveyance which conveys the estate even thought it is not the estate (1738: 146–7), might be the position with which the Wesleys found themselves in sympathy. The underlining belief is that consecration simply sets apart the elements for sacred use. The sacraments are 'enfleshed' physical contact points or instruments of the word. Certainly, this finds an echo in their *epiclesis*, pleading that the elements might be '. . . fit channels to convey Thy love' (*HLS* 72/2). More of this will be discussed in a later section on the role of the Spirit.

What happens at the eucharist is that we are invited to stand before the crucifixion as in a 'time-warp'. The Wesleys would prefer the biblical imagery of looking behind the 'veil' (*HLS* 93/1). In Calvin's mind, the Holy Spirit lifts up the communicants to where Christ is, in heaven. Although *HLS* 57 verse three mentions an upward movement, 'how can heavenly spirits rise, By earthly matter fed . . .', further evidences of such understanding have proved hard to find. The verse could mean a rising from the sphere of the earthly and material by those who are destined for higher/spiritual matters. The Wesleys might not have planned to pen any theological insight into the location or movement of Christ or of the communicants in this hymn after all.[5]

With the Wesleys (as with Brevint), although Christ is in heaven as eternal priest and intercessor, one cannot help but feel that the movement is more sideways than upwards: with the removal of the 'veil' which blinds us, we can see Calvary just before us (*HLS* 3, 18,122). Quoting Brevint, the Wesleys insisted:

> . . . the main intention of Christ therein, was not, the bare Remembrance of His passion; but over and above, to invite us to His sacrifice, not as done and gone many years since, but, as to grace and mercy, still lasting, still new, still the same as it was first offered for us (Wesley 1745: 6).

The 'past historical event' has become what Ole Borgen (Stacey 1988: 71) called 'the Eternal Now', brought about by the Spirit. Thurian speaks of a situation where 'the past event became present or rather each person became a contemporary of the past event' (1966: 19). The remembrance (*anamnesis*) is

---

5.   Some Wesley scholars have tried to show John Wesley's indebtedness to Luther and Calvin. Hildebrandt's *From Luther to Wesley* aligned Wesley to Luther. Cell in *The Rediscovery of John Wesley*, Sanders and Parris, presented Wesley in a Calvinistic mould. Yet it must be admitted that John never refers to Calvin in his discussions of the sacraments (Staples 1991: 228). Outler considered the attempt to make John a theological heir of Continental Protestantism as 'a notion that would have astonished Wesley'.

There are a few instructive parallels between Wesley in the eighteenth century and Luther and Calvin in the sixteenth, but it is highly misleading to interpret him as their conscious debtor (Outler 1964: 119–120).

seen as a dynamic participation in the past event rather than a recollection made psychologically. The Wesley brothers acknowledged that the passion was 'in this mysterious rite brought back' (*HLS* 123/3). We therefore experience 'anew' the presence in the sacrament.

The eucharist is referred to by the Wesleys as 'a memorial of the sufferings and death of Christ' (*HLS* title of Section One). In the eucharistic hymns, this 'memorial' entails the believer 'arriving' at the foot of the cross to behold Christ's first and only sacrifice in reverence and adoration as it is happening:

> See the slaughter'd Sacrifice,
> See the altar stain'd with blood!
> Crucified before our eyes
> Faith discerns the dying God . . . (*HLS* 18/2).

There are times when the believer 'arrives' at the point of his death, beholding him 'as newly dead' (*HLS* 3/3), noting that 'still the blood is warm' (*HLS* 122/3). In his context of this heightened awareness of Christ's presence at the eucharist, the encounter takes place between the communicant and Christ in a dynamic and personal way.

Finally, it must be said that there is a place for mystery in Wesleyan eucharistic theology. McAdoo observed that Brevint is in the Anglican tradition from Andrewes onwards through such as Bramhall, Thorndike, and Taylor in refusing any mandatory definition of what Hooker calls 'the manner How' (McAdoo 1994: 252). Reading the Wesleyan eucharistic hymns, I believe the same can be said of the Wesleys. Issues like:

> How the bread His flesh imparts,
> How the wine transmits His blood . . .
>
> . . . How we the grace receive
> Feeble elements bestow
> A power not theirs to give . . .
>
> How can heavenly spirits rise,
> By earthly matter fed . . .

(*HLS* 57 / 1, 2, 3)

have no answers except

> Sure and real is the grace,
> The manner is unknown . . .

> Thine to bless, 'tis only ours
> To wonder and adore
> (*HLS* 57 / 4).

Bowmer claimed that the brothers understood that the presence is close to the classical Anglican position which was 'content to insist on the "virtue" imparted in the sacrament and to leave the question of the "how" of the sacramental action ultimately unresolved' (Bowmer 1951: 91). While I would disagree with Bowmer's suspicion that the Wesleys held Calvinistic virtualist views[6] the statement about the second is fair. There is a recognition of the limitations of the human intellect to comprehend the works of God:

> God incomprehensible
> Shall man presume to know;
> Fully search him out, or tell
> His wondrous ways below?
> Him in all His ways we find;
> How the means transmit the power—
> Here He leaves our thoughts behind,
> And faith inquires no more.
> How He did these creatures raise,
> And make this bread and wine

---

6.   Virtualism has been defined by Stevenson as 'a tendency to see the Presence of Christ in his virtue and power in the elements, while the elements themselves remain bread and wine'. Stevenson would later say that the Wesleys in their eucharistic teaching were saved from virtualism by the very personal elements found in their eucharistic theology (1994:172f). The Wesleys' stronger and more personal expressions of the presence made it clear that Calvin's vague quasi-physical references to 'power' did not adequately describe the experiences of the eucharistic encounter.

Organs to convey His grace
To this poor soul of mine,
I cannot the way descry,
Need not know the mystery;
Only this I know—that I
Was blind, but now I see
(*HLS* 59/1–2).

For the Wesleys, the human response to this mystery is simply to accept the gift of the presence, the fruits of the encounter, and to give grateful thanks.

In the last chapter we saw the tremendous evidence of Wesleyan eucharistic revival and we asked: Was there a reason other than the Wesleys' effective efforts which motivated their people to respond in this way? Perhaps here lies the answer: the encounters the communicants had with the presence of the living Christ at the table. No power of intellectual argument, strategic organisation or determined leadership can compare with the impact of a dynamic and deeply personal experience which touches one's senses and emotions. Charles Wesley wrote of one communion service:

> Our Lord was made known to us, as He always is, in the breaking of bread. Let the Quaker and Orthodox dispute about the ordinance: our Saviour satisfies us a shorter way (*C W J* 25/5/1746).

Something happened at the table. That was why there was an eucharistic revival. This leaves us with the question, 'why then did that revival die?' We will explore this question in chapter 5.

2. Divine initiative and grace

Two other questions we raised in the last chapter were: 'why were the Wesleys so concerned about priesthood and sacrifice?' and 'why were the Wesleys so different from their contemporaries in their eucharistic requirements?' I believe that this had to do with the Wesleys' desire to redirect the focus from 'human work and activity' to 'divine initiative, grace and generosity'. Without eradicating the need for human action as a response to God's love, the weight of the Wesleys' teaching fell on who God is and what God does (his character seen through the work of Christ) and promises rather than what humans are or have been doing. This is seen very clearly through the way the Wesley brothers presented the theme of sacrifice and the role of the Holy Spirit in their eucharistic theology.

2.1 Christ's sacrifice and our offering

The Wesleys were strong on the subject of sacrifice. There are several sacrifices linked to the eucharist. Of the seven eucharistic sacrifices mentioned, the first two have to do with the direct work of Christ. The third has our participation in that we plead his sacrifice. The last four are our sacrifices to him.

First, there is Christ's sacrificial death on the cross, without which there would be no eucharist. Neville Shepherd, then a doctoral candidate at Bristol University, shared in an informal gathering that in his research on the views of the Wesleys on atonement he came to the conclusion that the position of the Wesleys was basically substitutionary. Shepherd's present research into Charles Wesley's teaching of the atonement has also led him to see that the second most used concept is that of Christ as sacrifice. The third concept is that of Christ as representative Adam. The *HLS,* which bears the names of the two Wesleys, certainly reflects this theological slant. The other categories which are present in lesser degree in the hymns are those that see the cross as ransom and as victory.

As the second Adam, the fully human Christ bears the full extent of the Father's wrath, receives the 'rage of sinful man' (*HLS* 2/2, 2/4) suffering at the hands of both (*HLS* 2/5). He offered himself as a ransom (*HLS* 132/1–2). He takes our sorrows and sins (*HLS* 156/2,133/1) by making 'expiation and oblation' (*HLS* 128/1), atonement (*HLS* 132/2) as a sacrifice that is sweet and pleasing to God (*HLS* 116/4). By doing this, he made it possible for us to begin anew, free from the 'seeds of pride and lust' and the desires of the world (*HLS* 135/4), living lives unto God.

Christ's sacrifice is a one-time event (cf *HLS* 122/1, 121/2), unrepeatable and complete (*HLS* 124/1). The Roman Catholic teaching about the mass gave the impression that the sacrifice was repeated at every celebration. Heirs of the Protestant Reformation like the Wesleys were always very careful to contend against this.[7]

Christ's sacrifice was voluntary and it was 'for all'. The Calvinists claimed that Christ died only for the elect. Against this position, the Wesleys preached salvation for everyone who would respond. The 'for all' theme echoes through many of the hymns: 'dead for all, for me He died' (*HLS* 164/4), 'Th' atonement Thou for all hast made' (*HLS* 79/2 cf. *HLS* 131/3, 30/7). The table is for the healing of all:

> Lord, I have now invited *all:*
> And instant still the guests shall call,
> Still shall I *all* invite to Thee . . .
> . . . That where *all* is there *all* should be.

While for the Roman Catholics love for Christ seemed to be more focused on Christ as a person whose character is expressed in his life, for the Wesleys love for Christ seemed to be more in response to his love expressed most vividly on the Cross. Yet to the Wesleys there is no romanticism or inordinate focus on Calvary. Christ, the work on the cross, the present work of Christ and the eucharist are inextricably linked. Who he is and what he does are one. Christ is the sacrificial lamb, the one sacrifice to appease God's wrath. Christ also is the revealer of

---

7.   To summarise the differences between the Wesleyan understanding of the eucharist as sacrifice and the Roman Catholic understanding, we need to focus on two key aspects: First, to the Wesleys, Christ's sacrifice for our salvation is a one-time, fully sufficient, unrepeatable and complete event. The impression given by the Roman Catholics during the time of the Wesleys was that the sacrifice was repeated at every eucharistic celebration. Second, the Wesleys taught that the church 'pleads' the sacrifice of Christ. It does not offer Christ to the Father as a mediating intercessor. The church's role is active in a receptive mode. The only other sacrifice offered at the eucharist is the offerings of the people in acts of self-surrender to God.

God's heart of love. Christ is the ascended yet perpetual priest-intercessor, the 'Master of the Feast' (*HLS* 84/3). Rattenbury says

> And although doing this (remembering Him) always involves a memory of Calvary, always shows forth the Lord's death till He come, it is Christ crucified, not the crucifixion of Christ which we are told to call to mind (Rattenbury 1948: 94).

Second, the eucharist is Christ perpetually offering himself to God, as high priest and victim, pleading as our advocate-intercessor:

> Before the throne my surety stands;
> My name is written on his hands.

> He ever lives above
> For me to intercede;
> His all-redeeming love,
> His precious blood to plead:
> . . . (His wounds) pour effectual prayers,
> They strongly speak for me . . . (*Collection* 194/1,
> 2, 3).

This theme, developed from the epistle to the Hebrews, is not new to the Wesleys. Non-juror Nelson's book, *A Companion for the Festivals and Fasts of the Church of England*, which John Wesley read in his pre–Aldersgate years, made reference to it (Nelson 1704: 467–8). McAdoo claimed that the theme of the heavenly altar and heavenly intercession, which had its roots in Irenaeus's thinking (McAdoo 1988: 69), continued through seventeenth century Anglican theology. It was at the heart of Brevint's understanding of the eucharist as both sacrament and sacrifice. It was also central to Taylor's eucharistic theology (McAdoo 1994: 246–7, see also McAdoo 1988: 67).

The Wesleys used time-transcending language in which the believer 'arrives' at the foot of the cross during the eucharist, during or just after the crucifixion.

Still the wounds are open wide,
The blood doth freely flow
As when first His sacred side
Received the deadly blow:
Still, O God, *the blood is warm*
(*HLS* 122/3. Italics mine).

George indicated that 'the idea that the blood still flows is a way of saying that the death is still efficacious' (1964: 154). What is unusual is that the Wesleys' desire to emphasise the 'still efficacious' nature of Christ's sacrifice led them to use metaphors beyond what Scripture described. They pictured Christ still standing before God's throne in many of the eucharistic hymns. In *HLS* 117/1, Christ 'still offer'st up Thyself to God'. The writer of the epistle to the Hebrews, however, has Christ the high priest seated after making his once and for all sacrifice (10: 12). The Scriptures are clear that the sacrifice was completed. All that needed to be done was done. George concluded that there is no inconsistency between the two spiritual states which they represent—namely, that he stands to plead, or he sits in triumph. With regard to Christ's continued intercession in a 'standing' mode, he referred to Hebrews 9: 24 where Christ entered heaven 'now to appear in the Presence of God on our behalf' and Revelation 5: 6 where 'a Lamb standing, as . . . slain' (George 1964: 152). Perhaps it would be fair to say that the interest of the Wesleys was not in denigrating Christ's victory or suggesting that the work of atonement was incomplete. The Wesley brothers wanted to emphasise his role in the present moment, as the active, effective and committed Intercessor those for whom he gave his life.

The third sacrificial act linked to the eucharist is that we plead his sacrifice as Lamb of God to God (*HLS* 118/4, *HLS* 14/1) praying for God to hear his blood interceding for us (*HLS* 14/1), to look at us 'through Jesus' wounds' (*HLS* 120/1), to 'behold Him' (*HLS* 121/1, 2, 119) as we 'spread before His eyes' (*HLS* 125/2) the one, eternal, not to be repeated, sacrifice of Christ. Rattenbury sees a kind of parallelism at work here. He says:

> . . . just as the Priest Victim in heaven pleads the
> cause of the sinful for whom He died, so on earth
> by means of the bread and wine, the tokens of His
> love, we plead the death of Christ
> (Rattenbury 1948: 109).

This 'showing forth' of his death is to God the Father and also to Jesus, pleading: 'O remember Calvary and bid us go in peace' (*HLS* 20/1–4).

When Stevenson identified the different Eastern church liturgical 'families', he found that the Egyptian school saw the putting of the elements on the altar as the only offering involved. The Antiochene one, however, had a rather elaborate commemoration and 'pleading' of Christ's sacrifice/oblation. It had a consecratory *epiclesis* as well. Perhaps the Wesleys were closer to this school liturgically. They displayed, in their eucharistic hymns, both characteristics of the Antiochene school (1984: 209–228).

The view of the eucharist as the sacrifice of Christ presented to the Father was not new in Anglican theology. The problem was how to disengage the term from the Roman Catholic understanding of the mass as the church offering Christ to the Father. It has to be made clear that the church can only plead or 'offer up' (*HLS* 125) the sacrifice of Christ. There is a need to hold on tightly two 'ground rules': commitment to the sole sufficiency of Christ's unrepeatable sacrificial death, pleading its effects on the present (Cocksworth 1993: 44) and admission of the church's actively receptive role in the salvific act. MacAdoo described Taylor's picture of the Offerer being offered 'as sacrificed' in conjunction with his perpetual offering to the Father in heaven (McAdoo 1988: 65). Bramhall called the eucharist a 'commemoration, a representation, an application of the all sufficient propitiatory Sacrifice of the Cross' (McAdoo 1988: 69). What is new is the weight the Wesleys gave to the emphasis that it is a sacrifice. It is true that they did not shrink back from referring to communion as a Christian sacrifice (*CWJ* 28/3/1738) nor from using the word 'altar' (*HLS* 18/2). Where Brevint in his original text had subtitled 'of the Holy Eucharist, *as it implies a Sacrifice*. And first of the Commemorative Sacrifice' (Brevint 1673: 71. Italics mine), the Wesleys while following the words of his subheading in their hymns (Wesley 1745: 98), changed Brevint in their edition of his work. They had it down as 'concerning the Sacrament, *as it is a Sacrifice*. And first, of the Commemorative Sacrifice' (Wesley 1745: 20. Italics mine). This is a stronger affirmation of the sacrificial aspect of the sacrament when we consider Brevint's rather tentative reference to the eucharist as a 'kind of sacrifice' (Brevint 1673: 74–75).

Where Brevint wrote:

> To men 'tis a Sacred Table, where God's Minister is ordered to represent from God his Master the Passion of his dear Son, as still fresh and still powerful for their Eternal Salvation: and to God *it* is an Altar whereon men mystically *represent* to him the same sacrifice as still bleeding and *still* sueing for *expiation* and mercy (Brevint 1673: 75–6) (italics indicate the words Wesley removed).

Wesley replaced the words 'represent' with the stronger word 'present' (Wesley 1745: 22).

Why this strong emphasis that it is a sacrifice presented to God? One possibility is that the Wesleys were writing against a background where the Roman Catholics had accused the Protestants of having no external sacrifices. Thus, the argument goes, the Protestants would have no priesthood and no church. Dr John Harding of Louvain was of that mind and he had a long-running controversy with Bishop John Jewel about the matter in the sixteenth century (Jewel 1847: 16, 410). The Anglican divines insisted that there is sacrifice offered at the eucharist. While they referred to the offerings of the people—prayer, alms, praise, thanksgiving, human lives (Jewel 1847: 410, Waterland 1738: 28)—Jewel and Laud both named Christ's own sacrifice as well. Even if the Roman Church would not recognise the other sacrifices as such, they could not ignore the latter. The issue of an external sacrifice spilled over to the eighteenth century (cf Waterland 1738: 55–56). This could have spurred the Wesleys to emphasise the reality of the holy eucharist as a sacrifice in which the effects of Christ's sacrifice are pleaded for. This they believed in strongly. We have to note that it was because they believed in an outward sacrifice like this that they held on strongly to an outward priesthood (Rattenbury 1948: 76.77). This understanding kept the early Methodist revival from being a lay movement in spite of its popular use of lay leadership. It also was the cause of John Wesley's ordinations which finally resulted in the separation of the Methodists from the Anglican Church.

Another outcome of the Wesleys' preaching regarding the 'pleading' of his sacrifice was they were able to affirm in a very strong way the present efficacy of Christ's unique unrepeatable and costly sacrifice of Christ made on the cross. This has powerful implications in a pastoral sense for their ministry. People caught in the cycle of addicting habits (like alcohol) or socially deprived situations (eg poverty leading sometimes to a life of crime) would need to be assured that every time they succumbed to ready temptations, there would still be fresh and 'plenteous grace' to 'cover all (my) sin' (*UMH* 479).

Does this mean that the Wesleys believed the church could 'activate' Christ's sacrifice by pleading for its application? If so, this is a problem, as Williams suggests:

> Who is the agent of the eucharist? . . . If Christ's sacrifice needs 'activation', this suggests that Christ is not now mighty to save by and through his accomplished work. It is he and he alone who pleads his sacrifice. Doctrines of eucharistic sacrifice transfer the agency to church or priest and thus immobilize Christ (1982: 3).

Although Williams was not referring to the Wesleys, his observation needs to be taken seriously. Just as prayer or the lack of it cannot be seen as 'turning on or off the tap' for God to act, neither can the plea or silence of the church be seen as the sole cause of 'activating' or 'not activating' Christ's sacrifice. This accusation might have had some weight if it had been directed against Roman Catholic eucharistic understanding during the time of the Wesleys. For the brothers, Christ is the intercessor. The church joins in his intercession. Unlike some aspects of late medieval Roman Catholic teaching, such intercession has no power to automatically claim any tangible benefits of his passion and certainly not to do so for anyone who might not be willing consciously to receive it. The Wesleys had often stressed the relationship between divine grace and human cooperation. All the believers are called to do is to commemorate the sacrifice before the Father:

> With solemn faith we offer up,
> And spread before Thy glorious eyes
> That only ground of all our hope,
> That precious, bleeding sacrifice . . .
> (*HLS* 125/2).

Although the next two lines sound as if the action of God is tied to the actions of the believer: '. . . Which brings Thy Grace on sinners down, And perfects all our Souls in One', the fourth stanza indicates that it is not an automatic 'cause and effect' action. God the Father is the one who has the final word. We simply offer the prayer, trusting in his grace:

> Father, behold Thy dying Son,
> And hear His blood that speaks above,
> On us let all Thy grace be shewn,
> Peace, righteousness, and joy, and love.
> Thy kingdom come to every heart,
> And all Thou hast and all Thou art
> (*HLS* 125/4).

Finally, through their strong teaching about the once-and-for-all work of Christ on the cross, his continuing work of presenting his sacrifice before the Father by his intercession for us and our pleading for the effects of his sacrifice, the Wesleys were able to underline their theme of the initiating, providing and sustaining grace of God in their eucharistic theology.

It is only with the grace of God as the backdrop that the Wesleys moved on to the fourth sacrificial reference: that of the eucharist as the offering of ourselves to him. This offering entails the giving of our very beings: our wills (*HLS* 133/5), our souls, bodies (*HLS* 153/2), our zeal, thoughts, desires (*HLS* 152/3). It is the offering of tears (*HLS* 152/2), sorrow for our sin, our mourning in grief and shame (*HLS* 133/2–3). It is our commitment to die to sin daily (*HLS* 141/6, 8; 135/1, 2):

> The feet which did to evil run,
> The hands which violent acts have done,
> The greedy heart and eyes,
> Base weapons of iniquity,
> We offer up to death with Thee
> A whole burnt Sacrifice.
>
> My hands I stretch out to Thee,
> My hands I fasten to the tree . . .
>
> No more may they offend . . .
> (*HLS* 149/1–2).

Luther and Calvin, Brevint and the Wesleys saw the believer first as recipient at the Table, then as the one who gives in response to God's love, ie first the 'sacrament', then the 'sacrifice' (Wainwright 1994: 13). Calvin, for instance, was very insistent on the gracious nature of the sacrifice, so much so that he would see that the application of Christ's passion is not when it is confirmed by new oblations but when we receive the fruits of it:

> (The Supper is) a gift of God which was to be received with thanksgiving . . . as widely as giving differs from receiving, does sacrifice differ from the sacrament of the Supper. But in receiving the gift we apply the once-offered sacrifice to ourselves (*Institutes* 4.18.7).
>
> This I say, is the way in which the sacrifice of the cross is duly applied to us: when it is communicated to us to be enjoyed and we receive it in true faith (*Institutes* 4.18.3).

The Wesleys, however, in comparison with the other two, displayed a stronger degree of concern about the response of the recipients. As insistent as they were about the prevenient and pro-active grace of God, they were passionate about human response to that grace. This is in line with their teaching about the eucharist as a relational sacrament. Since the encounter people have at the table is with a person (Christ), one's relationship with him would not be on a strictly utilitarian plane where the question, 'what do I get out of this?' is the only concern. The stress on human response to the grace and love of God in Christ testify to the existence of a personal relationship.

The fifth reference to sacrifice is on a more positive, pro-active mode: the offering of our willingness to live his life, identifying with him in his sufferings (*HLS* 134/3; 148, 149), 'panting' or full conformity to his likeness (*HLS* 130/1). This is described in two ways. First, as cheerful reception of perse-cution, chastisement, even martyrdom (*HLS* 142/6–7; 144/3–4). Wilson in *Many Waters Cannot Quench*, described the sufferings of the early Methodists. Opposition was experienced from the gentry, aristocracy, clergy, the university and some govern-mental authorities. Persecution was received at the hand of families, neighbours, employers. They had to contend with mob violence, public ridicule and written accusations (Wilson 1969: ix–x). John Wesley, commenting on Colossians 1: 24, spoke of the unity of suffering among Christians and how those sufferings arc united with those of Christ and used by him as testimony to others of gospel truth. Wilson felt that Wesley's conception of the Lord's supper took on special significance because Methodists were 'compellingly reminded of the relationship between their sufferings and those of Christ'. The Supper was, among other things, a strengthening reminder to the suffering Christian that there will be reward for his suffering and beyond the present is the hope of glory (Wilson 1969: 148–151).

Second, the sacrifice is expressed in forgiving foes, like Stephen in the book of Acts (*HLS* 144/4). John Wesley wrote in his *Journal*:

> I was well pleased to partake of the Lord's
> Supper with my old opponent, Bishop Lavington.
> O may we sit down together in the kingdom of
> our Father! (*JWJ* 29/8/1762).

The sixth aspect of sacrifice and offering the Wesleys taught is that of our goods. The Wesleys referred not to divestment of material things in the sense of voluntary poverty, but to the cultivation of a spirit of detachment quite akin to what we read in a part of *The Directions for Renewing our Covenant with God* in the *Covenant Service*.[8] The *Directions* read:

> . . . Make me what thou wilt, Lord, and set me
> where thou wilt . . . let my dwelling be upon the
> dunghill, my portion in the wilderness, my name
> and lot amongst the hewers of wood, or drawers
> of water, among the doorkeepers of thy house;
> any where where I may be serviceable; I put
> myself wholly into thy hands: put me to what
> thou wilt, rank me with whom thou wilt; put me
> to doing, put me to suffering, let me be employed
> for thee, or laid aside for thee, exalted for thee, or
> trodden under foot for thee; let me be full, let me
> be empty, let me have all things, let me have
> nothing, I freely and heartily resign all to thy
> pleasure and disposal . . . (Tripp 1969: 183).

One of the eucharistic hymns described it thus:

> Welcome whate'er my God ordain!
> Afflict with poverty or pain
> This feeble flesh of mine,
> (But grant me strength to bear my load)
> . . . Whate'er Thou send'st, I take it all,

---

8.   On 11 August 1755, John Wesley introduced to his people a service for corporate renewal of Christian commitment. A primarily New Year observance, the *Covenant Service* became linked with the celebration of holy communion for the Methodists and was held regularly mainly in London, Bristol, Dublin and Newcastle (Tripp 1972: 154).

Reproach, or pain, or loss . . . (*HLS* 143/3, 5).

Determin'd all Thy will t'obey,
Thy blessings I restore;
Give, Lord, or take Thy gifts away,
I praise Thee evermore
(*HLS* 145/5 cf Baker 1962: 131 *A Hymn at the Sacrament*).

It is noteworthy that the communion was associated with the *Covenant Service* on possibly all occasions (Tripp 1969: 31). They reinforced each other in the spiritual formation of Methodists.

Finally, there is the offering of our prayers and praise (*HLS* 161/2 cf *Collection* 493/3): in songs' (*HLS* 161/2), loud lifting voice and joy (*HLS* 162/2) as the 'stammerer's tongues are loosed to praise' (*HLS* 158/3). Around our altars, we are joined with 'listening angels, heavenly powers (*HLS*164/2), 'arch-angels' (*HLS* 161/2) and 'our Elder Brethren' (*HLS* 162/2) in praising God. We are not alone. The angelic hosts, the church triumphant, joins the church militant in the celebration of communion.

Although the Wesleys gave high place to thanksgiving and praise, they were not as strong as Calvin in stating it in the context of communion. Wallace noted that in the first edition of the *Institutes*,

> Calvin saw that an essential aspect of the Lord's Supper was the presence of such a willing sacrifice of gratitude to God on the part of the communicants, and he expressed himself willing to give this sacrificial and spontaneous response of thanksgiving the name of 'eucharistic' sacrifice (Wallace 1953: 215).

The Wesleys, on the other hand, did not appear very keen on the use of the word 'eucharist'. It appeared about eight times in Jackson's edition of John's *Journal*. These references were used mostly in his correspondence with Conyers Middleton, Jeremy Taylor and writings about the Roman Catholic Church. Charles seldom used the term in his *Journals*. This could be because the term was not among those more commonly used in the vocabulary of eighteenth century Church of England.

There is yet another aspect of this sacrifice of praise which we ought to note in the eucharistic hymns. Although Methodists were often rewarded with the experiences of Christ's presence at the Table, there were moments when they felt dry and abandoned. As we have noted in chapter one, Charles recorded some such experiences. In moments like these, the eucharist becomes in a very real sense a sacrifice of prayer and praise. As the Wesleys described it:

> And shall I let Him go?
> If now I do not feel
> The streams of living water flow
> Shall I forsake the well?
>
> Because He hides his face,
> Shall I no longer stay,
> But leave the channels of his grace
> And cast the means away?

They concluded with

> He bids me eat the bread,
> No other motive, Lord, I need
> No other word than Thine
> (*HLS* 86/1, 2, 5).

The Wesleys looked at the sacrifice of Jesus and the sacrifice we bring and asked, 'how can the two oblations join?'. For one is all holy and all divine. The other is 'human and weak, and sinful' (*HLS* 147/2). Their solution is to 'conjoin' (*HLS* 133/4), 'mix' (*HLS* 153/2) our sacrifice with his, and 'supported by His sacrifice' (*HLS* 152/4, cf 141/5, 140/3), our offering is presented to the Father, in, with and through him.

> Our mean imperfect sacrifice
> On Thine is as a burden thrown,
> Both in a common flame arise,

And both in God's account are one
(*HLS* 147/4).

In the end, perhaps the Wesleyan teaching is reflective of the Augustinian concept that we are able to offer ourselves only in so far as we are incorporated through communion 'in the supreme oblation of Christ' (Brilioth 1930: 284). Again, the theme of grace surfaces in Wesleyan eucharistic theology: it is through his grace that our offerings can be acceptable to him.

It might be helpful to note here that the sacrifice of ourselves mentioned by the Wesleys are not merely individual sacrifices:

Clothed in His righteousness, receive,
And bid me one with Jesus live,
Join all He sanctifies in one,
One cross, one glory, and one crown
(*HLS* 152/5).

As Rattenbury pointed out, the word 'we' appears in all the hymns.

There is no exception to the rule that the pronouns are plural in all the hymns of Eucharistic oblations (1948: 132).

The individual aspect of the corporate offering is obvious already in the personal nature of the hymns. Unlike Roman Catholic eucharistic theology (see chapter 3), the Wesleyan one did not subordinate the corporate element of the sac-rament to individualistic devotions—eucharistic or otherwise. If there was any prayer spirituality, it would be generated within the context of the liturgy and flow from there into the communicants' daily lives. Use of the *HLS* and devotional texts like Brevint's possibly provided this means of deepening one's eucharistic experience. The corporate element of the eucharist, so important to the Wesleys as it was to the reformers and to the Wesleys' Anglican forbears, meant loving God in love for one's neighbour expressed not only in worship but also in actual life situations.

Some themes about eucharistic sacrifice seem to be missing or have been left undeveloped in Wesleyan eucharistic theology. One is Irenaeus's teaching on the eucharist as an offering of creation, represented by the eucharistic elements. John Wesley could not have been unaware of, schooled as he was in the writings of the early Church Fathers. He had also included in his *Christian Library*, Nelson's *A Companion for the Festivals and Fasts of the Church of England*. In it was Nelson's answer to the question, 'What was the End and Design of Instituting the Sacrament of the Lord's Supper?' Nelson had written:

> To be the Christian Sacrifice, wherein the Bread and Wine are offered to God, to acknowledge him *Lord of the Creatures*; and accordingly in the Ancient Church they were laid on the Table by the Priest, as they are still ordered to be done by the Rubrick in the Church of England, and tendered to God by this short Prayer, Lord we offer thy own out of what thou hast bountifull given us, which by conservation being made Symbols of the Body and Blood of Christ . . . (1704: 467–8. Italics mine).

George sees the Wesleys as followers of Cyprian's theology which focuses on the passion of the Lord as the main sacrifice that is offered at the Table (George 1964: 152, 157). The second theme was the picture that St Augustine held—that the members of the body of Christ are being offered on the table as the eucharistic elements (Wakefield 1995: 146). Perhaps in the light of the special and urgent vocation of the Wesleys, namely, to convert people to Christ, their choice of focus in the eucharist on the passion and work of Christ rather than the redemption of creation was intentional. Williams indicated that Irenaeus had little interest in the imagery of 'propitiation by bloodshed' and that instead of the sin-offering understanding of the eucharist, Irenaeus's teaching on eucharistic sacrifice would be more that of the eucharist as thank-offering (Williams 1982: 10). Given the Wesleys' strong substitutionary beliefs about the atonement, it is understandable that they would choose to leave out

Irenaeus's eucharistic theology from their works. One puzzle, however, remains. We know that John Wesley was no admirer of Augustine. He had described Augustine's character sarcastically as 'a wonderful saint! As full of pride, passion, bitterness, censoriousness and as foulmouthed to all that contradicted him . . .' (*Sermon* 68). Yet dislike for a person would not be a good reason for not using his theology especially when it would have been a very powerful and effective image for eucharistic spiritual formation.

There is one more possible reason for why the Wesleys did not include the above themes. Both mentioned had one common thread: the focus is on what humans do. The use of these themes could well distract people from what the Wesleys wanted to highlight in their eucharistic theology: the central place and importance of the radical, active and hospitable grace of God.

2.2 The roles of the Holy Spirit

The Wesleys further strengthened the theme of divine initiative and work of grace by the roles they attributed to the Holy Spirit in the eucharistic service. The Wesleys mentioned the Holy Spirit (Ghost) at least thirty times in the *HLS*. Reference was made to the Spirit in 26 out of the 166 hymns (ie 15.66%). These hymns are found in four out of the five sections into which the hymns were divided.[9] This is quite impressive on three counts.

First, it is a high percentage considering that the hymns were about the passion, death and work of Christ as well as the Lord's supper, where the Son and the Father would be expected to take central place.

Secondly if we compare the *Hymns* with Brevint's text, noting that the hymns grew out mainly from the text, we see in Brevint that there was only one prayer directed exclusively to

---

9. References to the Holy Spirit in the *HLS:* From Section I: 5/1; 7/1; 10/4; 16/1, 2. From Section II: 30/4, 53/3, 71/3, 72/1; 75/3; 77/3; 78/6; 89/4; 92/1 (not counted but there is an allusion to the Spirit 76/1 cf Psalm 139). From Section III 93/4; 94/4; 112/1. None from Section IV. Section V: 130/2; 131/4; 137/7; 138/2; 150/1, 2; 151/1; 155/1, 6. Section VI 159/2; 163/7; 166/19, 20.

the Spirit (Brevint 1673: 54). In the three other occasions where the Spirit was referred to, the prayers was to the Father (*HLS* 53/1, 3), the Son (*HLS* 77) or to the Trinity (*HLS* 155). In the *HLS* however, prayer was made to the Holy Spirit alone on 6 occasions (*HLS* 7, 16, 72, 75, 112, 151). Three times he was addressed in prayer, along with the other two Persons of the Trinity (*HLS* 155/1, 155/6, 163/7).

Third, if we compare the number of references to the Spirit in the Wesleyan eucharistic hymns with those found in the Brevint text, one can see the weight the Wesleys gave to the place of the Holy Spirit. The Spirit was mentioned only ten times in Brevint (Brevint 1673: 12—twice, 21, 54, 79—twice, 103, 127—twice, 128). This is a mere third of the number the Wesleys had.

In Brevint's work, the Spirit, promised to the disciples (Brevint 1673: 21), was primarily seen as a teacher, an enabler and a sanctifier. The Spirit teaches us to perceive and consider Christ himself in other people, leading us to give of our own to serve them (Brevint 1673: 127) He enabled Jesus by being the one 'by whom' Jesus' offering to God was given (Brevint 1673: 12). He enables us to to perform the service we promise to offer to God (Brevint 1673: 103) and to do good moral work (Brevint 1673: 128). As Sanctifier, he is the Spirit of holy cleansing (Brevint 1673: 54). While he has a role in the life of the believer, his role in the eucharist seemed to be rather vague. Brevint presents it in a very weak manner: in a prayer addressed to Jesus, Brevint asked that the Lord bless the sacrament and 'send with it *some* influence of that Spirit . . .' (Brevint 1673: 79) The Wesleys strengthened it by saying, '. . . send with it *the* influence of the Spirit . . .' (Wesley 1745: 23), referring possibly to the specific tasks of the Spirit in the sacrament which he draws out in the *Hymns*.

In the *HLS*, the Spirit has four major roles, both in the believer's life as well as in the sacrament. He is, first, the 'Remembrancer Divine', being the 'Witness to His Dying 'and 'True Recorder' of Christ's passion (*HLS* 16/1–2). He is thus invited to help us remember and feel (even to the extent of groaning for it) Christ's suffering and work, applying the power of his salvation on our lives. He is also asked, in *HLS* 16 and *HLS* 7—both of which are in the (eucharist) 'as it is a Memorial of the Sufferings and Death of Christ' section—to witness inwardly in us that we may recognise and experience Christ and his work in the sacrament, his 'seal' (*HLS* 7/1–4).

He is the life-giver. In the sacrament 'as it is a Sign and a Means of Grace', the Spirit is called upon to do a quickening work (presumably in us through the elements) that we may 'feel' and 'sensibly believe' as we receive the 'tokens of Thy dying love' (*HLS* 30/4). This work might be said to be the conveyance of faith, which enables us to receive in our hearts the powerful effects of Christ's death, presence and divine love (*HLS* 75/3–4, 71/3 cf *HLS* 92/1). The end result of the fullness of his Spirit coming upon the believer would bring a store of blessings, 'love and power', 'present peace, future bliss', 'power to walk in all well pleasing' (*HLS* 78: 6–8) and 'joy unspeakable' (*HLS* 89/4).

He gives life not only to people but also to the institution of the sacrament and to the sacramental elements. There is a prayer to the Father (or the Son. The hymn did not make it explicit which of the two is invoked) for the descent of the Spirit: 'come in Thy Spirit down . . . Thine institution crown . . .' (*HLS* 53/3). The *epiclesis* on the elements found in *HLS* 72/1–2 was addressed to the Spirit directly:

> Come Holy Ghost, Thine influence shed,
> And realize the sign,
> Thy life infuse into the bread,
> Thy power into the wine.
>
> Effectual let the tokens prove,
> And made by heavenly art
> Fit channels to convey thy love
> To every faithful heart.

In the sections on the eucharist as 'Concerning the Sacrifice of our Persons' and 'after the Sacrament', the Spirit is seen in a further role as a kind of companion-sanctifier, involved in the believer's identity formation. He gives life to a Christian buried by the waters of baptism (*HLS* 130/2). As the Spirit of Christ was transmitted to the early church through the sacrament

(*HLS* 166/4), so that work continues through the sacrament, preparing us to live with God (*HLS* 159/2), filling us with divine love (*HLS* 77/3). His desire, passion and cry for partaking in the life of Christ (*HLS* 131/4, 137/7, cf *HLS* 166/19–20) find an echo in us. Our offering to God of ourselves is through the Spirit (*HLS* 138/2, 150/1) who sanctifies our offerings (*HLS* 150/2), helping us as a Spirit of contrition (*HLS* 151/1–2), leading us to obedience (*HLS* 150/2).

Finally, for the Wesleys in the *HLS*, the Spirit is the 'Assurance Giver'. In the eucharist 'as a Pledge of Heaven' the brothers have a picture of the 'loving Spirit' (*HLS* 94/4 and 93/4) who, somehow behind the scene, is working and leading the communicant actively in experiencing Christ at the sacrament. This Spirit is the seal or promise of the eternal bliss. Perhaps the assurance is rooted in the fact that the Wesleys 'put a face' on to the Holy Spirit by identifying him with Jesus in a very intimate way. In hymn 112/1, it is the 'eternal Spirit' who is said to have 'gone up on high'. This is a phrase which is more associated with Jesus in Ephesians 4: 8–9 ff. than with the Holy Spirit. Verses 2 and 3 of the hymn confirm that it is indeed Jesus whom the Wesleys were talking about here, yet the Spirit is referred to in his place.

When we study the number of times the references to the Spirit appears in each hymn section, we can see that the Wesleys put more weight on the Spirit as a 'companion-sanctifier' than in any other role. Thirty-three per cent of the hymns or three out of nine in 'after the Sacrament' section and 23.3% or seven out of thirty hymns in the section 'Concerning the Sacrifice of our Persons' have to do with this role. The Spirit as 'Remembrancer Divine' has 14.81% or four out of twenty-seven hymns. The Spirit as 'Lifegiver' in the section 'As it is a Sign and a Means of Grace' appeared in 13.84% or nine out of sixty-five hymns. The Spirit as 'Assurance Giver' and 'As a Pledge of Heaven', came out with thirteen per cent or three out of twenty-three hymns. Since the Wesleys saw Christian perfection or 'holiness in heart and life' as the goal for every Christian, this emphasis on 'companion-sanctifier' is very significant. The believer is not expected to work at sanctification alone. The Spirit does it, with the believer, during and after the sacrament. John Wesley echoed the position of the *HLS* when he wrote in one of his letters that the Holy Spirit is the 'immediate cause of all holiness in us' (JWW 13).

The only section of the *HLS* the Wesleys did not find a role for the Spirit was in the eucharist 'as it implies a Sacrifice'. biblical references play a major part in inspiring the contents of the eucharistic hymns. Could it be that there was no ready biblical reference to the Spirit in that particular aspect of salvation drama?[10] The main players in that scenario were the Father and the Son. Yet there were references in other sections about the role of the Spirit which could be appropriate in this particular section, eg when the Son offered that sacrifice, it was through the Spirit that the sacrifice was made (*HLS* 5/1). The Spirit speaks 'in the blood' (*HLS* 138/2), presumably not just to us but to the Father if we follow the biblical records. Yet the Wesleys probably wanted to focus on the Father–Son inter-action and they allowed nothing in which would distract the reader from the central issue.

The practice of having an *epiclesis* (invocation of the Holy Spirit's action) over the elements was observed in the Eastern rather than the Western church. At the Council of Florence (1438), the East held that the words of institution were merely the narrative which gives the dominical authority for the sacrament while the *epiclesis* was the sole formula needed for consecration. The West insisted that the words of institution sufficed. This became the battleline drawn between East and West (Maloney 1967: 464–5). The 1549 *BCP* had an *epiclesis*. Cranmer in the *BCP* of 1549 put these words before the words of institution: 'with Thy Holy Spirit and Word vouchsafe to bless and sanctify these Thy gifts and creatures of bread and wine'. The prayer was a combination of Eastern and Western views of consecration. The 'Word' mentioned here referred to the 'Words of Institution' (Clarke 1964: 342). This *epiclesis*

---

10. Most of the biblical passages the Wesleys used regarding sacrifice are taken from the book of Hebrews. Looking at the verses where the Holy Spirit is referred to in that book, namely Hebrews 2:4; 3:7; 6: 4;9:8;10:15, and even checking the *ENNT*, failed to surface any reference to the Spirit which the Wesleys could use on this theme (that they might not have alluded to somewhere else).

disappeared from the subsequent *Prayer Books* of 1552, 1559 and 1662. In contrast to their church's omission of the *epiclesis* from their eucharistic service (in the 1662 *BCP*), the Wesleys introduced the *epiclesis* in their eucharistic hymns.

The *epiclesis* in the Eastern church followed the words of institution. Deacon had his *epiclesis* after the institutional narrative, as it was practiced by the Eastern Church (Wainwright 1994: 10). Did the Wesleys follow this? Alexander admits that it would be impossible to find an answer based on the well-known epiclesis hymn *HLS* 72. However, from the structure of *HLS* 3/1, 4, he postulates that the liturgical order was institutional narrative, anamnesis, oblation, and epiclesis (1995: 47–8). If it is true that the Wesleys used the *epiclesis* hymns during their eucharistic celebrations and they had the hymnic *epiclesis* AFTER the words of institution, it could follow that the Wesleys shared the Eastern church's view regarding the epiclesis as the key factor in the consecration of the elements. This is an attractive proposition, but there does not seem to have enough evidence in the Wesleyan *corpus* to suggest (or deny) that it was put into actual practice.

John Wesley did not include the *epiclesis* in *The Sunday Service* liturgy (1784) he prepared for the Methodists in America. This has raised the question of how important the *epiclesis* is to the Wesleyan understanding of the eucharist. Would the Wesleys be basically in the Latin tradition which would see the words of institution as the main consecratory act, and the *epiclesis* as a useful but optional extra? Or did Wesley assume that the American Methodists would sing the *HLS*, including the two *epiclesis* ones, during their services? There is no doubt that the Wesleys believed that something actually takes place during the consecration. When they ran out of consecrated elements during an unusually packed eucharistic service, John Wesley wrote: 'I was obliged to consecrate thrice' (*JWJ* 4/11/1787). The question is: What did Wesley consider as the consecrating aspect of the service—the words of institution or the *epiclesis* (in hymnic or other forms)? Wesley in his revision of the *BCP* for the people in America had the rubric regarding reconsecration of the elements specify that the prayer of consecration was to be repeated. The usual practice (ie according to the rubrics in the 1662 *BCP*) was to repeat the words of institution. The prayer of consecration, however, included not only the words of institution (the institution narrative and the *anamnesis)* but preceded these with a prayer of thanksgiving for God's gift of Christ and a kind of preliminary *epiclesis* directed to the Father. White suggested that this rubric indicated a shift from 'the medieval and Lutheran attitude that the verba effected consecration rather than the whole act of thanksgiving' (White 1991: 21). I would add that it was a departure from their current Church of England eucharistic theology as well. Was there a significance to this? As an ex-missionary in a frontier situation, perhaps the pastoral Wesley could appreciate at that stage of his life that it would be difficult to introduce something radically new to people in already liminal (frontier) situations. Could the consecration prayer with thanksgiving and a preliminary *epiclesis* be Wesley's moderate alternative to introducing the *epiclesis* to the Spirit in this situation since this still fulfils his desire to stress the need for divine grace and action in the sacrament? It is a possibility.

Traditonally, the *epiclesis* has been on the elements, on the people and for the effects of the elements on the people (McGoldrick 1983/4: 54). The more ancient *epiclesis* would be prayers for the Spirit's descent on the people and for the effects of the sacrament. *Epiclesis* for the elements was not that common. The next chapter will look at some of these examples in depth, but it is appropriate for us to note here that the Mozarabic rites, the Gallican rites and the liturgies of St Basil and St Chrysostom include the *epiclesis* for the people as well as for the elements. The 1549 *BCP* favoured by the Manchester non-jurors, had a double *epiclesis*—which included a prayer for the elements. Perhaps their early close associations with the non-jurors led to their inclusion of not only the *epiclesis* and that particular *epiclesis* in the Wesleys' eucharistic hymns. The brothers would of course have been aware of the tradition of double *epiclesis* from their own readings of the Eastern liturgies. Selleck commented that John had knowledge of Orthodox liturgies as well as Collier's 'Reasons for Restoring Some Prayers' (1717), having read the book on the voyage to Georgia (1983: 117–8).

There were six Wesleyan eucharistic hymns with *epiclesis*. Some prayed for the effects of the divine descent on the sacrament for the people—for 'inner witness' to Calvary's event (*HLS* 7/1 cf. 16/1, 2; 75/3) for Christ to be seen, his love to be experienced (*HLS* 53/3; *HLS* 72/1, 2), for contrition (*HLS* 151/1). *HLS* 150 has a prayer for the people's sanctification. One was a prayer for the Spirit to descend on the elements (*HLS* 72) making them 'channels'to convey his love. The metabolist slant present in the liturgy of St Chrysostom where the Spirit was asked to 'make this bread . . . the Body of thy Christ, changing it . . .' (Clarke 1964: 119) was not found in their theology.

As we have seen earlier in this chapter, the Wesleys held that there is no inherent power in the elements. The elements, like the 'hem of Jesus' garment' which the woman touched (Wesley 1745:8) or the rock which Moses struck, are arbitrary instruments (Rattenbury 1948: 30). The *epiclesis* is what makes the common elements a meal for the church. There is no substantial change in the elements. They are changed, given perhaps relative holiness, in so far as they are now privileged to be special conduits of his love (*HLS* 57/2 cf 92/6). Nevertheless, 'the sign transmits the signified, the grace is by the means applied' (*HLS* 71/1 cf *HLS* 89/4). In contrast, the reformer Zwingli was fearful even about linking the Spirit to the sacraments. He had insisted that the Spirit does not need any channels, although he is free to use whatever he wishes, including the sacraments, on the senses of those with faith (Stephens 1986: 186–7, 191–2). The Wesleys were not afraid to link the Spirit with the sacrament nor, even more narrowly, the elements. Again we see the 'God–ward' focus of the Wesleys. Instead of concentrating on arguments having to do with human concerns and involvement, eg 'what constitutes consecration?' or 'when are the elements consecrated?', the Wesleys centred their attention on the one who consecrates: The Spirit of God. In the end, what matters to them is God authenticates the sign (*HLS* 11/4, 153/1). Could the Wesleys' creation of an *epiclesis-hymn* say something about their understanding of the value of created physical things, in that these can become very special channels of grace? Could it also say something about their concern for the immanence of God's presence in the here and now? More will be said about this in chapter 4.

We have already noted that the Wesleys had the *epiclesis* in their eucharistic hymns when their church removed it from their current *BCP*. We observed that the Wesleys had not just one but several *epiclesis*. There is a possibility that the *epiclesis* was located after the words of institution in the Wesleyan eucharistic service. If so, that points to an understanding which gives the Spirit a principal role in the eucharist. The great attention the Wesleys gave to the role of the Spirit in the *HLS* contrasted greatly not only with Brevint's text but also with the Western eucharistic tradition. It is true that they had the insights of people like Calvin who stressed the role of the Spirit in the sacrament. Calvin believed in the role of the Spirit, especially in connecting the worshippers to Christ in the sacrament. Communion with the body of Christ to Calvin is

> effected through the descent of the Holy Spirit, by whom our souls are lifted up to heaven, there to partake of the life transfused into us from the flesh of Christ (Wallace 1953: 206).

Calvin also remarked that

> No slight insult is offered to the Spirit if we refuse to believe that it is by His incomprehensible power that we communicate in the body and blood of Christ (*Institutes* 4: 17: 33).

Other than the disagreement the Wesleys would have with his use of spatial language to locate Christ, the believer and the Spirit, there would be no disagreement about the vital role the Spirit plays in the sacrament. The Wesleys also had, within their Church of England family, people like Taylor and Thorndike, Anglican divines who made the Spirit central to the life of faith and the working of the sacrament (Stevenson 1994: 174). Yet the evidence of a high degree of emphasis the Wesleys placed on the role of the Spirit raises the question, 'what was their motivation?'

Could it be that they intended the focus of attention in the eucharist to be God-orientated rather than human-orientated, ie it is seen more as God's action (in this case, the work of the Third Person of the Trinity, the Holy Spirit) rather than ours? We simply present ourselves and our gifts. We ask for him to do something with our offering. Without him, nothing happens. He is the one who needs to act. If this was the motivation of the Wesley brothers, they succeeded in affirming loudly and clearly one of the three key Wesleyan eucharistic themes: God's initiating, sustaining and active grace.

In the West, especially in the Roman tradition, a priest seen as *in persona Christi* says the formula for consecration and consecration is said to have taken place. The eucharist seems to be more institutionalised and static in that the focus is more on ordered action in response to a past commandment. Wesley was quoted as having said this:

> Settle this in your heart, that the *opus operatum,* the mere work done, profiteth nothing; that there is no power to save, but in the Spirit of God, no merit, but in the Blood of Christ; so that, consequently, even what God ordains, conveys no grace to the soul, if you trust not in Him alone ... (*Sermon* 16).

In place of this static picture, the Wesleys placed the Holy Spirit at the heart of the happening. Consecration is understood to take place by the direct, immediate action of the free Spirit of God descending upon the offerings of the elements and of the people. The dynamism of the event cannot be missed. In terms of time, the focus is not on a past institution. It is on the 'now-ness', the freshness, the 'present-ness' of the event. There is an open-endedness about this approach and the Spirit is free to do what he wills. This ties in with and underlines the Wesleys' teaching about the dynamic and personal presence of Christ which we have seen earlier in this chapter.[11] This again emphasises the theme of the pro-active, initiating grace of God.

3. The healing sacrament

3.1 Moving towards Christian perfection

The Wesleys utilised a therapeutic more than a legal framework to understand the divine-human interaction (Lindstrom 1946: 41). Sin was seen as sickness, salvation as healing of this sickness, Christian formation as long-term spiritual therapy towards full healing and wholeness defined as 'Christian perfection'. To the Wesleys, Christian perfection is the goal of the Christian life. Referred to sometimes as 'entire sanctification', 'scriptural holiness' or 'perfect love', Christian perfection simply means the state of living where there is 'holiness in heart and life', where one loves God and one's neighbour with pure intention (*Sermon* 112) and where one becomes conformed to the image of Christ. It is with this understanding that the Wesleys saw the eucharist as a therapeutic sacrament providing 'the medicine of immortality' for communicants as they seek to be healed of their present condition and become 'perfected in love'.

There is no doubt that the sacrament has a therapeutic role. The *HLS* has several references about healing. There was a prayer for the application of Christ's 'healing blood' (*HLS* 25/3) at the Table. Utilising the story of the woman with the flow of blood in the gospels, the hymns urged:

> Touch His sacramental clothes;
> Present in His power to heal,
> Virtue from His body flows
> (*HLS* 39/1).

Reflecting on the story of the man by the pool of Bethesda (John 5: 2ff), the Wesleys cried:

---

11. The Wesleys sometimes used the images of the Holy Spirit for Christ and vice versa (cf Christ's ascension and prayer to the 'Eternal Spirit, gone up on high'. In *HLS* 112/1 and 'the Spirit of His love' *HLS* 93/4).

> . . . when shall the means of healing be
> The channels of Thy grace to me?
>
> . . . O let the troubled waters move,
> And minister Thy healing love
> (*HLS* 58/1, 5).

The Lord's supper calls out to all with 'searching pain' whose conscience troubles them with their past sins. At the Table, they are called to

> Taste; and dismiss your guilty fear,
> O, taste and see that God is here
> To heal your souls and sin subdue.
> (*HLS* 9/3).

Emotional wounds and spiritual sicknesses are dealt with at the Table. Earlier in this chapter, we saw that there were times when people were healed physically at the sacrament as well. The sacrament *is* a place for healing.

For the Wesleys, communion is the chief means of grace for growing towards Christian perfection:

> The prayer, the fast, the word conveys,
> When mix'd with faith, Thy life to me;
> In all the channels of Thy grace,
> I still have fellowship with Thee:
> *But chiefly here my soul is fed*
> *With fulness of immortal bread.*
>
> *Communion closer far I feel,*
> *And deeper drink th' atoning blood;*
> *The joy is more unspeakable,*
> *And yields me larger draughts of God . . .*
> (*HLS* 54/4–5. Italics mine).

John Wesley, while referring to a Kempis's book, 'The Christian Pattern', wrote:

In the fifth chapter of the first book, and the forty
eigth of the third, we are directed how to read the
holy Scriptures: And the whole fourth book
instructs us how to make the Holy Communion
an effectual means of Christian perfection (JWW
14).

We know from John Wesley's writings that he was
influenced by a Kempis at one stage of his life and held the
author in high respect even in his latter years (cf *JWJ* 24/5/1738,
Sermon 55, JWW 2).

Holy communion and Christian perfection are linked in a
special way. When the Methodists sang the hymn 'Author of
Life Divine', they were reminded that he has set the Table to:

Preserve the life Thyself hast given,
And feed, and train us up for heaven.
(*HLS* 40/1).

Charles Wesley prayed:

O, wouldst Thou to Thy church return,
For which the faithful remnant sighs,
For which the drooping nations mourn!
Restore the daily sacrifice.

He then pleads for the realisation of the perfecting fruits of
such observance which is Christian perfection:

Now let the spouse, reclined on Thee,
Come up out of the wilderness,
From every spot, and wrinkle free,
And wash'd, and perfected in grace.
(*HLS* 166/16, 19).

The Wesleys were very concerned about the formation of
their people towards the goal of Christian perfection. If
communion was understood by them to be the chief means of
grace for growing towards that state, the Wesleys sought to

utilise the sacrament in a conscious and intentional way in their training/healing program.

The Wesleys were not the first to have such a therapeutic approach to life and to the sacrament. The 'salvation as healing' concept had some roots in the Eastern church (Tuttle 1989: 138–9) and there are evidences of it in the works of Anglican theologians (eg Hooker, cf Cocksworth 1993: 41) and in Stoddard's proclamation of the 'converting' qualities of the sacrament when he opened the Table to those who were in need of its grace but who were unable to fulfil some spiritual admission qualifications (Holifield 1974: 200, 214; Selleck 1983: 136). What would surface as unique to the Wesleys could be the way they clearly connected the therapeutic thread through issues of salvation, spiritual formation, the use of the eucharist in spiritual formation and eschatology. More will be written about this later: the historical sources for the Wesleys' therapeutic understanding of the eucharist and the Wesleyan understanding of Christian perfection will be explored in the next two chapters.

It would suffice for us here firstly to note that there is a therapeutic language and role found in the Wesleyan description of the sacrament. We have already seen the strong link the sacrament has to the process of growth towards Christian perfection. Our second task therefore is to see how this affects attitudes regarding the future.

Healing is often a process. It takes time. A eucharistic theology and practice which is very concerned about the memory of Christ's death or about the worthiness of its communicants would be more orientated towards the time-frames of the past and the present. An eucharistic theology and practice which is more concerned with the grace of God, the present dynamic work of Christ and the Holy Spirit at the table and the full healing effects of the sacrament on its communicants would not only be looking at the past and the present, but it would also have a very strong perspective about the future. There is hope. Yet this hope is not simply tied to a future set in a conceptually linear time-frame. The Wesleys' eucharistic eschatology has an ' already' and a 'not yet' dimension.

3.2 *The eschatological dimension*

Perhaps a picture of the early Methodists gathering for the covenant-cum-communion service on New Year's Day provides a clear image of the Wesleys' understanding of the holy communion as an eschatological feast. Here on New Year's Day they observe a linear time–bound event which drives home their mortality and the provisional nature of all things. Here at the Table time is transcended as the 'veil' of time past is pushed aside and they encounter Christ crucified before them on the cross. Here Christ stands as high priest, interceding for them. Here they plead the effects of his sacrifice. Here they receive fruits of the encounter with him, experience the in-breaking of the reign of God and the reality of the words 'heaven and thou (Christ) are one' (*Collection* 493/6). It is here in the covenant prayer of self-surrender and total abandonment that they underline what they are verbalising in the communion liturgy: that their lives are not their own. They belong to and have begun in Christ. Living in Christ, their life will exist beyond the bonds of time in a quality that they cannot yet imagine. Heaven is both 'a present reality and a future hope' for them (Macquiban 1998: 3), experienced at the table. The covenant service simply emphasises what is true of every eucharist.

The Wesleys used several words to describe this 'already' and 'not yet' nature of the sacrament. Three of the most used were: earnest (*HLS* 103/2) veil (*HLS* 44/4, 93/1) and taste (*HLS* 101/1). Quantitatively, though not qualitatively as much, these are words that indicate 'partial-ness', 'incompleteness'. The earnest is a partial payment, the veil hides the depth of the mystery and a taste awaits the full meal (Brevint 1673: 56–57). Wainwright commented that Wesley more than Brevint used the word 'taste' with regard to the eucharist. The word 'is much rarer in eucharistic liturgies and theologies than one might have expected' but he added that it had the value of undeniably expressing the relationship between the 'already' and the 'not yet' (Wainwright 1981: 196).

The fourth word used is pledge (*HLS* 100/2–3). Since Brevint and both Wesleys were more concerned with the divine action in the sacrament than was Zwingli, they did not use the word to indicate the believer's oath of allegiance to God. Instead, it is used of the sacrament as God's guarantee of his faithfulness, so needed by us on this side of eternity. Pledge is a terminal image in their understanding. A pledge has to be returned to him who gave it on that day. It would no longer be needed then (*HLS* 111/3, 100/5 cf *HLS* 12/4).

Caught as they were in polemics against the Roman Church and with each other, the reformers did not do much to restore the teaching of the eucharist as a sign of the Kingdom feast. Issues like sacrifice and the mode of Christ's presence at the sacrament took centre stage until the Wesleys published their eucharistic hymns (Wainwright 1981: 56). Indeed, the Wesleys called communion the 'Supper of the Lamb' which we begin 'in faith' to eat (*HLS* 97, cf *HLS* 111). It is 'the type of the heavenly banquet' (*HLS* 107/1).

The provisional nature of the sacrament, the time-transcending 'realised eschatology' served as a source of assurance as well as a promise of hope for believers. Assurance is in the gift of the sacrament, the sign of his faithfulness and the table of his promised presence. The hope is in the coming 'Marriage Feast' (*HLS* 114/7), where sadness and sorrow will be no more (*HLS* 95/3), where we shall 'retrieve His nature' (*HLS* 32/2) regain His image, rise to his stature (*HLS* 102/3 cf *HLS* 111/2), ie be fully the whole persons which God had intended us to be. There, united with those above (*HLS* 165/4), our 'elder brethren' (*HLS* 98/7) and the martyrs (*HLS* 106), 'perfected into one' with them (*HLS* 104/2, 111/2), we join the camp of heaven, both saints ('church triumphant' in *HLS* 96/2) and angels (*HLS* 105, 106), singing and celebrating. There will be much joy, love and praise as we banquet on his richest love (*HLS* 93/2). Such is the glory to come, the ecstasies unknown (*HLS* 101/4). When and how that will be, we cannot foresee (*HLS* 156/6) but it *will* come. The Wesleys expect it to be sudden with apocalyptic effects on the world (*HLS* 93/2, 3, 98/6, 93/3). Less traumatically, the individual's communion with the divine is seen as growing until 'the Ray shall rise into a Sun, the Drop shall swell into a Sea' (*HLS* 101/4).

> Nourish us to that awful day
> When types and veils shall pass away,
> And perfect grace in glory end;

Us for the marriage feast prepare,
Unfurl Thy banner in the air,
And bid Thy saints to heaven ascend
(*HLS* 44 / 4).

Wesleyan eucharistic theology has in its eschatology an answer to the tyranny of time and mortality. It provides assurance of God's faithfulness. It gives hope for the future. The healing has begun and will be completed. One of the strongest themes which bursts out of the eucharistic hymns is that of joy. Over and over again, the hymns sing of that. I have counted at least forty-two words with references to joy/enjoy, happiness and cheer/cheerfully in the *HLS* (omiting words like bliss, rapture, gladness and feast).[12] These are present in about a quarter (twenty-five per cent) of the 166 eucharistic hymns. This is in direct contrast with the communion liturgy found in the 1662 *BCP* which can be accused of displaying a noticeable lack of eschatological themes as well as being inordinately penitential in tone. The feature of joy can be described as one of the unique contributions of Wesleyan eucharistic theology and spirituality.

It must be admitted that although John Wesley did write and preach about what are traditionally termed as 'The Last Things', heaven and hell, death, judgment, resurrection, not much of what he has mentioned about these (with the exception of heaven with themes like reunion with others who share the faith, celebrative feasting, removal of pain and suffering, enjoyment of God's presence) is directly linked to the eucharist. That he believed in the existence of hell, the wrath of God against sin and sinners, the resurrection of the body, there can

---

12. References in the *HLS* to joy/joyful: 28 times *HLS* 9/4; 10/3; 11/2; 21/1; 56/4; 62/8; 81/2; 91/3; 92/4; 43/3 (2 times); 95/4; 99/3; 102/1; 109/1; 112/1; 115/2; 116/4; 125/4; 130/3; 131/3; 157/4; 158/3; 160/1, 5; 162/2; 164/8; 166/22; happy/enjoy: 8 times *HLS* 4/3; 11/2; 96/1; 98/8; 102/3; 108/2; 113/2; 155/5; cheer/cheerfulness: 6 times *HLS* 9/1; 61/3; 62/2; 86/6; 158/2 160/1.

be no doubt.[13] There are hints of judgment in the *HLS* where we see 'the Judge in glory come' (*HLS* 98/4) staining the skies with

> . . . deepest red,
> Dies the land and fires the wood
> Turns the oceans into blood
> (*HLS* 98/6, cf. 93/3).

Also there are very mild allusions to resurrection: 'suffering and curse and death are o'er'(*HLS* 93/4). Since death is not a strong theme in the Wesleys' eucharistic theology, the hope of resurrection fails to stand out as strongly as one would expect. What Wainwright observed about the approach of *HLS* 40/1 could be true of Wesleyan eucharistic theology. He said:

> An advantage of this approach (which focuses on the eucharist as food for eternal life) is that it may express continuity and growth in the eternal life which Christ already gives and which will be perfected in heaven; but it leaves out of account the element of rupture that is represented by human death and by the expected resurrection and judgement at the *parousia* of Christ (1981: 111).

Indeed, if one criticism can be levelled at Wesleyan eucharistic theology with regard to eschatology, it would be that it avoids (intentionally or otherwise), the discussion on the darker side (destruction and judgment) which precedes the banquet. Another unexplored area is that of the redemption of creation. John Wesley did write at length about it in the sermon 'The General Deliverance' but he failed to provide it with any

---

13.   John Wesley was aware of the fear of hell (cf *JWJ* 30/12/1742). He warned people about the place (*JWJ* 6/4/1772; 22/4/1772) and of God's judgment (*Sermon* 118; *Sermon* 88, *Sermon* 51). He was more concerned to invite people through the mercy and love of God than to dangle them over hell (*Sermon* 15). Both Wesleys were very interested in death: their lives were constantly threatened, they had ample interaction with dying people (eg *JWJ* 3/11/1738) and they collected death-bed stories.

sacramental links. Some reflections on these omissions will be made in chapters 4 and 5.

Having looked at the three key themes of Wesleyan eucharistic theology—the dynamic encounter with the presence of Christ, the tremendous grace of God and the eucharist as a joyous therapeutic sacrament—we begin to understand why the Wesleyan revival was not just an evangelical but an eucharistic one.

3
Sources of Wesleyan Eucharistic Theology and Spirituality

1. The search for sources

There are four main areas where one can look into for influences on the Wesleys' theology and spirituality. They are: the books read by the Wesleys, the significant people in their lives, the impact of some experiences they underwent, and the general theological and spiritual trends of their day.

Green in *The Young Mr Wesley* appended a list of books (not exhaustive) read by John from 1723 to 1734 (1961: 305–319). Campbell's book *John Wesley and Christian Antiquity*, especially his Appendix 2 (1991: 125–134) and John Wesley's own *Journals*, letters and other works (including the fifty volumes of *A Christian Library* he edited) add more to our knowledge of John Wesley's resources. I have found that Charles's written records were not as well documented as his brother's. However, his *Journal* does provide some insights into the books that he was familiar with (Appendix E), although one has to excavate quite deeply to find the other sources. It might be possible to assume that the influence on Charles, especially with regard to books and experiences would be quite similar to that on John, since the brothers were very close despite certain strong disagreements throughout their lives.[1] For example, John read George Herbert's poems while still a curate at his father's church (Tuttle 1978: 105). In 1733, he published *Select Parts of Mr Herbert's Sacred Poems* (a collection of twenty-three poems from Herbert's *The Temple*). In 1744, he included several poems from *The Temple* in his *Collection of Moral and Sacred Poems*. Herbert's poems, though not mentioned in Charles's journals, affected both 'the imagery and texture' of Charles' hymns (Morris 1969: 375–383).

---

1. John and Charles disagreed strongly regarding the ordinations which John performed. The brothers also held slightly different positions regarding Christian perfection (cf chapter 4).

At least two of Herbert's poems have been adapted by Charles for his *HLS* (*HLS* 160 from *The Banquet* and *HLS* 9 from Herbert's *The Invitation*). Sometimes, it is not possible to distinguish with finality the Wesleys' works from each other's. The joint publication of the *HLS* for example, does not indicate to the reader which section or hymn was which brother's input or preference.

Significant people played a role in shaping the brothers' lives. Both Wesleys were influenced by their parents, especially their mother. Elder brother Samuel probably played quite a part in Charles's formative school years since he was his guardian. Sally Kirkham, sister of fellow holy club member Robert Kirkham, was a good friend of John's in his early years as a Fellow of Lincoln College. He paid several visits to her family at her father's rectory in Stanton some forty miles from Oxford, sometimes accompanied by Charles (Davies 1976: 43). She was almost John's spiritual director, providing him with spiritual conversations and readings. Deacon and others like Law and Taylor (the latter two more through their books) left their imprints on the Wesleys as well.

Experiences also shaped their theology and spirituality. Positive encounters affirmed some beliefs and practices. Negative ones brought out responses and reactions which affected their theology and spirituality too. Some of the effects of John's encounter with the mystics and the interaction of both Wesleys with groups as varied as the Manchester non-jurors, Moravians, deists, the mystics and the Roman Catholics will be looked into in this chapter.

The Wesleys were men of their times. The general theological and spiritual trends during their time would have had some effects on them as well. In this chapter, some of these trends will be explored.

There are limitations in the attempt to trace the sources of Wesleyan eucharistic theology and spirituality. Firstly, there exists the cross-fertilisation of some materials: the *BCP* itself, for instance, had several sources ranging from the Fathers of the early church to the continental reformers. Who is to say by which route influence on the Wesleys came—via the *BCP* or directly through one of the *BCP's* sources? Second, the Wesleys might have read an author without receiving any significant impact on one occasion, while the writings of another on the same theme might have spoken to them on a later occasion. Which author was the source then? Again, the combination of the opinions of several authors, friends or experiences might have built up a particular belief. What the Wesleys read, composed or edited could sometimes not be clear proofs of their full agreement with the documents. John edited, for example, *A Christian Library*, but when it was published,

> a hundred pages were left in that he had scratched out; so that the work cannot be taken as an authoritative statement of Wesley's doctrinal teaching (Green 1906: 62, item 131).

Some information John included in *A Christian Library* was not reflected in his eucharistic theology or spirituality. For example, in Nelson's *A Companion for the Festivals and Fasts of the Church of England: with collects and prayers for each solemnity,* there was a section alluding to the idea that creation is offered to God through the offering of the sacraments (1704: 467–468). In Wesleyan eucharistic spirituality, there is no such orientation.

Aware of the limitations of this study, I will try to do two things. First, I will list the key sources of Wesleyan eucharistic theology and spirituality. Whether they are from books, from experiences with significant people or encounters with theological/spiritual trends of their time, the input the Wesleys received can be placed into three source categories: Scripture, church tradition in general and the Anglican heritage in particular. We will look at these categories and note their effects on the Wesleys. Second, I will highlight and reflect on instances where the Wesleys departed from or developed their own thought apart from their sources, revealing their unique theological or spiritual concerns.

2. Scripture

Baker wrote of Charles:

> His verse is an enormous sponge filled to
> saturation with Bible words, Bible similes, Bible
> metaphors, Bible stories, Bible ideas (1962: xxv).

Both Wesleys' writings attest to this fact. *Sermons, Journals,*
letters are rarely without scriptural references. The *HLS* are
tightly packed poetic descriptions of scriptural events and
teachings (references to the Old Testament in the *HLS* include:
Melchisedec 46/1, 2; Job 145/4; Rod of Moses 27/2, the practice
of Exodus 21: 6 in 80/3. New Testament references include
Lazarus 68, Blind man 59/2, Man by pool of Bethesda 58,
Emmaus 29, Christ as Second Adam 114/4). Lindbeck's
observation could be an apt picture of the Wesley brothers:

> For those who are steeped in them, no world is
> more real than the ones they create. A scriptural
> world is thus able to absorb the universe. It
> supplies the interpretive framework within which
> believers seek to live their lives and understand
> reality. Scripture creates its own domain of
> meaning and the task of interpretation is to
> extend this over the whole of reality (1984: 117).

The tendency of the Wesleys, especially Charles in his
hymns, to let the Old Testament be interpreted by the New
Testament was noted by Ward, a scholar of medieval studies.
She felt that Charles stood in the tradition of the biblical
exegesis where the gospel was the key to understanding the
Scriptures. Every part of Scripture was seen to contain some
aspect of the good news about the person of Christ, although
such meaning was often hidden (1992: 14). One thinks of the
exposition of Isaiah 63:1–6 in *HLS* 17/1–4 as an example of
this.

Another interesting characteristic in that tradition is that
'Scripture was not considered well read' unless it was read

both in public congregational/liturgical settings as well as in private devotional situations (Ward 1992: 15). Communal affirmation as well as individual appropriation of the Scripture text were equally important. The devotional aspect strengthens the union of head and heart, a practice so evident in all the Wesleys' eucharistic hymns (cf *HLS* 58 which is an exposition and a moving personal appropriation of John 5: 1–18). This style in turn shaped their eucharistic theology and spirituality. One of the principal media through which the brothers appropriated the Scriptures was the Anglican *BCP* (Selleck 1983: 342). Several psalms, with a passage each from the Old and New Testaments, some canticles from the gospels (eg the *Benedictus, Magnificat*), specific readings from the gospel and epistles are the combined offerings of its daily liturgies of eucharist, morning and evening prayer. The Wesleys had been schooled in the medieval style of interpreting Scripture through the use of this book. Although John was free to use alternatives to the passages given in the lectionary for his preaching, he was said to use the lectionary quite often, finding it edifying to his hearers (Selleck 1983: 907).

According to Jones, John Wesley considered the Bible as the supreme authority for Christian teaching. John cites it more often than all the other authorities combined. Other authorities —namely, reason (which never opposes Scripture), Christian antiquity (especially those practices and beliefs held during what Wesley considered the 'purest' age of the church when Christians were living according to scriptural teachings), experience (especially of those whom John considered real believers) and the Church of England (primarily in its Scripture-based homilies and liturgy)—are subordinate to Scripture. Jones argued that for Wesley, authority was not constituted by a 'quadrilateral'[2] but by a 'fivefold but unitary

---

2.   The Wesleyan 'quadrilateral' was first surfaced by Outler to describe the four 'authorities' in Wesley's theological writings—namely Scripture, Tradition, Reason and Experience (Outler 1991: 86). Williams noted that while Scripture is primary, the other three were equally important (Williams 1960: 23–38). An updated discussion on it

locus comprising these' where each dimension is inter-dependent on the others. Scripture, however, is least dependent on the others. John Wesley's interpretation of Scripture was not in the least enamoured with doctrinal speculation but was intensely concerned with his consuming soteriological interest (1995: 216–219). Jones discovered that in practice Wesley relied more on the entire Christian tradition (especially resources from the early church and the Church of England) than his stated conception of Scripture would seem to allow (1995: 218), and it is to these that we turn our attention now.

3. Church tradition

Before we look at each section of church tradition for the imprints on the Wesley brothers, it would be helpful to note what has been done in terms of scholarly research thus far. There has been quite a number of studies done regarding the historical sources of the Wesleys. The earlier investigations concentrated on the Wesleys' (more of John's than Charles's) links with Western theology. Roman Catholic influence were claimed by Piette (1937), Todd (1958) and in recent years by Frost (1980) and Berger (1991, 1995). Tuttle focused his research on Wesley and the Roman Catholic mystics (1969). Hilder-brandt (1951) concentrated his attention on Luther, while Cell (1935) on Calvin. Cannon then repudiated the claim of positive Calvinist influence (1946) and Outler dismissed the idea that John Wesley owed any major debts to the continental reformers (1964: 119–120). The Wesleys' Anglican roots were investigated by Allchin (1965), Borgen (1972/1986) and Selleck (1983). The 'high church' aspect of the Wesleys was explored by Bowmer (1951). Towlson (1957) and Podmore (1998) looked at the Moravian input, while Maldwyn Edwards, SG Dimond, Gordon Rupp (Newton 1964: 3), Newton (1964) and Monk (1966) the Puritan heritage.

---

is found in Gunther's *Wesley and the Quadrilateral: Renewing the Conversation* (1997).

The interest in the Eastern sources of the brothers' theology and spirituality flowered with Outler's suggestion that John Wesley owed his idea of Christian perfection to Gregory of Nyssa and the other Cappadocians through the Macarian *Homilies* (1964: 9–10, footnote 9). A number of doctoral dissertations soon emerged, looking into the Wesleys and the works of Gregory of Nyssa (Robert Sheffield Brightman 1969), John Chrysostom (Kelly S McCormick 1983) and themes associated with the Wesleys and their Eastern sources. The latter work was carried out by Campbell (1984), Arthur C Meyers (1985) and Lee (1991). Bondi wrote two articles on the possible links (1986; 1987). All acknowledged the influence of the Eastern Fathers and most agreed that the influence was not as strong as earlier suspected. Bouteneff noted that 'it is no longer possible to press the idea of direct influence so far'. He also observed that the Wesleys have often cited patristic literature inaccurately as well (1999: 2). Meistad sought to summarise the findings when he pointed out that while the Wesleys' general theology was rooted in both traditions, they followed their Eastern mentors in soteriology and cosmology (1999: 1).

3.1 The early church
It is hard to ascertain the full nature of the debt the brothers owed to the early church—especially the church of the first five centuries. Yet one is never in doubt of that debt. Although Charles did not mention any early church source in his journals, it is inconceivable that he had not read some of them as part of his preparation for the priesthood in the Anglican Church. John certainly was familiar with the Fathers of the church. Green mentioned a few primary sources including Justin Martyr's *First Apology*, Lactantius' *de Morte,* and Augustine's *Confessions* among John's early readings. Secondary sources include Johann Lorenz von Mosheim's *A Concise Ecclesiastical History* (which was read by John in its Latin version) and Cave's *Primitive Christianity: The religion of the Ancient Christians* (1672) (1961: 305–319). John's knowledge of the early church was evident in his writings, especially in his letters to Dr Conyers Middleton and Bishop Smallbrooke about extraordinary gifts of the Spirit being operational during the time of the early church. His

Christian Library included 'readers digest' versions of the writings of John Lawrence Mosheim and Cave as well as the epistles of Clement (to the Corinthians), Polycarp (to the Philippians), Ignatius (to the Ephesians, Magnesians, Trallians, Romans, Philidephians, Smyrneans and to Polycarp), the *Homilies* ascribed to Macarius and records of two martyrdoms (Ignatius and Polycarp extracted from the *Epistle of the Church of Smyrna*). He had read many books about the life and practices of the early Christians: Claude Fleury's *The Manners of the Ancient Christians* and William Whiston's *Primitive Christianity Reviv'd* (1711) being two of them. The latter had the *Apostolic Constitutions* in English (2nd volume) and Greek (3rd volume). Several devotional books John read also made frequent references to the primitive church's eucharistic practices, eg Robert Nelson's *A Companion* (1704), Waterland's *A Review* (1737) recalled the purpose of and obligation to receive the sacrament.

In a sense, John Wesley's interest in the early church, especially the pre-Constantinan period, was not a surprise. Church leaders of his era displayed similar interests too. The Wesleys' association with the non-jurors meant that there was more reason for them to do so: the *Apostolic Constitutions* was used by Deacon, Clayton and others to supplement and revise the liturgy and practices of the existing *BCP* (ie Deacon's 1734 *A Compleat Collection of Devotions* which was used by John Wesley on his voyage to Georgia) (Wainwright 1994: 7). The *Constitutions*, thought to be a fourth century document, was later discovered to be post-Constantinian and Arian. Book VIII of the *Constitutions* contained the Clementine liturgy which has references to the eucharist and Wainwright has noted its imprint on *HLS* (Wainwright 1994: 7–8).

One of the most interesting findings that has surfaced in recent years was the fascination John had with the Eastern church. In *On Laying the Foundation of the New Chapel*, after claiming that Methodism was nothing less than the religion of the Bible and of the early church, John asserted:

> . . . the religion of the primitive church of the
> whole church in the purest ages . . . It is clearly

> expressed, even in the small remains of
> Clemens Romanus, Ignatius, Polycarp, it is seen
> more at large in the writings of Tertullian,
> Origen, Clemens Alexandrinus, Cyprian and
> even in the 4th century, it was found in the
> works of Chrysostom, Basil, Ephrem Syrus and
> Macarius (*Sermon* 132).

Campbell pointed out that from that list, only Clement of Rome was Western. The rest were Eastern Mediterranean Christians.[3] It seems significant that the great leaders of the Western church like Augustine, Jerome and Ambrose were not among those listed, although he did use them in *A Christian Library* and as ammunition to battle against people like Middleton. What the Wesleys received from these Western Fathers was possibly imbibed less consciously through their Anglican heritage (eg *BCP*, *Homilies*). The Eastern impact possibly came more directly through secondary sources (eg Cave) and through associations with the non-jurors and their writings/practices.

Some influences of the Eastern church can be detected in the *HLS* (e g *HLS* 21 with Gregory of Nazianzus' *Miracle of Crucified God, HLS* 43 and 81 to the *Apostolic Constitutions*) (Wainwright 1995: ix). Young commented that the Wesleys seemed to share some 'commonalties' with Macarius, namely, practical theology, the drive towards Christian perfection as the goal for the Christian life, the emphasis on incarnation, the role of the Spirit as the generator of perfection and the emphasis on the love of God (1999: 8).

---

3.   The second century Apostolic Fathers were Clement, Ignatius of Antioch and Polycarp of Smryna. The third century ones were Tertullian from Roman North Africa, Carthage, Origen from Alexandrian tradition, Clement of Alexandria, Cyprian from Roman North Africa, Carthage. The fourth century leaders were John Chrysostom of Constantinople (educated at Antioch), Basil the Great of Palestine (Caesarea), Syrians Ephraem Syrus and Macarius (Wesley had thought that Macarius was one of the fourth century Egyptian monks).

There are eight areas in which one can trace the influence of the early church on the Wesleys' eucharistic theology and spirituality. The first has to do with the *epiclesis*. We noted in chapter 2 that while the Western church placed greater weight on the words of institution and had less interest in the *epiclesis*, the Wesleys included several *epiclesis*-style hymns in the *HLS*.

Prayers for the descent of the Holy Spirit upon the communicants and for the effects of the sacrament upon the people are more common in most liturgies: Roman Catholic liturgical scholars have found early evidence of these forms of *epiclesis* but none before the fourth century for the *epiclesis* on the elements (Cooke 1967: V: 465). Other scholars argued that the third century *Apostolic Traditions of St Hippolytus* had a petition for the descent of the Spirit upon the elements without specifying the nature of the change that is to be effected in them (Cross 1974: 463). In the Eastern church, this *epiclesis* can be found in the Mozarabic and Gallican rites and is especially predominant in the Byzantine rite as typified by the liturgies of St Basil and St Chysostrom (Cooke 1967: V: 465f). The Wesleys included a prayer for the Spirit's descent on the elements themselves in the *HLS* (*HLS* 72).

While the Wesleys could have received the inspiration for having an *epiclesis* and for the *epiclesis* prayer on the elements from the Syrian *Apostolic Constitutions,* one can argue that John Wesley could have easily picked it up directly from Chrysostom's liturgy in some of his readings. As we have already noted in chapter 2, John Wesley had some knowledge of Orthodox liturgies and was familiar with Collier's *Reasons for Restoring Some Prayers* (1717) which contained some early church prayers from the Eastern church (Selleck 1983: 117–8).

The second contribution of the early Eastern church would be the understanding of Christian perfection as *teleiosis* and sin as 'sickness'. As we have seen earlier, Outler had hinted that the Eastern Fathers, especially the Cappadocians, pseudo-Macarius and Ephraem Syrus, were responsible for John's theology of sanctification. We have also seen that subsequent studies made indicated that there was little possibility of a direct link. John Wesley could have come to appreciate the Eastern church's portrait of Christ as a doctor who offers medicine to release

Christians from the power of sin (Cousins 1989: 223) through a variety of individuals, eg Lutheran Johann Arndt (1555–1621) who was said to have memorised the fifty Homilies of Macarius (pseudo-Macarius). Arndt's *True Christianity*, which presented this therapeutic view, was included in John's *Christian Library* volumes I and II.

Although John consistently removed passages referring to the Eastern concept of divinisation or deification—*theosis/apotheiosis*—(and to the ascetic life) in his edition of the *Homilies*, it could be seen that that reflected his caution regarding the use of those words (and to that brand of ascetism). Deification, though common in traditional Eastern theology can be subject to controversy in other settings (Campbell 1991: 66). It would not be wise to interpret that John Wesley was averse to the concept of *theosis* since his understanding of Christian perfection bears the marks of the Eastern Fathers. More about this will be said in the next chapter, but suffice it to note here that the Fathers' emphasis on grace–filled, persevering growth in love (a more progressive kind of perfection as compared to the Western linear 'completed perfection' understanding), for example, emerged in John Wesley's teaching on Christian perfection (Tuttle 1989: 138–9). Since this Christian perfection was the goal for which the eucharist was the chief means of grace, this third contribution of the early church does affect Wesleyan eucharistic theology and spirituality. The Eastern understanding of salvation from sin perceived more in a therapeutic rather than in a juridical way (as in the West) could have opened the way for Wesley to see communion as a 'converting' and hence healing sacrament.

Not all early church contributions came from the Eastern church. The third contribution, the practice of mixing water with wine in the chalice, was observed by the non-jurors. The Wesleys followed the practice. The mixed chalice was first found in Justin Martyr's *First Apology* (chapter LXV), was also present in Irenaeus' *Against the Heresies* (V.1.2) and Cyprian's *Epistle 63: To Caecilius*. Cyprianic interpretation of the mixture of water and wine was that it represented the association of the faithful and their sins with the atoning sacrifice of Christ (*Epistle 64, 13*). Wainwright in his *Introduction* to the *HLS* (Kimbrough

1995: x), observed that Brevint took this interpretation while the Wesleys took St Ambrose's interpretation (from *De Sacramentis)* —that the wine, standing for the blood, represented justification; the water, sanctification (*HLS* 37/3, 4). Hence even at the Table, the Wesleys were able to proclaim (in a rather visible way) their doctrine of salvation which stressed the link between justification and sanctification and underline that the sacrament is both a converting and a convincing ordinance (*JWJ* 27/6/1740) where one receives several benefits of his passion (*Sermon* 101). More about the Wesleys' understanding of salvation will be explored in chapter four.

We have to note here that John did not include the mixed chalice practice into the liturgy that he adapted for the American Methodists. It could not be that he stopped believing that the theology of justification and sanctification could be symbolised as well as preached at the table. Perhaps as an older and wiser ex-missionary who had experienced his frontier congregation's confusion and disapproval when he tried to introduce practices like this in his earlier days, Wesley decided to dispense with the mixed-chalice practice, entrusting the message of justification *and* sanctification to be proclaimed primarily by his preachers there.

The fourth contribution of the early church was the practice of extemporary prayer during the eucharist. Justin Martyr's *First Apology* (chapter LXVII) had this: 'the president (of the eucharist) offers prayers and thanksgivings according to his ability . . .' That was the whole liturgy. The extemporary prayer was expected from the bishop in the *Apostolic Tradition* of Hippolytus as well (chapter 10: 3). The result was that for the Methodists the Wesleyan eucharistic celebrations were a blend of the formal and the informal, the liturgical and the free, paralleling the Wesleys' teaching of using both the ordinary/ instituted means of grace and the extraordinary means of grace. The first attest to the faithfulness and unchangability of God, the second, to the freedom of the Spirit to create, renew, revitalise.

Fifth, the brothers' ideal of having communion weekly if not daily was rooted in the practice of the primitive church (cf chapter 1). The teaching could have been first imparted to them through their reading of Cave (Campbell 1991: 96).

The sixth link: Wainwright highlighted the similarity between the oblation theme found in *HLS* 118 and the manual acts of the celebrant during the institution narrative found in the Apostolic Traditions of Hippolytus as well as in the Alexandrian liturgies of St Basil. These speak of the sacrifice of Christ as a 'memorial of Christ' shown to the Father, cf *HLS* 116, 121, 123, 124, 125, 126 (1996: 6).

The connection between the eucharist and care for the poor was an ancient one. In Justin Martyr's *First Apology* (chapter LXVII) immediately after the eucharistic celebration, there was a collection for the poor. Could the brothers have been inspired by this, seeing their concern for the poor as a logical outflow of their eucharistic life? Could this be the seventh debt the Wesleys owed to the early church?

Finally, the worldview of the early church with regards to supernatural happenings left an imprint on the Wesleys. It can be argued that their worldview is similar to the one found in the Scriptures, but I believe that when the Wesleys saw the early church holding on to this cosmology, it did make a difference in their theology and spirituality. For example, we note that John Wesley's letter to Middleton displayed his evident store of patristic knowledge. In the letter, John quoted a story by Cyprian in which the 'heathen Magistrates' gave a Christian infant food that has been offered to an idol. The child was 'seized with convulsions and vomiting' on reception of that. A woman who had apostatised took consecrated elements. She too had convulsions and vomited. This to Wesley was an example of the supernatural power inherent in the sacrament and that such 'surprising' and 'unexpected' (unexpected by natural human logic) happenings *do* take place (JWL 19).

We must not imagine that John Wesley was blind to the faults of the early church or accuse him of blindly following their precepts and practices. He openly acknowledged that the Fathers in their works displayed 'many mistakes . . . many ill–drawn conclusions'. Yet he affirmed that he did

exceedingly reverence them, as well as their
writings, and esteem them very highly in love. I
reverence them, because they were Christians,
such Christians as are above (I have) described.
And I reverence their writings, because they
describe true, genuine Christianity, and direct
us to the strongest evidence of the Christian
doctrine . . . (JWL 19).

There were some concepts/practices of the early church
which the Wesleys did not use in their eucharistic theology and
spirituality, eg the 'offering of creation' theme and the use of
reserved consecrated sacraments in the homes of early
Christians. Perhaps the first was laid aside because the teaching
of it could take the spotlight away from the soteriological focus
of the eucharist. Perhaps the second was rejected because the
Wesleyan understanding was of the '*dynamic* Presence of Christ
at the eucharistic service itself'.[4] The Wesleys adopted and used
only whatever they felt would revive the church of their day.[5]
Their respect for the traditions of the church was probably
second only to their respect for Scripture. Tradition was not
equal to Scripture in authority but it had quite a high place. One
major area in which the Wesleys did not take up from the early
church was the penitential disciplines with regard to the Lord's
supper. For example, John was aware of Nathaniel Marshall's
Penitential Discipline of the Primitive Church (1714), having read it
in 1734 (cf Campbell 1991: 30). In Georgia, he had tried to
impose some of the preparation for communion and excommunication rules of the early church on his unsuspecting
parishioners. We have seen in chapter 1 that even though the
Methodists subsequently had strict rules to govern their
societies, John did not require the same degree of penitential

---

4.   Wesley omitted this in his abridged edition of Cave in *A Christian
      Library*. Could it be that he wanted to avoid the danger and abuses of the
      'reserved sacrament' practices found in the Roman Church?

5.   Campbell in his book *John Wesley and Christian Antiquity* made a case
      for John Wesley's programmatic use of Christian antiquity for reviving
      the church.

preparation where reception of communion was concerned. He believed in communion as a 'converting ordinance'. With regard to excommunication, however, it must be remembered that the Methodists were not often in any position to excommunicate their erring members since they were merely a group within a larger Anglican framework (unless of course, a Methodist happened to be the celebrant). This they did not fail to do later on, when they had their own communions, by using their 'class ticket' system (a parallel to the ticket could be found in the commendary letters of the early church mentioned in *Apostolic Constitutions* [Book II: chapter LXVIII]). Their restoration of repentant members to the communion table did not require as stringent a program as the early church did. Again, it could be because of the Wesleyan view that communion itself is a means of healing (just as salvation is seen as healing in the Eastern tradition), not just a means of blessing where only the worthy can receive.

3.2 *The medieval church*

Among the readings of Wesley, one finds the Middle Ages less represented than those of the primitive church and those after the reformation. The *Christian Library* had only a few writings from that period. The contributions to eucharistic theology and spirituality of those who were represented there or in the brothers' writings could be described as 'devotional' (or 'discipleship building') and 'Christocentric'.

The brothers' study of a Kempis's *Imitation of Christ* enriched their devotional lives, bringing to John a deep desire to develop inward holiness. He quoted the man several times (eg in *Sermons* 55, 73, 79, 117, JWL 15, JWL 20). Charles recommended the reading of it to his daughter (Wesley 1849: II. 278) and quoted him to his Roman Catholic hearers, urging them to repentance and to experience the love of Christ (*CWJ* 20/9/1744, 27/9/1744).

Another person who impressed John Wesley in the area of Christ-centred devotion and discipleship was St Francis of Assisi (cf *JWJ* 7/3/1736, I: 179). John also read St Bernard's *Meditations* (Green 1961: 312).

In the Wesleys' eucharistic teachings Christ was central. One sees the human Christ on the cross, bleeding for the sins of the world (while one cannot forget at the same time the divinity of the One who now stands as the risen priest-intercessor before the Father). Some scholars have noticed a similarity of style between the Wesleys' tendency to focus on the humanity of Christ and the preferences of devotional literature during the Middle Ages (Ward 1992: 26). While the early church focused on the risen Christ or the *Christus Victor* and the Greek-orientated church on the pre-existent being, this interest in the human Jesus with the imitation of him as the main thrust of spirituality, was more evident among the monastics of the Middle Ages (Cousins 1989: 375). The devotional works read by the Wesleys could have resulted in the rather warm and personal nature of the brothers' eucharistic theology and spirituality. Devotion was to the wounds of Christ as symbols of his love (Hodges 1966: 43), seeing the wounds as 'clefts on the rock' (using both the symbolism of St Bernard and the *HLS)* (Ward 1992: 27). His wounds became effective pleas not to us for pity but to the Father for redemption of sinners (Ward 1992: 26). In the hymns of the Wesleys, one sees the 'Protestant crucifix' (Rattenbury 1948:16) with the suffering of Christ displayed in one's full view. Did the Wesleys receive this vision directly from those writers of the Middle Ages? Or could the medieval input come more from people like Brevint and the other Anglican devotional writers of their day? Stevenson, for example, found Aquinas's three-fold scheme of 'memorial, food and pledge' in Brevint's *Christian Sacrament and Sacrifice* and in the Wesleys' ordering of their *HLS* (Stevenson 194: 101). Bett thought that Charles Wesley seemed to be directly dependent at times on Aquinas and Adam of St Victor (Bett 1913: 39–70). Berger did not find this evidence compelling and she argued that the similarities between Charles and these writers could be the result of his drawing on traditional images and terminology rather than borrowing directly from specific writers (1991: 216–7).

There is no doubt that the Anglican tradition (including the *BCP*) offered the Wesleys the riches of the church of the earlier ages.

3.3 Post-medieval period: Roman Catholic devotional writers and saints

Scholars see the end of the fifteenth century as the close of the medieval period. For the sake of the flow of this study, we will now look at the period after that—the sixteenth and seventeenth centuries and the influence of Roman Catholic devotional writers and saints on John Wesley. There will be a separate section for those traditionally considered 'mystics' in the church.

John Wesley was familiar with a number of Roman Catholic devotional writers and saints. Although he did not seem to have any acquaintance with St Teresa of Avila or St John of the Cross's works first-hand, he might have received aspects of their teachings via John of Avila, a mystic who was a trusted counsellor and confessor of St Teresa and who had been associated with the early Jesuits in Spain (Cross 1974: 745). He read Brother Lawrence some time before 1754. Both brothers read Francis de Sales (Green 1961: 315; cf JWL 21, *Sermon* 107; Heitzenrater 1985: 267). John knew about St Robert Bellarmine (*Sermon* 20), St Bonaventura (JWL 21, JWL 22), St Francis Xavier, St Ignatius of Loyola (*JWJ* 16/8/1742) etc. Both brothers read books by Jansenist Pasquier Quesnel (JWW 17) and Blaise Pascal (*Sermon* 84; JWW 17; Berger 1991: 207). John was familiar with the martyrdom story of the monks from the order of *de la Trappe* (*JWJ* 21/12/1747).

David Butler highlighted the point that about five per cent of the *Christian Library* recommended by Wesley to his preachers to form their theology, spirituality and ministerial life are those written by or about Roman Catholics. He commented:

> The amount of Catholic literature recommended by Wesley is fairly small, but perhaps substantial for its time by the standards of the 18th century (1995: 157).

While John Wesley included life stories and writings of several Roman Catholics in his *Christian Library*, he also made it a point to edit out the distinctively Roman Catholic teachings found in these works, eg assistance of the saints, penance etc (Butler 1995: 156).[6]

What we have seen in this section is John Wesley's surprising knowledge and appreciation of these Roman Catholic resources. The contribution of these to Wesleyan eucharistic spirituality would be indirect: many of these people mentioned provided him with teachings on and examples of committed discipleship and a glimpse of what holiness in Christian life is like.

3.4 Main trends of eucharistic theology and spirituality

At the time of the Wesleys, there were five major theological positions held about the eucharist. These were represented by the official Roman Catholic eucharistic teaching and by the writings of the refomers: Luther, Zwingli, Calvin and Cranmer. There were also those who adhered to variations of and/or developments from these views, eg the Puritans and the theological successors of Cranmer in the Church of England. The positions differed primarily on the question of how literally Jesus' words, 'This is my body', 'This is my blood' are linked with the communion elements of bread and wine. In some instances, the issue of contention was over the nature of that 'body' in the consecrated bread and wine (ie in what sense the body of Christ is present in the elements if Christ is now ascended and sitting at the right hand of God the Father).

3.4.1 Roman Catholic eucharistic theology and spirituality

Present in the *Confession of Berengar* (Bettenson 1963: 147–8), transubstantiation became the official position of the Roman Catholic Church at the Fourth Lateran Council (1215). The Council of Trent (1545–1563) confirmed this teaching in the face

---

6. The Wesleys had six key theological problems with the Roman Catholic Church. They include issues regarding the papal office, 'idolatry' of the Roman Church, the issue of how sins are forgiven in the Roman Church, the undermining of Christian perfection by intolerance and lying on the part of the Roman Catholics, the beliefs about the afterlife and the teachings about the sacraments (JWW 15, 16).

of the Protestant reformation. In 1965, transubstantiation was reaffirmed in the encyclical *Mysterium Fidei* (Cross 1974: 476).

Central to the concept of transubstantiation is the belief in the real corporeal presence of Christ in the consecrated bread and wine. Aristotelian metaphysics had provided a philosophical basis in which all matter is understood to have a core identifying quality (termed 'substance' of the matter) and a specific character (termed 'accidents' present in the matter). The table's 'accidents', for instance, is its colour, shape, make and size. These are observable distinctives. Its 'substance' is the 'tableness' of it which distinguishes it as a table from a chair or a lamp. Christian Aristotelians believed that the 'substance' of the matter is located within the object itself, put there by God as part of the creative act. At the eucharist, the 'accidents' of the bread and wine remain intact after the consecration. Bread and wine look, taste and feel like bread and wine. The 'substance' of the eucharistic elements, however, has changed. The body and blood of Christ have replaced the 'substances' of the bread and wine. Christ therefore, is corporeally present when the communicant receives the consecrated elements.[7]

In Roman Catholic teaching also, the work of Christ on the cross and the Mass (the eucharist) are seen to be on two different time-frames. There was the sacrifice on the cross at Calvary. There is the sacrifice of the mass where Christ is offered up to the Father anew every time a mass is celebrated. The eucharist thus became a propitiatory sacrifice which could be offered on behalf of special intentions, eg to release a soul from purgatory. Just as some of the offerings in the Old Testament did not require the shedding of blood (they were burnt or eaten), the whole of Christ's life was seen to be offered up at the mass as an 'unbloody sacrifice'.[8]

The focus of Roman Catholic eucharistic spirituality is Christ in the bread and wine. Bread and wine are identified

---

7.   Stookey's book *Eucharist: Christ's Feast with the Church* (1993:136–8) is one of the best books on the eucharist which I have read. It provided the basis for this section.

8.   See *Doctrine Concerning the Sacrifice of the Mass* in the documents of the Council of Trent, chapters 1–2 (Leith 1973: 437–439).

with Christ: belief in transubstantiation provided a clear physical and tangible focus for prayer and devotion. The goal of the Christian life is understood as holiness or closeness with God. Since masses are said daily, the eucharist was the main means of formation for the majority. However, in reality, most Roman Catholics, at least, during the Middle Ages, rarely received the eucharist more than once a year. The decline in eucharistic reception began in the fourth century (Taft 1989: 423) and by the medieval period, eucharistic piety was primarily 'a piety of presence'—'seeing and worship' and not 'tasting and feeling' (McCue 1989: 430). The 'feast' quality and the participatory aspect of the sacrament were diminished. Eucharistic spirituality became more visual and passive.

Supplementing spiritual formation were guide books on eucharistic devotions, teachings of religious communities committed to such practices, hagiography with eucharistic models and the para-liturgical services of the church, eg visits to the blessed sacrament, public processions linked with the *Corpus Christi* festival, a thirteenth century development and the exposition/benediction of the blessed sacrament which originated in the fourteenth century (Cross 1974: 349, 157–8). With the rise of eucharistic adoration, eucharistic spirituality moved beyond its communally orientated liturgical setting to become a more individually orientated prayer spirituality.

The communal aspect of the eucharist was not lost. As the eucharist could be offered to ease the situation of those in purgatory and special intentions could be made for the living as well as dead, it was seen as very powerful instrument for the church's mission and ministry.

3.4.1.1 The Wesleyan response

First as heirs of the reformation, the Wesleys would reject the transubstantiation of the Roman Catholic Church. As we mentioned in the last chapter, John considered it to be against Scripture, antiquity, reason and the senses. In his comments on 1 Corinthians 10:17, 11: 26–28 (*ENNT*), John wrote:

> . . . it is not said, 'This is changed into my body'
> but, 'This is my body'; which, if it were to be

taken literally, would rather prove the substance of the bread to be his body. But that they are not to be taken literally is manifest from the words of St Paul, who calls it bread, not only before, but likewise after, the consecration (JWW 16).

As Church of England clergymen, both Charles and John accepted the transubstantiation–condemning Article 28 of the *Articles of Religion* found in the *BCP* (1662: 706). The 'superstition' of the doctrine had 'consequences hurtful to piety' (JWW 18).[9] Although transubstantiation would not be the means by which the Wesleys would explain the presence of Christ at the sacrament, they had, with their followers, a great sense of expectancy for the experience of his presence at the eucharistic gatherings.

Second, the Wesleys held that the eucharist, central to worship in both Roman Catholic and Wesleyan eucharist spirituality, had to be accompanied by the preaching of the word.

---

9.   The main issues of contention can be summarised when we identify the Wesleys' fears by asking the question: 'What is at stake here?' ie what were the Wesleys trying to protect? The answer would be four basic tenets of faith: First, the Christ of the Scriptures (not papal decrees and interpretation of tradition) as central in worship and as sole authority for faith and life. Second, Christ's centrality in the work of salvation which must not be shared by any other human agency, be they living beings here or holy beings in the hereafter. Third, unadulterated love for one's neighbour seen in attitudes and actions towards the other who might differ from oneself in matters of theology. Finally, perception of one's self as a helpless sinner before God; perception of God as the sole initiator and provider of salvation; of others as valued beings with dignity; of the world where one's senses are honoured and not disregarded in the name of dogma (JWW 15, 16) Granted that the Wesleys' understanding of the Roman Catholic Church might be limited and somewhat biased, their almost unexamined wholesale adaptation of the Protestant polemic materials uncritical (eg Butler 103, 108, 124, 127, 115), the key issues of contention with the Roman Catholic Church and the main concerns of the Wesleys remain (cf *CWJ* 2: 131).

Third, unlike Roman Catholic eucharistic spirituality, the Wesleyan model could not simply be a prayer spirituality (which encourages adoration of the consecrated elements and passivity in the reception of them). Actual active participation was required, non-communicating attendance was forbidden. Without the eucharistic devotions of the Roman Church, the spirituality of the Wesleys would be grounded solidly in the context of worship. The Wesleys did not subordinate the corporate element of the sacrament to individualistic devotions. If there was any prayer spirituality linked to the eucharist, it would be generated within the context of the liturgy and flow from there into the communicants' daily lives. Use of the *HLS* and devotional texts like Brevint's possibly provided this means of deepening one's eucharistic experience.

Fourth, for both the Wesleys and the Roman Catholic Church, the corporate aspect of the sacrament was further enhanced by the practice of intercession. The Wesleys experienced 'the spirit of intercession' during the sacrament for living people (*CWJ* 27/4/1746). Charles did record once that there was 'strong intercession for departed friends' during their eucharistic celebration (*CWJ* 10/3/1745). However, for the Wesleys, prayers at the eucharist were not seen as 'tapping into the benefits of Christ's death' in an automatic way, with the church playing the role of intercessor. Christ is the intercessor. The church joins in his intercession but has no power to cash into any tangible benefits of his passion for another who might not be willing to receive it consciously.

The influence of the Roman Catholic Church on Wesleyan eucharistic theology and spirituality can be described as mostly a 'negative contribution'. By this I mean that the Wesleys' eucharistic positions were in some ways the outcome of their negative responses/reactions to what they perceived to be Roman Catholic errors in eucharistic theology and spirituality. The result was an eucharistic position which had three key features: a solidly cross-centred Christology, a strongly corporate/community-orientated outlook (cf eucharistic piety cultivated in a worship-based context/the practice of intercession for the body of Christ) and the firm union held regarding word and sacrament, faith and active participation. The first would influence how the Wesleys perceived Christ at the table, the second would be incorporated into the Wesleys' understanding of therapeutic formation and the third would help keep the balance of grace and works in Wesleyan eucharistic theology and spirituality.

3.4.2 *The eucharistic theology and spirituality of the continental reformers*

The continental reformers were concerned about different issues. Luther, the principal mover of the Protestant reformation, wanted to affirm the real corporeal presence of Christ in the consecrated elements. He saw the eucharist as a means of union with Christ in the most intimate way: the communicant touches Christ physically, thus enabling the emergence of believing, spiritual faith within oneself (Cocksworth 1993: 21). The reformer in German-speaking Switzerland, Zwingli (1484–1531), focused his attention on the worshipping believer at the eucharist. He wanted to maintain God's sovereignty rather than tie God down to ecclesial activities. He wanted to be sure the freedom of the Spirit to do as he pleases is not compromised. He wanted also to safeguard the belief that faith in Christ was absolutely essential in the Christian's relationship with God and would not allow for any thought which might lessen the role of faith (Cocksworth 1993: 22). The Genevan reformer Calvin (1509–1564) dealt with the question of how the union between the believer and Christ takes place at the eucharist.

Luther did not accept the Aristotelian philosophy which underpinned the transubstantiation theory. He believed that it is possible for Christ to be bodily present in something without having to change the substance of the object. He drew a parallel from Christology which affirmed that the deity of Christ shared the properties of his humanity and that his humanity shared those of his deity *(communicatio idiomatum:* communication of properties), without diluting or changing the other. Thus at the eucharist, the real bodily coporeal presence of Christ can be and is present with, in, and under the consecrated elements (consubstantiation) (Luther 1972: 29: 35).

Luther believed that it is possible for the resurrected and ascended body of Christ to be at the right hand of the Father and also be at the eucharist because of his body's ubiquity (omnipresence) (Stookey 1993: 53). All that is asked of the believer at the eucharist is faith in Christ's work and the willingness to receive. The only sacrifice the believer offers is that of prayer, praise and thanksgiving. Given the strong Roman Catholic background of 'indulgences for sale' against which Luther rebelled, one can understand why Luther was strongly against the idea of any other kind of human offering beyond these. The focus is not on the individual's work (as in intercession or adoration). The praise and self-offering come later, as response to the gift received. In the eucharist, Christ offers us with himself to the Father in heaven. Given Luther's strong emphasis on the role of faith in the believer's relationship with God, one asks the question: why is there need for the sacrament? Luther simply states that it is a matter of obedience. One's role is not to justify the decisions of God but to respond to them (Cocksworth1993: 20).

Zwingli asserted that Christ's presence is not unique to the eucharist. He is already present in the hearts of believers who are members of his body on earth. Nothing objective happens to the eucharistic elements. Jesus' 'this is my body' is to Zwingli a metaphor. 'Eating His body' means simply 'to believe in Him' (Bromiley 1953: 205). Zwingli believed that Christ's body is an authentically human one and is now in heaven (Cocksworth 1993: 24).[10] Zwingli believed that to the elect, the eucharist is a sign of grace already received, facilitating the contemplation of faith (ie it is not a means of grace, a sacrament). The eucharist is simply a memorialistic service: one remembers Christ's death by a ritual enactment of the Last Supper (Berkhof 1979: 367–8).

---

10. Zwingli met with Luther, Philip Melanchthon, Martin Bucer and J Occolampadius in 1529 at Marburg for a conference called by Philip of Hesse. The conference was aimed at achieving unity between the Swiss and Saxon reformers. At this Colloquy of Marburg, Zwingli and Luther strongly disagreed with each other on the issue of the eucharist: the former could not accept Luther's 'consubstantiation' position (Cross 1974: 869).

It has a place in building up the faith of the believer as well. In a letter to Fridolin Lindauer (October 1524) Zwingli described the human person as having both an 'outward' and an 'inward' man. He understood that the sacraments are given for the instruction of the former who receives and understands through the senses. (The latter lives by the light of faith and is not affected directly by sensory input). The 'sensory' experience that the 'outward' man experiences can confirm the person's certainty of a spiritual truth or fact (Stephens 1986: 182). The eucharist was not central in Zwinglian spirituality. Zwingli's eucharistic spirituality—if it can be called that at all, was primarily communal. The eucharist is a fellow-ship meal which provides the opportunity for believers to gather in mutual support of each other, to remember and to publicly reaffirm their faith. Zwinglian theology could foster a very rational spirituality which has little place for 'supernatural' intervention either in one's life or in the world. It is no wonder that the deists adopted Zwingli's theology of the sacrament.

Unlike Zwingli, Calvin believed that the eucharist is a sacrament, a real means of grace. It is not merely a 'spiritual–mental' contact which builds up faith in the believer (Cocksworth 1993: 25). Calvin rejected the physicality of the body represented by the Roman Catholic and Lutheran positions. He did not believe that there are any changes in substance in the communion elements. The change is spiritual: the consecrated elements now have spiritual virtue and effect. The 'power' ('*virtus*') and 'benefit' of the whole of Christ—his divinity and His humanity—is now there. '*Virtus*' is not something separate or different from the body of Christ. In this 'Virtualist' under-standing of the eucharist, Christ is present and the effects of his presence are felt. There is no transfusion of coporeal body substance—but a transfusion of life (Wallace 1953: 200, 202,208). The believer who receives the consecrated elements by faith, receives Christ spiritually (Receptionist position). The unbeliever who partakes receives nothing but an empty, useless figure while incurring judgment for eating unworthily.

What makes the communion possible is the Holy Spirit, who descends and lifts the communicants up to heaven to partake of the life of Christ in a spiritual manner (*Institutes* 4: 17.30; LCC 21.1401). Wallace considered Calvin 'inconsistent' in using the words 'ascend' and 'descend'. However, he said that Calvin would use 'descend' as long as it is clear that Christ's body is in heaven and the descent is seen to be spiritual and heavenly 'by His Spirit' (1953: 208–9). To Calvin, the body of Christ remains in heaven with all his human properties and divine properties intact (*Institutes* 4: 17.26). In union with Christ, the believer shares in Christ's one sacrifice and in his eternal priesthood before the Father's throne. The only sacrifice required of the communicant is thanksgiving (Wallace 1953: 215).

Calvin was against the propitiatory concept of the Roman Catholics, nor did he believe that the sacrament is an 'application of the once–offered sacrifice'. The focus was to be on the giftedness of the sacrifice, not on the work to be done by the communicant. He reminded the communicant of the commemorative character of the eucharist and that Christ's command is simply, to 'take'. The thanksgiving he felt that would be appropriate should be expressed not only in prayer and praise but also in faith and charity towards others (Wallace 1953: 214–6).

Calvin could not identify a distinct gift of the sacrament except to say vaguely that Christ reveals himself in a 'special way' there (Cocksworth 1993: 26). Even if, as Calvin put it, the whole of Christ is present with his 'power' and 'benefit', yet his eucharistic spirituality did not appear to be as personal as the other two. This lack of physicality and a somewhat detached approach could affect the communicant's attitude towards the physical world, the self and God. Calvin's receptionism and predestinarianism put more onus on the communicant to ensure worthiness at the table, even if at communion the believer receives the help of Christ in dealing with the still defective areas of life. It also puts the communicant in a communal setting where accountability is to and for the faith community.

3.4.2.1 The Wesleyan response

Luther's description of Christ's body as being the same as the one he had on earth and his ubiquity idea sounded absurd to the Wesleys (cf *ENNT* Matthew 26: 26, 28; *HLS* 63/2).

The Wesleys would not accept Zwingli's position. For them, the eucharist is a means of grace, a sacrament. There is a place for memorial but it is not a 'mere memorial' (cf Wesley 1745: 13). The *HLS* attest to the Wesleys' strong belief in Christ's presence at the table. While Zwinglian eucharistic spirituality was primarily rational, the Wesleyan one was more experiential.

With Calvin, the Wesley brothers would see the sacrament as a means of grace. Calvin's insistence that the change that takes place in the elements is not in substance but in spirit would probably be affirmed by the Wesleys, although the Wesleys' understanding of Christ's presence might be expressed in stronger and more personal terms than that of 'power' (*'virtus'*). Sanders believed that John Wesley shared Calvin's idea of 'spiritual presence' (1966: 6–7). Borgen would refer to the Wesleys' experience as 'living presence' (Borgen 1986: 69).

In Calvin's mind, the Holy Spirit lifts up the communicants to where Christ is, in heaven. We have stated that while the Wesleys saw Christ in heaven as eternal priest and intercessor, the movement is 'sideways' rather than 'upwards', in that the 'veil' which blinds us is removed and we can see Calvary before us (*HLS* 3, 18, 122). As a predestinarian, Calvin believed that the sacrament was for the elect. The Wesleys invited all who needed to come (Wesley 1997: 3,13). It was a converting ordinance. Calvin was more concerned with the giftedness of the sacrifice. The Wesleys, with the response of the recipient. The *HLS* has a section on 'concerning the Sacrifice of our Persons' which encouraged the self-offering of the communicant. Where Calvin could not find a specific role for the eucharist, the Wesleys had one: it was the primary means of grace for growing into Christian perfection.

Wesleyan eucharistic spirituality appeared more warmly personal and confident than Calvin's with regard to the believers' relationship with Christ, the world and the self. Its focus on the objective grace of God freed the communicant from anxieties which predestinarianism and receptionism would engender.

It is tempting to postulate how the reformers could have influenced Wesleyan eucharistic thought. The Wesleys seemed to owe little to the reformers except to Luther's 'justification by faith' teachings (cf *C W J* 17/5/1739. 6/6/1738,11/6/1738, 24/5/1738). As footnote 6 of chapter two indicated, Calvin was never referred to in John Wesley's discussion on the eucharist and the great Methodist theologian Outler himself debunked the possibility of the Wesleys owing the reformers any conscious theological debt. It is more likely that elements of Luther/Zwingli/Calvin's eucharistic thought filtered to the Wesleys through the Wesleys' Anglican heritage, eg through the *BCP*. The Wesleys' responses were thus greatly coloured by their heritage's positive adaptations of and negative reactions to the reformers' positions.

Two stark differences characterise the Wesleys in relation to the Continental reformers: the Wesleys' eucharistic theology and spirituality seem to be more 'activist' than those held by the Continental reformers. This orientation contributed to the Wesleys more 'robust' concept of grace (ie in the face of divine gift of love, the passivity of the human's receptive role is balanced by the encouragement of human responsive in pro-active works). In the eucharistic teaching of the Wesleys, the Presence of Christ is presented as more personal and intimate, even surprisingly dynamic, than in the writings of the reformers.

It would be possible at this juncture to look at Cranmer's eucharistic position and subsequent developments in eucharistic thought within the Church of England. However, we are following not just a chronological scheme (early church —medieval period—reformation—post-reformation) but one which maintains denominational and sectarian categories (eg Roman Catholicism, positions represented by Luther, Calvin, Zwingli) as well. In line with the latter structure, I will first look very briefly at three groups which had some influence on the Wesleys' thinking. Two of them are 'children' of the refor-mation—the Moravians and the Puritans. The third are the mystics—a mixed classification of those who can be described as such from both Roman Catholic and Protestant circles. After looking at these, I will turn to exploring the eucharistic positions within the Church of England from the time of Cranmer to the time of the Wesleys.

3.5 The Moravians
The Moravians were the descendants of the Bohemian Brethren who settled in the estate of Count Nikolaus Ludwig Graf Zinzendorf. Gathered into a religious community at Herrnhut under his leadership, their missionary zeal led some of their people to journey to America. It was on the ship *Simmonds* that the Wesleys first encountered them. John was so impressed with the fact that the Moravians, including their children (unlike all those on that ship including himself) were not afraid of the storm and were praying and singing during that frightening episode (*JWJ* 25/1/1736). It was a Moravian, Peter Bohler, who challenged John and Charles with the gospel of grace (JWL 3). Bohler started a 'religious society' at Fetter Lane in London.[11] In later years, his teachings regarding the need for Christians to have absolute faith and his setting aside the means of grace (eg the eucharist) in favour of waiting on the Lord for a direct divine encounter led to the separation of the Methodists from the English Moravians.

At first glance, it would be difficult to see how the Wesleys would be indebted to the Moravians in the area of eucharistic theology or spirituality. We know that the Wesleys parted company with the English Moravians primarily over the issues of the use of means of grace (to the Wesleys, these are the means by which God has chosen to create and to continue the faith) and of Christian perfection; (the Wesleys allowed for 'degrees of faith' and encouraged people to work actively towards Christian perfection, the English Moravians believed

---

11. Podmore's (1998: 29–96) investigation into the accounts of several people (including the Moravians) provides a more accurate picture of the Fetter Lane situation. However, since the study of this thesis is about the Wesleys' theology, what is being presented is from their perspective.

that either one has absolute faith or one has none at all). Perhaps the intensity of their disagreement with the Moravians regarding the means of grace resulted in the strong emphasis the Wesleys placed upon the sacrament of the Lord's supper. This could be the Moravians' first contribution to Wesleyan theology and spirituality. Second, in an ironical way, two of the key means by which the Wesleys propagated their eucharistic faith were possibly learnt from the Moravians. Towlson credited the Moravians with imparting to the Wesleys the practice of hymn singing (Towlson 1957: 246). Some of the *HLS* hymns reflect the Moravian hymnic style which wore a darker shade of emotions (some might call this the 'blood and wounds' school) familiar also to hymn styles found during the Middle Ages and in Saumur (Morris 1969: 382 cf. *HLS* 20; 85/3). John Wesley was familiar with how the Moravians used testimonies of their members to reinforce their teachings. We have noted in the last chapter how testimonies of experiences at the Table were used by the Wesleys to encourage reception of the sacrament. Third, as mentioned in chapter 1, John Wesley paid a visit to the Moravian community in Herrnhut and on one occasion he was turned away from the Table because they considered him a *homo perturbatus*. We recall also that the Moravians had strict restrictions as to who could come to the table. One can postulate how John Wesley could have been affected by that episode in his life and how that could have tempered his eucharistic theology and spirituality, especially with regards to divine grace and eucharistic requirements. Fourth, the weight the Moravians gave to personal faith and the respect they gave to experience as an authority (albeit under Scriptural authority) for beliefs and action provided the Wesleys with a basic evangelical foundation and a heart - orientated faith (cf Podmore 1998: 42). Finally, we observe that Clifford Towlson had listed (among other things) the band system, love feast and the watchnight service (1957: 246–247) as the contributions of Moravianism to Methodism. In our next chapter we will see how some of these practices were used by the Wesleys to cultivate eucharistic spirituality.

3.6 The Puritans

The Puritans were the more extreme English Protestants who had been influenced by the Calvinists in Geneva. They insisted on having scriptural warrant for all public worship practices, focused on preaching and rejected any use of what they considered to be Roman Catholic forms. Some were for presbyterian government, others for congregationalism, but most were against episcopacy (Cross 1974: 1146–7). The grandparents of the Wesleys were nonconformists although their parents returned to the Church of England. The upbringing Susanna Wesley had in the home of her father Dr Samuel Annesley included education in Puritan writings (including Richard Baxter's books), methodical keeping of timetables, regular times for meditation, self-examination and the keeping of the Sabbath. Susanna passed this heritage on to her children. Among the scanty list of readings we have of Charles Wesley, we know that he was familiar with Bunyan's *Pilgrim's Progress* (*CWJ* 8/3/1744). John Wesley read the Puritan writers, and abridged, edited and published several of them in his *Christian Library*. These include works by Robert Bolton, John Preston, Richard Stibbes, Thomas Goodwin, Thomas Manton, Isaac Ambrose, Nathanael Culverwell, John Owen, Joseph Allein, Samuel Rutherford, John Bunyan, Richard Baxter, John Flavel, Stephen Charnock, John Howe, and Samuel Annesley (Newton 1964: 7). He also read Daniel Neal's *History of the Puritans* which he recommended as a textbook for Kingswood students. The largest single tradition represented in the *Christian Library* edited by John Wesley was that of the Puritans. They influenced John Wesley in theology, pastoralia, family piety and ethics (Newton 1964: 9). The *Covenant Service* of the Methodists (which we refered to in chapter 2) had its roots in the work of Puritans Joseph and Richard Allein.

Most Puritans (some exceptions include John Goodwin) were Calvinists, and Wesley found that he disagreed with them not only over their Calvinism but over their love for controversy (JWW 19) and their views regarding Christian perfection. Unlike some of the Puritans, Methodists gave more weight to the place of feelings, especially the experience of inward assurance (Rack 1997: 3).

The Puritans were not unanimous about their sacramental positions: while some Puritans 'sub-ordinated or even rejected the sacraments in favour of the Word', eg the Quakers, the Pilgrim Fathers, Separatists, Ranters and Seekers (Cocksworth 1993: 56), and some held Zwinglian views about the eucharist (eg Richard Crakanthorpe 1567–1624) (Dugmore 1942: 59), many of those who followed Oliver Cromwell saw the eucharist as a sacrament, a means of grace. These focused not on the benefits of his passion but on Christ whom one really received at the table and who furthered one's union with him there (Cocksworth 1993: 50). They held that something happened to the elements at consecration and included in their liturgy the sanctification of the elements and a prayer for the Spirit to work effectively in the lives of the communicants. To them, Cranmer's liturgy in the *BCP* did not have an adequate prayer of consecration (Cocksworth 1993: 48).

There was a great deal of concern about worthiness of reception because they sought to keep the faith and the sacrament pure by being a church of discipline and of the Spirit's presence. Before the service itself where the communion would be served to those seated at a special table, there would be the examination of communicants (Stevenson 1994: 167). They practised 'closed' communion. At the other end of the spectrum, we have Puritan Stoddard who developed the idea that communion is a converting ordinance in response to the pastoral needs of baptised Christians unable to testify to the experience of grace required for admission to the sacrament (Holifield 1974: 200, 214). Selleck raised the possibility that the Wesleys could have been aware of Stoddard or of the Erastian controversies which gave rise to this teaching (1983: 136).

The Puritan contribution to Wesleyan eucharistic theology and spirituality was in providing him with an understanding of the value of maintaining strict devotional disciplines and lifestyle. Its legacy of the covenant service enriched Wesleyan eucharistic spirituality. Perhaps the memory of Stoddard's experiment in grace could have contributed to Wesley's 'eucharist as converting ordinance' idea.

One other note: although John Wesley did read and abridge some books by the Pietists (eg *Nicodemus* by AH Francke), it was probably through his associations with the Moravians and the Puritans that pietism with its concern for evangelical preaching, family worship, group Bible studies, and revival in spiritual life was filtered through to the Wesley brothers. The *ENNT* which John Wesley published was John's adaptation and plagiarisation of Pietist Johannes Albrecht Bengel's *Gnomon*.

3.7 The mystics

Berger suggested that Charles Wesley might have read some of the books studied by his brother John and the Oxford small groups, eg those by Antoinette Bourignon, Jeanne Marie Guyon, Francois Fenelon, Nicholas Malebranche, Miguel de Molinos, Alfonso Rodriguez and Johannes Tauler. He could also have read some of the Roman Catholic mystics John included in his *Christian Library* (1991: 207). The *Library* contained extracts from Fenelon's two letters to the Duke of Burgundy, parts of Spanish Quietist Molinos' work—*Spiritual Guide* and Bourignon's preface to her *A Treatise of Solid Virtue*. Both Guyon and Fenelon were suspected of 'quietism' in the Roman Catholic Church. John Wesley had reservations regarding Guyon's (spelt 'Guion' sometimes by him) reliance on inward inspirations and impressions rather than the Scriptures (*JWJ* 5/6/1742; 27/8/1770). While he found Fenelon's *Telemachus* rather long-winded, though sensible (*JWJ* 7/1/1760), he quoted Fenelon's words on simplicity at least twice (JWL 23, 24).

There were two groups of mystics who had great influence over John Wesley. First were those of the more passive tradition—the contemplatives who would travel on the *via negativa* road. These include Tauler, Molinos, the author of *Theologia Germanica*, Malebranche, Bourignon, the Rhineland mystics and, in later years, Law, who was influenced by Jakob Boehme. These were more speculative and pantheistic in their philosophy, aiming for the deification of the soul, and had no appreciation of the use of the means of grace like the sacraments. They spoke of blind obedience to God and the need to go through the 'dark night of the soul' (Tuttle 1989: 108). John was an avid reader of these mystics,[12] especially in the years prior to Aldersgate. In his letter to his brother Samuel, John wrote:

> I think the rock on which I had the nearest made shipwreck of the faith, was, the writings of the Mystics, under which term I comprehend all, and only those, who slight any means of grace (*JWJ* 23/11/1736).

However, when he published the 1739 *Hymns and Sacred Poems*, he gave credit to the mystic writers in the preface of the book saying that some verses were written 'upon the scheme of the Mystic divines' (*JWW* 20).

Although the mystic writers of this tradition were against the means of grace, Wesley did receive from them lessons in perseverance, disinterested love, and prayer (Tuttle 1989: chapter 6). Some of these fruits could have surfaced in the *HLS* and in the eucharistic spirituality of the brothers, eg obeying Christ by going for constant eucharistic reception and disregarding one's lack of warm feelings during reception could have come from Fenelon's idea of 'disinterested/pure love'.

The other group of mystics which enjoyed the favour of John Wesley were mostly those from the counter-reformation. They were ascetical but not as contemplative or introverted as the first group. There were strong moral, intellectual and activist strains in them. We already looked at one from before the reformation: a Kempis. Those after the reformation were de Sales, Brother Lawrence, John of Avila and people like Gregory Lopez (1611–1691), a missionary to Mexico and Marquis Gaston Jean Baptiste de Renty (1611–1648), a French nobleman. John saw de Renty and Lopez as examples of holiness and models of Christian perfection like John Fletcher (*Sermon* 133). He called them 'real inward Christians' even when he admitted that they had 'wrong opinions and (were) Romanists' (*Sermon* 55). Even Bourignon could not compare with them

---

12.   See Tuttle's *John Wesley and the Roman Catholic Mystics*, a PhD dissertation presented to Bristol University in 1969.

(JWL 25). He included their life stories in his *Christian Library*, removing the more Roman Catholic beliefs and practices of these men from his accounts. These active mystics provided Wesleyan eucharistic spirituality with concrete human models of eucharistically centred Christian discipleship.

John Wesley admired Lopez, having read about him in 1735. He appreciated Lopez's life of union with God. After 1738, John returned to reading Lopez's life again and again. When he dined in luxury at Bath, John judged himself by wondering what Lopez, a Spaniard who spent the last 34 years of his life as a hermit committed to a life of simplicity in Mexico, would have thought of it (*JWJ* 15/10/1755) and with regard to the sacrament.

De Renty was a saintly councillor at the French court. Charles read de Renty's life by St Jure (see Appendix E). John Wesley saw in de Renty certain parallels to his own ministry and work: both had outreach to the poor, both were involved in the formation and running of religious societies (de Renty had them in Paris and Toulouse), de Renty had the experience of the constant presence and fullness of the Holy Trinity (which perhaps John saw as a proof of perfect love), they both shared a simple spartan lifestyle and a stringent use of time. The understanding of detachment from worldly goods even while having them (*HLS* 145/5) could have been inspired by de Renty's example. De Renty was also cautious about outward visions and was, like Wesley, involved in experimental medical practices (Duffy 1993: 1–19). The man 'had an incredible esteem for the Holy Eucharist' and communicated three to four times a week (St Jure 1795: 6), a practice which we know John observed as well. De Renty not only engaged in self-examination and other spiritual disciplines, but he also visited the poor, the sick and the imprisoned. Chapter 8 (Section II) of St Jure's book reported him as begging for the poor (1795: 45). Could Wesley have followed this eucharistically centred examplar of his when he begged for the poor in London in his old age (*JWJ* 4/1/1785)? In 1758, John Wesley claimed that de Renty's *Life* was his favourite book. He quoted most from it in his later life (Butler 1995: 142–3). Wilson expressed his surprise and wrote:

It is ironical that one of the greatest Protestant leaders of time should have turned to the Counter Reformation for his staple food (1968: 152–172).

4. The Anglican tradition

4.1 Cranmer's eucharistic theology and spirituality

The focus of English Reformer Archbishop Cranmer's eucharistic theology was purely 'receptionist', centring on the faith of the communicant. He was more concerned about the relationship of the presence of Christ to the worthy believer than to the consecrated elements. He differed from Calvin in the weight he gave to the faith in the communicant. For Calvin faith is merely the prerequisite, the eucharist mediated Christ directly. The eucharist cemented the communion between Christ and the believer. For Cranmer the eucharistic elements stimulated faith, giving the communicants the assurance they need. This faith in turn facilitates the communicants' communion with God (Cocksworth 1993: 29). How Christ is present was not Cranmer's main concern. Content to leave it as a mystery, his *Articles of Religion* in the *BCP* can be interpreted as holding to a 'virtualist position' (like Calvin's) with regard to the question of the presence of Christ in the consecrated elements. With regard to the believer, it was understood that those who receive it 'worthily' received Christ's spiritual presence (a 'receptionist position'). Those who receive un-worthily received damnation (cf *Articles of Religion* Number 25).

Cranmer's eucharistic spirituality was corporate and liturgical. Avoiding the temptation to specify the nature of the presence, he left the worshipper with a sense of mystery and expectation, awaiting a spiritual touch from the divine in the eucharist. The worshipper, coming with limited faith, will receive that increase of faith which would make his communion with God possible. This in some ways took the sting out of the absolute necessity to be a 'worthy' communicant where unworthiness would bring damnation.

4.2 The Book of Common Prayer[13]

The old adage *'lex orandi (est) lex credendi'* (the law of prayer is the law of belief) held true of the Wesleys. It is possibly accurate to assert that other than the Scriptures, the Anglican tradition was the other primary source of the Wesleys' eucharistic theology and spirituality. The corporate and liturgical spirituality of the *BCP* kept Wesleyan eucharistic spirituality from being simply individualistically devotional (without losing the latter element).[14] The anti-Roman Catholic diatribes of the *Articles of Religion* there ensured that their theology (and thus their spirituality) was solidly within the Protestant tradition. The *BCP's* Christocentric focus, the biblical understanding of substitutionary atonement (Selleck 1983: 214–226), it's 'embryonic' doctrine of sanctification and perfection (eg in the Collect for Purity of Heart), its idea that the eucharist is a 'converting ordinance' (cf *Article 15* in the *Articles of Religion* which states that the sacrament has a task of 'quickening' one's

---

13.   The first *BCP* came out in 1549. It restored the *anamnesis'* central position, introduced an *epiclesis* where both the Word and the Holy Spirit were invoked, and sought to avoid the use of the concept of sacrifice for the sacrament. As the compromise document between those who held the traditional faith and those who had moved more towards the continental reformers' theological orientations, it failed to please both. The second *BCP* came out in 1552. It was more 'reformed' in character. The 1553 *BCP* of Queen Mary restored the ancient services. The 1559 *BCP* was based on the reformed one. The next significant publication came in 1662, the edition which was used by the Anglican Church during the time of the Wesleys (Cross 1974: 320).

14.   John Wesley published in 1733 *A Collection of Forms for Prayer for Every Day of the Week*. This collection was reprinted twelve times during his lifetime. He adapted the eucharistic prayer of confession for a devotional evening prayer:

> O almighty Lord . . . I . . . cast myself down before thee, humbly confessing my
> manifold sins and unsufferable wickedness. I confess . . . I have sinned grievously
> against thee by thought, word and deed particularly this day .
> . . (Selleck 1983: 182).

faith) and its belief in the sacrament as a real means of grace were inherited by Wesleys (Selleck 1983: 291–3), affecting their eucharistic theology and spirituality.

The Prayer Book was the source of Wesleyan eucharistic liturgy. John admired the liturgy there for its simplicity and solemnity as compared to the Presbyterian style (*JWJ* 16/6/1764). John altered the eucharistic liturgy for use by Methodists in America. Very few significant changes were made. Most changes had to do with adapting to the situation of independent America (eg in the prayers for rulers, no mention about table location), simplifying the rules and liturgy (eg in not requiring communicants to inform the minister the day before of intention to communicate, removing unnecessary words) and giving place to three distinctive Methodist developments (ministers were called 'elders' not 'priests'; extemporary prayer were provided for at the end of the service and the long didactic confession exhortations were removed in view of the mutual examination and confessions in Methodist societies). John Wesley also removed one quotation from Tobit from the offertory sentences and replaced the long Nicene Creed with the simpler Apostles' Creed (White 1991: 125–139). Selleck concluded that the reason for the removal of the second post-communion prayer could be because it was not as 'high church and priestly' as the first: 'it sounded too much like Calvinism for Wesley's Arminian plate' (1983: 386–7). George (1976: 103, 105) and Harmon (1974: 140) believed that the first editions of the service (1784) included instruction regarding the manual acts for accompanying the consecration. Wesley omitted the Nicene Creed because his Apostles' Creed would have been said at morning prayer. He did not include what the non–jurors would have liked.

Liturgy shapes theology. The *BCP's* Arminian orientation, the combination of 'free form' extemporary prayers and formal liturgy which affirmed the union of heart and head in the worship of God, the visual element (which affirmed the use of senses) provided by the manual acts—all these were absorbed into Methodist eucharistic theology and spirituality. In the *HLS*, some links with the *BCP* can be discerned. *HLS* 105 has the echoes of the *Sursum Corda,* 163 of the *Gloria,* 20 of the *Agnus*

Dei. HLS 157/4 corresponds with the sentiments of the post-communion prayer ('Here we offer and present unto Thee ourselves, our souls and bodies . . .').

The *BCP* influenced the Wesleys' eucharistic practices. Although John was not insistent that dissenters (or the Methodists in America) should kneel as the Anglicans would as they come for communion (cf *BCP* of 1662), the general Methodist practice was the same as that of the Anglicans. John's preference was clear, yet he noted that when he administered to about two hundred communicants at Norwich, 'a considerable part of them were dissenters', he left it up to each one to use whatever posture they wanted, knowing that if he had required them to kneel, 'probably half would have sat'. The result was that on that occasion, all but one knelt for the sacrament (*JWJ* 18/3/1759). Kneeling was an expression of humility and reverence. Cosin, an Anglican divine, said that kneeling expressed 'inward reverence and devotion of our souls' (1855: 345–346). Could these be the reasons for John's preference? It would certainly reflect the theme of grace in Wesleyan eucharistic spirituality to picture the communicant coming to the Father as one who is a much loved yet a needy sinner.

4.3 Developments after Cranmer

Although Cranmer's first *BCP* (1549) did not depart far from Anglicanism's Roman Catholic roots except avoiding the presentation of the mass as a sacrifice (Sykes 1988: 273–4), later versions of the *BCP* showed greater influences from the Reformed tradition (eg the ones in 1552, 1559). The Church of England after Cranmer developed further his eucharistic theology. Stimulus for change was wrought by many causes —some of which were the social and political happenings in England (Dugmore 1942: 2).

Cocksworth postulated that there were three significant shifts. First, a more significant role was given to the consecrated elements. Second, the focus was more on the experience rather than the manner of the presence of Christ in the eucharist. Third, there was deeper exposition about the sacrificial aspects of the eucharist (1993: 34).

There seems to have been a lot more discussion on the role of the consecrated elements than the two other areas. The Prayer Book of 1559 strengthened the link between the presence of Christ and the consecrated elements. In 1573, the Church Com-missioners ruled that there was a need for supplementary consecration.[15] This was enshrined in the Canon Laws of 1603 and reflected in the liturgy in 1662. In contrast to Calvin who had the reading of the institutional narrative so that the congregation could hear Christ's eucharistic mandate, the Anglican leaders now addressed the words at the elements as well (Cocksworth 1993: 34). There was an understanding that something did happen to the elements. Both Jewel and Hooker went beyond Cranmer's position. Cranmer had seen that the elements helped to create the faith which made communion with Christ possible. Now the consecrated elements were seen to be the means by which communion with Christ was made possible. Hooker wrote that

> the elements are changed in use that they become causes instrumental upon the receipt whereof the participation of His body and blood ensueth (Hooker 1940: 322).

Andrewes in his 1618 Christmas Day sermon described the elements as vehicles of the Spirit, conveying Christ to people. Consecration set apart the elements for sacred use. There was no substantial change in them, hence Christ in the eucharist was 'truly present and to be adored' but the sacrament was not to be adored (Dugmore 1942: 41).

Nevertheless, Anglican church leaders were careful lest there be misinterpretations. Jewel wrote:

> First, we put a difference between the sign and the thing itself that is signified. Secondly, that we

---

15.   The 1573 Johnson Case revolved around the question on whether there was a need for supplementary consecration. Johnson interpreted Cranmer as saying it was unnecessary. The Church Commissioners disagreed with him (Cocksworth 1993: 34–6).

seek Christ above in heaven, and imagine not Him to be bodily upon the earth. Thirdly, that the body of Christ is to be eaten by faith only, and none likewise (1847: 449).

. . . the sacrament bread is bread, it is not the body of Christ: the body of Christ is flesh, it is no bread. The bread is beneath: the body is above. The bread is on the table: the body is in heaven. The bread is in the mouth: the body in the heart. The bread feedeth the outward man: the body feedeth the inward man. Such a difference is there between the bread, which is a sacrament of the body, and the body of Christ itself (1847: 1121).

While Cranmer was vague and diffident, some of his followers were more definite: they had no anxiety about putting 'The Body of Christ is given . . . ' in the *Articles of Religion* 1563 and 1571. Hooker moved from Cranmer's Virtualism. He wrote:

. . . this bread hath in it more than the substance which our eyes behold . . . what these elements are in themselves it skilleth not, it is enough that to me, which take them they are the body and blood of Christ (Hooker 1836: 462).

Those who wanted to see more objectivity in the sacrament, however, taught that reservation of the elements meant that consecration was permanent, the faith or lack of it on the part of the communicant did not affect anything of what God was doing. Adoration was not of the elements but of the presence that had joined itself to the elements. John Johnson (1662–1725) (1714: 341–342) and Robert Nelson a non-juror (1665–1715) and author of *The Great Duty* of *Frequenting the Christian Sacrifice* (1707) were of that opinion (Nelson 1909: 477).

The Manchester non-jurors as a group also shared this view. They stood for frequent celebrations of communion and they insisted that the spiritual (not corporeal as held by Roman

Catholics) presence of Christ's body and blood is there with the elements, brought upon by the *epiclesis* prayer (Dugmore 1942: 146–7, 153).

The fear of the practice of adoration of the consecrated elements had been expressed by Cosin (1594–1672). Cosin denied that the consecrated elements had the nature of a sacrament when it is used outside its original eucharistic purpose appointed by God. He therefore stated that it would not be possible or right for the elements to be reserved and carried about (Dugmore 1942: 108). Christ was only present to those who communicated. As Patrick, Bishop of Ely, wrote in *The Christian Sacrifice,*

> And this indeed the bread and wine are changed, not by abolishing their substance, but by turning them to this Divine Use (to which they are deputed by prayer according to Christ's institution) to render to us spiritual grace of the broken Body and Blood shed of our Saviour (1753: 141–350).

Waterland (1683–1740), like Cosin and Patrick, taught that the elements are not changed in substance (unlike Roman Catholic beliefs) but held that they are changed by consecration only for the specific use of communion. In chapter 2 we recorded Waterland's belief that the elements gained relative holiness because of the consecration (1738:127–8). Waterland utilised St Bernard's illustration of comparing sacraments with instruments of investiture and described the elements as a deed of conveyance which conveys the estate even though it is not the estate (1738:146–7). The elements convey Christ and therefore can be called by the name of what they are set apart to convey. Waterland disagreed with the non-jurors that the divine was united with the elements. If this were so, unworthy communicants would receive Christ with the elements.

The emergence of the deists in the early eighteenth century brought yet another challenge to Anglican eucharistic theology. More about the deists will be written in the next section. We note here that Waterland's accusation against deists was that they were Socinians who believe in bare commemoration (1738:148–9).

The second theological shift since Cranmer's time was that many in the Church of England wanted to emphasise the reality of communion with Christ without having to pinpoint exactly the mode of that possibility.

> Sith we all agree that by the sacrament Christ doth really and truly in us perform his promise, why do we vainly trouble ourselves with so fierce contentions whether by consubstatiation, or else by transubstantiation the sacrament itself be first possessed with Christ, or no? (Hooker 1836: 353)

In this light, people like Jewel and Hooker spelt out the unique role of the eucharist in the life of the church: Hooker believed that the eucharist

> creates the righteousness of Christ in the moral, spiritual and bodily life of the individual as the believer is united more deeply and more really in the life of Christ by means of the elements through the activity of the Spirit (1940: 234–236).

While the word taught the mind through hearing, the eucharist marked the believer physically and was an effectual means, not just the seal of the word (Hooker 1940: 234–236).

The third noticeable shift was that the theologians who came after Cranmer developed more deeply the sacrificial aspects of the eucharist. They were not for the Roman Catholic understanding of propitiatory sacrifice: there was only one sacrifice—Christ's. There would be no repetition of his sacrifice. The only repetition was the memory, a commemoration of the sacrifice, brought to mind by the Holy Spirit (Andrewes 1841: 301). On the human level, this memory became for the believer an invitation to follow the example of his life (Jewel 1845: 493). On the divine level, Laud and

Andrewes saw the eucharist as a commemoration to God. Christ was offered up as sacrificed (Taylor) and his past sacrifice pleaded its effects on the present, interceding for us (Cosin) (Cocksworth 1993: 44).[16] Waterland saw the sacrifice of the eucharist as commemorative, participative (Waterland 1737: 475–478) and applicative:

> . . . it is not barely or performing the conditions that finishes our salvation but it is our Lord's applying his merits to our performances that finishes all (Waterland 1738: 105).

Patrick (1625–1707) described it as a commemoration, or 'shewing forth' in two directions: Godward—where Christ's sacrifice is shown to the Father and manward—where it is shown to the world to tell of Christ's death for all (cf Patrick 1753: 161–2).

The three developments in English eucharistic theology brought about a corresponding shift in eucharistic spirituality. Firstly, Christ became more identified with the elements: eg the Puritans requiring 'valid' consecration, Hooker and Andrewes moving beyond a mixture of virtualism and seeing

---

16. The accusation of the Roman Catholics that the Protestants do not have a proper priesthood because there was an absence of a material sacrifice. engendered a debate within the Protestant ranks regarding eucharistic elements. Were the elements sacrificed in addition to Christ's sacrifice? If they were, then there would be a material sacrifice offered up at communion. John Johnson believed that Christ offered himself in the eucharist by and with the elements. The church followed his example in offering the symbols, a material sacrifice. Johnson was accused of being a papist. Waterland mused that he could have made a cause for Protestant priesthood being proper without opting for a material but by speaking of a spiritual sacrifice (Waterland 1738: 53–55). Dr Mede wrote *The Christian Sacrifice* in 1672, referring to the bread and wine as a material sacrifice like the *Micha* of the Old Testament Law. Although he rejected the Roman Catholic understanding of material sacrifice, he was misunderstood and attacked as a papist. Added to the confusion, the Jesuits started claiming him as a supporter of the Roman cause as well (Waterland 1737: 467–8).

the elements in an instrumental way, Waterland's insight of the elements having 'relative holiness', Cosin's belief in their special 'set apartness' because of Christ's spiritual presence, Johnson and the non-jurors affirming the permanent nature of the consecration. The stronger the link between Christ's presence and the elements, the more positive the affirmation of the material goodness of all creation: for these creatures would be seen as being capable of a deeper degree of sanctity and union with the divine.

The second shift was the movement to focus on the experience rather than the manner of Christ's presence. This shift signalled the deepening of a more intimate spirituality where head and heart, theology and spirituality are conjoined. Brevint's treatise *Christian Sacrament and Sacrifice* with its interflow of theological reflection and prayer is a good example of this.

When stronger links are made between the consecrated elements and the presence of Christ, the importance of the believer's faith in relation to what happens to the elements is lessened. This third change and its stress on the 'applicative' sacrificial aspects of eucharistic theology meant the focus was more on a grace–filled relationship with the divine, not so much on the response of the communicant. Yet we note that the official position of Anglican eucharistic theology was still receptionism and there still existed a great concern about adequate preparation and worthy reception of the sacrament. One senses that there was a constant tension in English eucharistic theology between focusing on the divine work of grace and focusing on the human response.

4.4 The deists, latitudinarians, moralists and non-jurors

Four groups around that time in Anglicanism also affected the Wesleys' eucharistic theology and spirituality, namely the deists, the latitudinarians, the moralists and the non-jurors. Deism was 'natural religion' and, as a result, 'minimised' the value of biblical revelation (Sykes 1962: 60–61). It eroded the corporate understanding of the church as the body of Christ, focused on the beliefs shared by all religions and placed little demands on the people in terms of commitment to the faith.

Sincerity, not dogma, was most important (Selleck 1983: 43, 44). Bishop Hoadly (as reflected in his sermon *The Nature of the Kingdom of Christ*) and Samuel Clarke (as represented in his book *Scripture Doctrine of the Trinity*) were proponents of these positions. Law and Waterland battled against them, the latter accusing them of being Socinians or Arians with regard to Christ's divinity (Selleck 1983: 45–46).

Latitudinarianism developed from the Cambridge Platonists, the theological liberals of their day, seeking to give more latitude in the imposition of the laws of the Church of England on dissenters. Loyal to the episcopacy and Anglican liturgy, they also wanted freedom to explore philosophy and theology in a scientific, reasonable way. Religion had to do with conduct. Public worship was to adore God and to inculcate 'the duties of people living in society' (Sykes 1962: 257–258). Faith thus became intellectual and the inward operation of the Holy Spirit which might supersede reason was negated (Selleck 1983: 23–4). Tillotson, a good but unemotional preacher and Benjamin Hoadly (who expressed Zwinglian sympathies in his anonymously published *Plain Account of the Nature and End of the Sacrament of the Lord's Supper* [1735]), were Latitudinarians (Stevenson 1994: 181). Deism as well as latitudianarism arose around the eighteenth century as a reaction against the years of religious intolerance, the fairly current experience of Puritan commonwealth rigidity and uncertainties regarding James II's Catholic orientation. Religious enthusiasm was discouraged in deism, lest violent and intense passions were stirred up again to the detriment of the community. The result was that Anglicanism became more individualistic, cerebral, anthropocentric (rather than Christocentric) and chiefly practical (rather than mystical or spiritual) in orientation.

Wesleyan eucharistic theology and spirituality, in contrast and possibly, in response to these two movements, sought to be personal though not individualistic, careful to maintain the corporate element in the inner as well as the outer life of the believer. It spoke to both heart and head, to the emotions, not only to the intellect. It was very Christocentric and open to the

Spirit's vibrant, suprising, life-changing initiatives in people's lives within and outside the eucharistic services.

The two other movements affected Wesleyan eucharistic theology and spirituality in a more positive way. Moralism or 'holy living' religion represented by Taylor and Law was one of these. They stressed the need for conscious and serious discipleship, seeking to instil piety through disciplined prayer, worship, study of Scripture and conscientious, worthy reception of communion. The virtue of moderation was exalted, and control of one's emotion even as one loves God, was important (Taylor 1844: 158–9).

The moralists were fearful of the atmosphere of antinomianism which prevailed in their day. Their stress on human autonomy and responsibility led them to emphasise human effort (and in the case of the sacrament, worthy reception). Preparation manuals abounded. As a result, there seemed to be a shift in their theology from the Protestant 'justification by faith' to something more 'catholic' —sanctification by effort. John Wesley would complain of the *Theologica Germanica* (though not an Anglican work but one highly recommended to him by Law, who stood in the moralist school): '(in it) I remember something of Christ our Pattern, but nothing express of Christ our Atonement . . . '(JWL 26).

Justification by faith and salvation by grace sometimes became casualties of the moralists' teachings.[17] This was John's bone of contention with Law whom he read, corresponded with and revered for years.[18] Charles who said of Law, 'All I knew

---

17. Allison observed that Taylor was inconsistent: in his sermons and theological writings, he would put the onus on human effort almost to the point of saying it was the basis for God's acceptance. In Taylor's written prayers, however, 'forgiveness and pardon precede any necessity of obedience and in spite of disobedience and lack of virtue' (Allison 1966: 88–9).

18. John Wesley was introduced to Law in 1732. He read Law's books (cf. *JWJ* 1/2/ 1737). Law got drawn towards the teachings of quietist Joseph Behmen, which Wesley considered confusing, 'dark and indeterminate' and unscriptural about the nature of God (JWW 21). John turned against Law, calling him a mystic who denied justification by faith and the imputation of the righteousness of Christ (*Sermon* 20). Yet he credited

of religion was through him' (*CWJ* 17/10/1736 and 18/10/1736) also had problems with Law's theology (Appendix E).

Both Law and Taylor contributed to the Wesley brothers' singleminded and intense dedication to God. They were all very Christocentric. These too surfaced in the eucharistic theology and spirituality of the Wesleys. However, the Wesleys reacted against Law's intensity and Taylor's strictures about the worthiness of communicants.[19] Wesleyan eucharistic spirituality was, especially in the hymns, joyous and world-transforming, not world-denying. Instead of saying that those who receive communion without faith were like the 'dead' who have 'no portion' of the meat offered to them in the graveyard (Taylor 1667: 143), the Wesleys said that communion was not 'dry breasts' and, to whoever comes, the sacrament has the potential to convert.

The last group of influential Anglicans were the non-jurors. As we have seen in chapter 1, the non-jurors had very high views of the sacraments and the patristic roots of the church. Like the moralists, they were very concerned about preparations for worthy communion and preparation manuals abound among them.

Perhaps the greatest contribution of the non-juror community towards Wesleyan eucharistic spirituality was through the work of Brevint (1616–1695). Brevint's book

---

Law with sowing the seed of religious faith (*Sermon* 68) in the people of England. He indicated that there was some truth in the people's perception that Law was 'Methodism's parent' (*Sermon* 107). John was introduced to Taylor's *Rule and exercises of holy living and dying* by Sally Kirkham. Taylor inspired him to keep a concise record of his activities throughout the day, and use ejaculatory prayers and provided the materials for Wesley's rules (twelve of them) for helpers and for the united Societies.

19. It was remarkable within the Anglican circles of their time. However, some Puritans, eg Baxter, displayed willingness to learn from Roman Catholic spirituality while rejecting papist theology. In that sense, what the Wesleys did was not unprecedented.

inspired most of the eucharistic hymns written by the Wesleys (Wainwright 1745: vi). The Wesley brothers appended an edited version of his book as a preface to their *HLS*. While the Wesleys received inspiration from Brevint, Brevint received his formation at the French Calvinist school at Saumur. Stevenson believed that Brevint could have been influenced by Philippe du Plessis-Mornay's *De l'institution, usage et doctrine du sainct sacrement de l'eucharistie en l'e`glise Ancienne* (1598). Mornay's style was to put Christ on the cross at the centre, inviting the worshipper to view him through Biblical images and references as the sacrifice (Stevenson 1994: 105–6). The Wesleys could have inherited this style from him.

The influence of the non-jurors (including Brevint) on Wesleys' eucharistic theology seemed to be in four areas. First, they underlined very strongly the centrality of the eucharist for the Christian life. Second, they directed the Wesleys, perhaps more than other existing groups at that period (possibly because of their close association with the Wesley brothers), more deeply to the primitive (including the Eastern) church for their understanding and practice of the eucharist. Third, they inspired a greater understanding of the role of the Holy Spirit in the act of *epiclesis* upon the elements. It must be admitted that in this area the Wesleys probably inherited the emphasis more from the non-jurors in general than from Brevint. However, the *HLS* does not have any evidence that the Wesleys went as far as the non-jurors did about the permanency of the change in the elements. Finally, the Wesleys probably learnt from the non-jurors the importance of the theme of eucharistic oblation. Wainwright saw the idea of oblation reflected in *HLS* numbers 116, 118, 121, 123, 124, 125, 126 where the Wesleys spoke of the 'memorial of Christ' shown to the Father (Wainwright 1996: 6).

Tracing possible sources of their eucharistic theology and spirituality even within the Anglican tradition can prove rather daunting. There are so many routes one can take and so many possible influences that one can explore. Samuel Wesley, the father of John and Charles, for example, was a member of the Society for Promoting Christian Knowledge (SPCK). John was a member as well. The SPCK produced books and pamphlets for the spiritual nourishment of its members and encouraged the development of the interior life. They held frequent celebrations of the eucharist (Selleck 1983: 145). This could very well have been a formative discipline which the Wesleys could not forget in later life.

The Wesleys were prolific readers. They could have assimilated the deep sense of love for Christ from the moralists and the non-jurors (especially Brevint and Ken) and some idea of Christian perfection from John Norris (John described him as 'a lover and a witness of Christian perfection' JWW 22). As to practices regarding regularity of reception, they could easily have picked up from Cave's *Primitive Christianity* (1672), Nelson's *A Companion to Festivals and Fasts* (1704) and Waterland's *A Review of the Doctrine of the Eucharist as laid down in Scripture and Antiquity . . .* (1737) that the eucharist was celebrated every day (Cave 1753: 218) 'while the Spirit of Christianity was yet warm and vigorous' (cf *HLS* 6), always at every public assembly (Nelson 1704: 466) and that Christians have an obligation to receive (Waterland 1737: 562–600). John Wesley probably adapted Nelson's argument against those who felt that frequency of reception would diminish reverence for the sacrament (cf Nelson 1704: 471–2).

One notes as one reads the *HLS* that there are certain similarities between them and a few other Anglican works. Patrick in *Christian Sacrifice* pointed to four things which 'makes the true feast'. To him, they were: 'select persons, choice place, choice time, choice provisions' (1753: 197). *HLS* 80 proclaimed: 'His presence makes the Feast'. Was hymn 80 inspired by Patrick's writing? Could the Wesleys be commen-ting on the difference between what they considered to be the central focus of the eucharist and that of the 'preparation schools'—the brothers focusing on Christ's presence and not on the preparations?

Although the style of the hymns does not fundamentally change their theology and spirituality, the style does make the difference in affecting the reader or singer and the effective rendering of the message. Charles Wesley's hymn imagery and texture, with its dramatic, vivid, 'abrupt speech patterns', 'startling imageries' through association of unusual objects and a sense of 'religious melancholy' (compared with Isaac Watts's

more spacious and optimistic hymns), have been linked to
George Herbert's influence. Watts was Calvinist and non-
conformist and had a deep sense of the sovereignty of God.
The Wesley's and Herbert shared the same Anglican Armenian
heritage, with great concern for the interior spiritual life
(Morris 1969: 375–383). The hymns of the Wesleys were hence
more personal, reflecting the warmth of the divine-human
relationship.

4.4.1 *The Wesleyan response to eucharist theology and spirituality in the Church in England*

Eucharistic influence on the Wesleys was primarily Anglican
because of their family background, education and orientation.
The brothers moved beyond Cranmer's receptionist position
and were affected by the three 'shifts'in Anglican eucharistic
theology. They had the *epiclesis* — one for the congregation, one
for the elements (*HLS* 7, 72)—in their eucharistic hymns
(influenced no doubt by their non-juror friends and/or their
knowledge of the Eastern church). The inclusion of the *epiclesis*
reflected their understanding of the link between the elements
and Christ's presence. We have noted that the Wesleys seemed
to share Andrewes' position that the eucharistic elements are
the 'vehicles of the Spirit, conveying Christ to people' (with its
underlining belief that consecration simply sets apart the
elements for sacred use, cf *HLS* 63/2) and Waterland's imagery
of the elements as the 'deed of conveyance' (cf Johnson and
Nelson). Yet the brothers would not go as far as the non-jurors
to say that the consecration was permanent and they did not
agree to the reservation of the elements: they were content to
leave the issue of the presence of Christ at the Table as a sacred
mystery (*HLS* 50/1–2, 57/4), they were strong in their understanding and use of sacrificial language for the sacrament. In
possible reaction to the deists and latitudinarians and in line
with Brevint's style, Wesleyan eucharistic theology and
spirituality reflected an intimacy and warmth, wedding both
the heart and the head. While they inherited from the SPCK, the
moralists and the non-jurors a strong emphasis on discipline
and spiritual formation, the Wesleys were strong on themes
regarding sacrifice and oblation which in turn put the spotlight

more on God's grace than on the place of human response and worthiness.

5. Closing observations

First, one of the strongest impressions I had in working on this chapter was that the eucharistic theology and spirituality of the Wesleys were birthed from a remarkably enriched womb, nourished by the traditions stretching through centuries of church history, particularly from the heritage of the first five centuries, the reformation and post-reformation period. These sources cut across sectarian and theological barriers. The breadth of the Wesleys' exposure to eucharistic teachings from many traditions reveal not only their depth of knowledge but also their openness and capacity for gleaning the riches from a variety of resources.

Second, it has been surprising to see how many of those who have influenced the brothers are from the Roman Catholic Church—ie those in the medieval period, those in the post-medieval period and the mystics of the more active school. Considering the era the Wesleys were living in, where there existed deep suspicion of Roman Catholicism, the input the brothers chose to receive from there was quite remarkable. It must be noted that the influence was not eucharistic in nature but had to do primarily with issues about holy living and models of serious spirituality, affecting indirectly the nature of Wesleyan eucharistic spiritual formation.

Third, the Wesleys came from a tradition where the importance of the eucharist in Christian worship and life was strongly affirmed: ie from their early church and Roman Catholic (medieval, post-medieval and counter-reformation) sources, right through to the continental reformers (with the exception of Zwingli) and their Anglican heritage (especially the non-juror connection). It is therefore little wonder that they rejected the dissenting voices of the English Moravians and the mystics of the passive school who dismissed the use of the sacrament (among other 'means of grace') in favour of 'waiting on the Lord' for a divine touch. These represented a theology totally alien to their upbringing.

Fourth, in chapter 2 I identified three key Wesleyan themes. Regarding the first theme ('the presence of Christ' in the eucharist), there seemed to be two major forces which moulded the Wesleys' position. One can be described as a 'negative' current. It is negative in the sense that the Wesleys could have developed their own eucharistic theology and spirituality in reaction against it. This negative current came from the rather impersonal, cerebrally-orientated theologies of the deists and the latitudinarians. (One could say that the more 'technical' eucharistic language of Calvin and the more 'mechanical' *ex opera operato* concept of the Roman Church has the same 'impersonal effect' on the theology of Christ's sacramental presence.) It came from the strong focus on the horizontal relationship (relationship between communicants/believers to the detriment of divine action at the sacrament) held by Zwingli and it came from the moralists' legalistic tendencies. The second force, what I would call the 'positive' current (positive in the sense that the Wesleys agreed with it and developed it further), flowed from the medieval church, the mystics, the Moravians and from their post-Cranmer Anglican eucharistic theology (especially that which is found in Brevint's treatise). This latter current provided the resources for the Wesleys to centre in on the very dynamic divine-human relationship at the Table. In opposition to the direction of the 'negative current', the Wesleys held a very warm, personal and intimate understanding of Christ's eucharistic presence at the eucharistic service. This intimacy does not cloud out the sense of mystery which Cranmer and Hooker acknowledged in the sacrament. It further enriches it. The post-Cranmer Anglican theologians with their bold linking of Christ's presence to the consecrated elements (in varying forms) not only contributed to the sense of divine immanence and warmth but also to the affirmation of the physicality of created things.

It was perhaps in reaction to the stringent eucharistic requirements of most of the groups the Wesleys grew up with, their positive exposure to the teachings about *epiclesis* and sacrifice from their Anglican tradition, from the early church and mostly through the non-jurors, that the Wesleys developed their very strong second theme—that of divine grace. This tremendous grace demands no heavy load of penitential disciplines from the early church (no matter how revered that period was held by the Wesley brothers themselves). The call for strong pro-active response to that grace by the Wesleys contrasted greatly with that era's Roman Catholic passivity and the reformers' rather quiescent receptivity.

The therapeutic role of the eucharist—the third theme —along with its 'sin as sickness; salvation as healing; goal is Christian perfection' concepts—was possibly developed from their readings of the Eastern Fathers through the influence of their more 'catholic' Anglican friends, the non-jurors. Attractive though it might sound, I have yet to discover any mention in the writings of both brothers regarding Stoddard who had explored the 'converting ordinance' idea. As we shall discern in the next chapter, the methods for applying this 'therapy' (through Christian formation) were possibly borrowed from the early church, the Moravians, the moralists and the SPCK. Their corporate (as opposed to 'individualistic') approach of their formation, their concern for the poor in their eucharistic spirituality had roots in their readings of the early church, their training in Anglican communally-orientated liturgy (which in turn owed some debt to the continental reformers) and the examples set for them by some of the Roman Catholic 'active mystics'. The urgency to get people 'on' this therapeutic treatment came from their strongly Protestant heritage where soteriological issues were paramount.

Fifth, granted this bird's-eye view of the sources of the Wesleys and how they shaped the brothers' eucharistic teachings, we can discern that the strongest influences came from the early church (more from the Eastern than Western tradition) and primarily from their Anglican heritage. It was through their Anglican non-juror friends that much of the treasures of the early church were opened to the brothers.

Although the Wesleys were nurtured by their Anglican heritage, I believe their faith in the freedom of the Spirit of God to work however he wishes led them to grow apart from their heritage on a few counts. Selleck listed two: one, the Wesleys believed that all means convey God's grace not only to believers but also to unbelievers; two, they also believed that God can and does work outside the means although he does not abandon the means he appointed (1983: 309–310). I want to add a third: where Anglicanism thrived on liturgical spirituality tied to prescribed texts, the Wesleys allowed and encouraged a Spirit-led spontaneity in their meetings through enthusiastic preaching, enthusiastic singing, extempore prayers, sharing of testimonies and an openness to supernatural 'happenings' (God-encounters which they had read about both in Scriptures and in the accounts of the early church) during those periods.

4
Wesleyan Eucharistic Spirituality

---

1. Defining Wesleyan eucharistic spirituality

What is Wesleyan eucharistic spirituality? Spirituality has to do with action (practices) and it has to do with attitudes (beliefs and theology). Our working definition states that spirituality is an 'existential and experiential response' to a call to move 'towards a goal of wholeness (however that is defined)'. The call and the goal forms one's character and colours one's total perception of life. Based on that definition, five questions will be asked of Wesleyan eucharistic practices and beliefs/theology to explore the inherent nature of Wesleyan eucharistic spirituality. They are:

- Who is the one who issues the 'call'?
- What is the nature of the movement—ie if it is a response, what kind of a response is it?
- What is the goal, ie how is the goal of wholeness understood?
- How is formation done?
- How is perception of God, self, others, world and time affected by the spirituality?

In Wesleyan eucharistic spirituality, God in Christ is identified as the one who calls. Grace plays a very major role in the response: we are supported all the way by the grace of God as we actively grow towards the goal of wholeness. Christian perfection as taught by the Wesleys is the goal or 'wholeness' sought. Intentional and intensive formation takes place through the eucharist, developing certain virtues. The formation affects the way one perceives God, self, others, the world and time, creating for the Methodist a particular worldview and thus a particular way of life.

165

2. The centrality of Christ's presence

First, Wesleyan eucharistic spirituality is Christocentric. Although the Wesleys were strongly trinitarian, Christ's presence in the eucharist is central to Wesleyan eucharistic theology. If spirituality is first 'a response to a call' (as the working definition of this thesis states), the one who initiates the whole spiritual enterprise in Wesleyan eucharistic spirituality is the Christ who issues that invitation which prompts a response.

Second, the person of Christ, not just the work of Christ, is important. Who he inherently is puts the value on what he does. Christ is always seen from the perspective of his present state of glory. His divinity is stressed even as his humanity is affirmed in the historical event at Calvary.

Third, the focus is solely on the Christ who comes. The Christocentric focus of Wesleyan eucharistic spirituality' might acknowledge the 'set-apartness' of the consecrated elements to be vehicles of the divine presence, but it would not allow for such close identification of Christ with the elements as to have reservation and adoration of the consecrated elements.[1]

This theme of 'the dynamic presence of Christ in the eucharist' which emerges in the study of Wesleyan eucharistic materials points to the fourth distinctive feature of their spirituality. The spirituality of 'the presence' is a spirituality of immanence.[2] The spirituality of immanence comes through the

---

1.   Two forms of Christocentric eucharistic spirituality come immediately to mind in comparison with the Wesleyan model. The first comes from the Roman Catholic counter-reformation tradition. The second is that of the Tractarians, who were the precursors of the Oxford Movement. The Tractarians shared with the Wesleys the concern for frequent communions, the sacrament as a definite means of grace and the desire to imitate the eucharistic practices of the early church. They differed to a certain degree in their theological understanding of whether consecration affects the elements permanently. Like the Roman Catholic counter–reformation representatives, they practised eucharistic adoration.

2.   To those who are familiar with the Myers-Briggs Type Indicator (MBTI), a personality profile test which indicates preferences of people

Wesleyan eucharistic language (from both their hymns and their writings), characterised by the sense of intimacy, immediacy and engagement.

Intimacy is relational: Christ's presence is experienced as intensely personal. Instead of the question, 'What is there?', the focus of the Wesleys regarding the eucharist was 'What is happening here?' The attention is shifted from the questions about the change or non-change in the sacramental elements to the Christ who is there and the experience of the people as they commune with him. John Wesley's interest in 'feeling' and relational types of words surfaced very clearly when he edited Brevint's *Christian Sacrament and Sacrifice*. Where Brevint prayed for the Lord to 'dispose my mind' (Brevint 1673: 19), Wesley inserted 'prepare my heart' in its place (Wesley 1745: 8). Brevint invited the worshipper to 'lay our liberalities with that same mind and thought'. Wesley changed the last two items to 'such faith and love' (Brevint 1673: 127; Wesley 1745: 32). Wesley replaced Brevint's phrase '. . . holy Thoughts . . .' (Brevint 1673: 126) with 'Let him draw out of the good measure of his heart, fire and frankincense, that is, such Zeal *and Love* as may raise good, moral works into religious sacrifices' (Wesley 1745: 31 Italics mine).

Immediacy as expressed in time-orientated terms concentrates on the 'now-ness' (cf *HLS* 126/5, 13/2, 116/5, 117/1),

---

for either Extroversion or Introversion, Sensing or Intuition, Thinking or Feeling, Judging or Perceiving, the immanence and transcendence-orientated spiritualities I mention would correspond with the preference for either the Sensing or the Intuition faculty respectively. The sensing faculty is more concerned with facts, details, history and with what can be perceived by the senses in the here and now. The intuition preference is interested in future possibilities (rather than actual realities), transcendence and mystery, imagination and the 'overview vision' (cf Goldsmith 1994, Briggs Myers 1980, Keirsey 1984). Spiritualities of immanence need not be Christocentric. The Zwinglian concentration on the more 'anthropocentric' aspect of communion might engender a feeling of immanence because of its location in the concrete and experienced fellowship of believers. However, it lacks the sense of divine immanence which would be very strong in Christocentric spiritualities which emphasise the presence of Christ at the Table.

the freshness and the 'present-ness' of the event of Calvary, experienced at the eucharist. What is happening at the eucharist is happening *in* time *now* rather than in the distant past or in the possible future. Communicants become contem-poraries of Jesus' life and passion through what can be called *'anamnetic'* remembering. In such a remembering, the barriers of time are put aside and what has taken place in history there and then is telescoped into the here and now where his present presence and power are manifested. Past-orientated mem-orialistic understandings of the eucharist can lead to sentimen-talism about the cross. This danger is not present in Wesleyan eucharistic spirituality because of the dynamic participatory mode of the experience for the communicant.

Engagement speaks in concrete, material terms through the reverence given to the role of concrete sacramental elements (seen through the use of the *epiclesis* hymns) and in the stress on actual physical consuming of those elements as part of the eucharistic encounter. Wesleyan eucharistic spirtuality has a very strong place for the use of the physical senses (as we shall see in the section 'Seeing life through the eucharist').

In contrast, a spirituality of transcendence and of the 'mys-terious other' tends to look more to the future, the general, the unknowable greatness of God. In Wesleyan eucharistic theology it must be admitted that there is place for transcendence too—the place of mystery in the sacrament, the timeless-sness/eternity which the communicant encounters and the active work of each person of the divine Trinity which cannot be fully comprehended by human minds. Although there is a tension between the transcendent and the immanent aspects in their theology and spirituality, at the end of the day, however, one senses that the stronger preference was for immanence. A comparison of the hymns of Isaac Watts and those of the Wesleys shows up the fundamental difference. The Wesley hymns, especially about the eucharist, were warm and personal, engaging the singer in the present, calling forth an immediate response from the person. Watts's hymns paint on a wider canvas. The greatness of God, of his creation, his sovereignty, is never far from Watts's reflections, even when the matter at hand is Christ on his cross (Manning 1942: 83, 84, 97).[3]

Calvin saw the Holy Spirit playing a major role in the sacrament. He struggled with the question: 'How is the individual believer connected with Christ in the eucharist? How is it done?' (Cocksworth 1993: 24). His answer was to say it is done by the power of the Holy Spirit who 'descends' and lifts us up to where Christ is. Calvin's use of spatial and time–linked concepts regarding the presence of Christ and his use of the word *'virtus'* sometimes as an almost quasi-physical matter creates an impression of distance and space in the divine –human interaction. While the Wesleys accepted the strong role of the Spirit in linking the believer to Christ at the sacrament, their preference for relational-type language brought to the surface a question which called for a deepened personal under-standing and experience of the Spirit's work: 'What is the Spirit doing in and for the believer at the eucharist here and now?' The role of the Spirit in their theology further underlined their strong preference for a spirituality of immanence.

Wesleyan eucharistic spirituality is both Christocentric and immanence-orientated. What are the benefits of eucharistic spirituality being either christocentric or with an 'immanence' orientation? First, a spirituality that is Christocentric (as opposed to being patricentric or pneumacentric) provides a clear human model (ie Christ) to follow, especially when growing towards 'Christian perfection'. Second, when the focus is on the Son who is strongly linked to the history of the world and of time (as compared to the focus on the Creator–Father with his attributes of omniscience, omni-presence etc), the sense of 'rootedness' in this world is further concretised. This not only enhances the sense of immanence but also encourages the communicant to be committed to the service of Christ to

---

3. This eucharistic spirituality of immanence which we have found in the Wesleys is not common in most Protestant traditions which do not share certain Roman Catholic eucharistic beliefs regarding the effects of consecration on the elements. The Wesleyan eucharistic spiritual tradition may provide some bridges for the dialogue between Roman Catholics and Protestants.

humankind. Third, a Christocentric spirituality that is tied in to the sacramental celebration (rather than allowing solitary eucharistic devotions) would have the potential to build up corporate life of the Christian community. Fourth, a Christocentric spirituality that demands physical participation (in this case, in the actual partaking of the consecrated elements) as an act of relating with the divine touches the psyche of many cultures where meals are strong symbols of and bridges to more intimate fellowship.

Finally, a spirituality of immanence provides a sense of expectancy in the communicant. It answers the question—very relevant in the days of the Wesleys when they had to deal with the deists—'does God care?' not with cerebral answers but with God's personal presence in Christ. It is existential and experiential. A Christocentric spirituality of immanence does not mean the absence of a theology of transcendence but presupposes it. Faith in the divine identity of Christ and of the reality of his incarnation are the foundations of this spirituality.

If spirituality is 'a response to a call', the spirituality of immanence engages the communicant in making a present response. What kind of a response is it then?

3. The primacy of grace: sacrament before our sacrifice

Grace is primary in the eucharistic spirituality of the Wesleys. The strong place of grace can be seen in three areas: first, in the Wesleys' theology of Christ's sacrifice; second, in the major role they gave to the Holy Spirit at the eucharist; and third, in the Wesleys' teaching on the requirements for communion.

In the Wesleys' theology of Christ's sacrifice, the brothers affirmed, as did Brevint, that the divine gift is given first. The sacrament is instituted for us to receive the gift: Christ and 'all other benefits of his passion'. We then respond to that gift through our offering (ie the sacrifice of ourselves). Sacrament thus precedes our sacrifice. Wainwright observed that this is a 'soundly Protestant thought ', in line with the teachings of the reformers and the early Fathers of the church (Wainwright 1994: 13).

The Wesleys, like Brevint, were anxious to avoid the idea of the Roman Catholic Church of their day, that the church can 'offer up' Christ to God. The sole sufficiency of the ultimate sacrifice of Christ is affirmed: what we can do is simply to plead his sacrifice as Lamb of God (ie we receive that grace offered to us and plead for its efficacy). As John Wesley described it thus in the *ENNT*: *Do this in remembrance of me:*

> The ancient sacrifices were in remembrance of sin: this sacrifice, once offered, is still represented in remembrance of the remission of sins (1 Corinthians 11: 25).

The pleading of Christ's sacrifice is the first of the acts which we can do in response to his work. It is simply the reception of the grace proffered. It is only after Christ's sacrifice is made, after we see him continually offering himself to God the Father for us and after our response in pleading for the effects of his sacrifice to be made effective in our lives, that we can respond in self-offering, giving him our selves, committing ourselves to live his life, giving him our goods, our prayers and our praise of thanksgiving. Our constant need for his grace is underlined by the 'pleading for the effects of his sacrifice' and the sacrifices we offer 'in, with and through him' at every eucharist.

In their teaching on the role of the Holy Spirit in the sacrament, the Wesleys highlighted further that not only is the initiative of relating God's but also that the whole process of relating (between God and humans) is undergirded by God's good pleasure. They did this through the use of the *epiclesis* and through the identification of four key roles of the Holy Spirit in the eucharist: 'remembrancer divine', assurance giver, the life-giver and most importantly, the companion sanctifier. These are the roles of one who actively accompanies Christians in their pilgrimage of faith and discipleship. These strong roles attributed to the Spirit concentrated on God's gracious works rather than on human action. Without the Spirit even with the right eucharistic formulas and priestly credentials, the ritual would be empty, conveying nothing to the communicant.

Earlier, we have seen that in spite of the strong tradition of using preparation manuals and teaching the need for adequate preparation for the sacrament, the Wesleys gradually came to encourage their people to set aside their fears of judgment and with joyful expectation receive all that the Lord wants to give them at the Table, just as they are. They were concerned that too much emphasis on preparation resulted in people neglecting the very sacrament which could be a means of healing to them. Adequacy of faith is not the issue, but an openness to receive from God, relying on the merits of Christ. Prayer and self–examination would be good, but they are not absolutely essential. Even children are welcomed at the Table on the same terms.

Wesleyan eucharistic spirituality is a grace–filled spirituality. Undergirding that strong grace–centred orientation lies one very important point of Wesleyan theology: salvation is seen in terms of healing. The language of healing is warmer and more welcoming than the language of the law courts. Its concern is not so much on justice and judgment (although there still needs to be an element of these in the therapeutic model), but on restoration and life. As it has been mentioned before, the eucharist is seen as a therapeutic sacrament.

The Wesleys called for responsible reception of the grace of God. In their teaching about the eucharist as 'sacrifice', there is a place for self-offering, be it in terms of one's goods, one's adoration and praise or one's life. Reverence is called for and the place of Table discipline is not overlooked with the practice of issuing tickets only to those who are seriously keeping the faith. Yet what we offer to Christ is offered only 'in, with and through Him'. The only way the 'two oblations', one divine and holy, one human and marred (cf *HLS* 147), can join is if one is 'cast' onto the other and offered as one with the other (cf *HLS* 134, 137/3–7, 141/7–8). Even at that point, we are not left on our own. Christ continues to intercede for us as our priest-intercessor before the Father (*HLS* 129). Thus, to the end, we encounter grace again.

The Wesleys demanded and enforced disciplined disciple-ship upon their followers. Theirs was certainly not a passive spirituality. Even in their teaching about Christian perfection, John avoided the danger of putting everything on human effort by stating that Christian perfection can be the instantaneous work of God in a person's life, not just a gradual growth through disciplined effort supported by divine grace.

4. Christian perfection as the goal

4.1 What is Christian perfection?
In chapter 2, we noted that the Wesleys saw Christian perfection as the goal of the Christian life and holy communion as the chief means of grace for growing towards Christian perfection. How then did the Wesleys understand Christian perfection? John Wesley saw the doctrine of Christian perfection as the 'grand depositum' which God had lodged with the people called 'Methodists'. It was for the sake of propagating it that God raised up the Methodists (JWL 27). Some of the key works on this subject published by John Wesley are: *A Sermon on Christian Perfection* (1741), *Thoughts on Christian Perfection* (1759), *Cautions and Directions to the Greatest Professors of the Methodist Societies* (1562), *The Scripture Way of Salvation* (1765) and *A Plain Account of Christian Perfection 1725–1765* (1766).

To understand Christian perfection, we have to look at the Wesleyan *'ordo salutis'*. The Wesleys saw the universal human problem as sin. There is, first, original sin or the inclination to sin. This is a state of being, inherent in being a descendent of Adam (*Sermon* 2). Following the Eastern tradition of the church, John Wesley saw sin as sickness rather than in the juridical images of the Western church (*Sermon* 44 cf Lindstrom 1946: 41). This sickness is passed on from one person to the next, one generation to another. Secondly, sin is also what people do as a result of what they are, through intentional, willful and voluntary acts stemming from any other motive than love (*Sermon* 28). Thirdly, sins can be committed through honest misjudgment and ignorance. Such mistakes might be made even when done with love as the basis for action. There is a tension between pure intention and flawed performance (*Sermon* 40). In John Wesley's earlier writings, he did not list this third category as 'sins'. In his later writings (*Thoughts on Christian Perfection* and A *Plain Account of Christian Perfection*) he modifies this earlier view of sin by saying that even mistakes and misjudgments need forgiveness because they do not meet up with God's high standards and because they can lead us to damnation. Grace and forgiveness are still needed for such actions.

The work of Christ on the cross justifies the repentant sinner, giving pardon, forgiveness of sins, acceptance by God. After justification, the power of sin is broken but total freedom from sin is still lacking (JWW 23).

Salvation consists of both justification *and* sanctification. At the moment of justification, sanctification begins. Sanctification is the process of growing towards perfection of love for God and neighbour. Charles preached it as the growth towards 'utter domination over sin, constant peace, and love, and joy in the Holy Ghost, the full assurance of faith, righteousness and true holiness' (*CWJ* 26/9/1740). Entire sanctification or Christian perfection is the full restoration of the *imago Dei* in the individual. The Wesleys believed that Christian perfection is possible for all human beings, even with their limited minds, imperfect knowledge and flawed bodies ('infirmities').

The Wesleys spoke of Christian perfection in relational terms. First, perfection is loving God. It is full consecration /surrender, loving him with all one's heart, soul, mind and strength, open for him to mould, renew and recreate. There is a pure desire to do his will because of love. As one walks in his presence in uninterrupted daily communion with him, one is transformed in one's inner being and behaviour. The tendency to sin slowly dies. Perfection is therefore a state, an atmosphere in which one lives in close proximity and openness to God. Second, Christian perfection is loving people with pure intention. This state of loving God and one's neighbour (cf *Sermon* 112), which can be described as 'holiness in heart and life' or the restoration of the *imago dei* in the person, is received by grace through faith. It is not an impossible demand from an angry judge but it is a call, an appeal, an offer and a gift from God (*Sermon* 43). Christian perfection has to do with one's entire being: one's thoughts, words and actions.

Heitzenrater claimed that one of the most common ways in which John Wesley expressed the nature of Christian perfection and the marks of a true Christian is through his use of the phrase: 'having the mind of Christ and walking as he walked' (Philippians 2: 5; 1 John 2: 6). Heitzenrater noted that this is the most repeated biblical phrase in John Wesley's published sermons (Meeks 1995: 58). The growth into full 'conformity with Christ' begins at one's baptism (*HLS* 130/2) and continues for Christians as they constantly

> ... pant for full conformity
> To our exalted Head ...
> (*HLS* 130/1 cf *HLS* 154/3, 129/3).

Rattenbury wrote of the Wesleys' position there (reflected in *HLS* 154, 131 for example) as saying:

> If (a man) drinks the chalice of salvation, it is to enable him to quaff the cup of challenge; if he would share all the glories of the redeemed, he must not shrink from being crucified like the great Apostle on the Cross of his Redeemer. So a man must reach full conformity with the mind of Christ to realise the deepest meaning of the blood which atoned for the race and for him, and which continues to be the blood of sprinkling and cleansing (1948: 202–203).

All his life, John sought Christian perfection. As early as 1734, he wrote:

> I take religion to be, not the bare saying over so many prayers morning and evening, in public or in private; not anything superadded now and then to a careless or worldly life; but a constant ruling habit of soul; a renewal of our minds in the image of God; a recovery of the divine likeness; a still-increasing conformity of heart and life to the pattern of our most holy Redeemer (JWL 28).

Heitzenrater commented on this lifelong theme of John Wesley:

> The idea of imitating Jesus, the great exemplar is not only the primary motivation of Wesley's social ethic at Oxford, it is a central and persistent theme throughout his ministry (Meeks 1995: 59).

John Wesley believed that Christian perfection is possible here and now in this world, before one's death. He spoke with an expectancy that as one works towards Christian perfection to be realised in one's life in a gradual way, it can come as an instantaneous happening after years of growth in grace. In *Scripture Way of Salvation*, John urged his hearers to expect it any-time. Where Brevint in *The Christian Sacrament and Sacrifice* wrote in hope that Christ might 'in part' make his disciples holy (Brevint 1673: 63), Wesley edited it to say that Christ might *now* make His disciples holy (Wesley 1745: 19). Outler commented that this expectation of the divine intervention is another way of 'celebrating the sovereignty of grace' (1964: 253). It must be noted that Charles and John had slight differences regarding Christian perfection. Although in the earlier years Charles agreed with John that Christian perfection can be a reality here and now, his more realistic and discerning judgment of people's character and his deeper self–awareness led him to see that the possibility exists only in the next life (Hodges 1966: 27).[4] The brothers were, however, agreed on the same goal and the same means of pursuing the goal.

The Wesleys taught that Christian perfection is dynamic. Growth, stagnation or regression is possible in this state. They were thus in line with the Greek church's understanding of *teleiosis*. The Latin equivalent is *perfectio*, referring to an ongoing process of perfecting rather than the Latin *perfectum* which refers to a finished work. Christian perfection is not sinless perfection. Even when one is 'perfected', one is still not free from temptations, agony, distress or the characteristics of one's

---

4. Some examples of Charles Wesley's more cautious and discerning nature: cf *CWJ* 15/12/1739, 26/8/1739, 5/2/1743, 13/6/1743, 2/10/1744.

own personality—like having favourite foods. The person still needs to receive forgiveness and intercession from Christ and needs to be supported by the means of grace (both the institutional and the prudential ones). The 'perfected one' must watch and pray, avoiding pride, enthusiasm, sins of omission, schism, antinomianism and would desire nothing but God. The Wesleys did not share the Calvinist belief in the 'perseverance of the saints'. It is as one continues in this state of loving God and one's neighbour that one's tendency to sin slowly 'dies' and sin is rooted out from the person's life.

One can know when one becomes perfect. Signs of perfection are: an awareness of death of sin within oneself and the experience of the renewal of love for God and for people. The person is joyous and prayerful, giving thanks to God for all things. To John Wesley, Christian perfection is not a private matter. One is called to share with the community one's experience of Christian perfection, not only to be judged by them on whether it is indeed true that one has received that gift/state (the fruit must be evident in one's life) but also to encourage them in their Christian walk. There is accountability, assurance and a supportive system (ie in the bands, classes, societies) for all to grow towards this goal. In short, if Christian perfection is a gift of grace, human effort is required to avail oneself of it and community support is vital to keep one growing and remaining in that state.

4.2 Challenges and possibilities of this understanding of Christian perfection

In my working definition of spirituality for this thesis, I indicated that spirituality is a response to a call to move 'towards a goal'. In Wesleyan eucharistic spirituality, the goal is clear. It is Christian perfection as described by the Wesley brothers. A spirituality with a goal like that has certain challenges and possibilities. The first challenge is that the tension must be constantly kept between human effort and divine grace. The intentionality and intensity of commitment to a focused, achievable (albeit grace-bestowed) goal has to preserve the delicate balance between the understanding of the freedom of human beings to cooperate with God and the freedom of God to do as he wills in the process of salvation. The Wesleys feared antinomianism. They fought the Calvinists because they saw, in their understanding of the Calvinist predestination, the seeds of destruction for any effort to grow in holiness (*Sermon* 110). Human dignity and personality could suffer where divine arbitrariness is supposedly exalted. Calvinists, in turn, feared what they felt was the Wesleys' over-emphasis on the ability of humans to participate in their salvation. It felt like pelagianism to them, doing damage to the doctrine of the sovereignty of God. The place the Wesleys gave to the primacy of grace in their eucharistic spirituality, and the expectancy of the possibility of a divinely bestowed (and immediate) sanctified state, put the danger under control.

The second challenge is to correct the slightly accommodative attitude John Wesley had toward infirmities and disabilities. While John Wesley had real concerns about human health and even tried to alleviate physical suffering through his *Primitive Physick* (a handbook on home-tested cures), his setting up of dispensaries and his healing-orientated experiments with the use of electricity, it must be said that he saw Christian perfection mainly in a moral and spiritual light. I would venture to question if Christian perfection does not have a stronger implication on the physical sphere of one's life. Should salvation (in Greek, *sozo*, the very word used for physical healing) not be a call to wholeness of the whole being —including physical wholeness? Perhaps the lack of resources in depth psychology and the psychosomatic nature of many illnesses limited the Wesleys' vision on the matter.

There are at least three positive aspects of this goal-orientated spirituality. One strength could be said to be in the focused nature of their goal. They provided a concrete, achievable 'roadmark' for their people (I use the word 'road-mark' instead of the 'destination' because of the dynamic nature of the state of Christian perfection). Growth, movement, effort could thus be encouraged and affirmed under the grace of God. Discipleship called forth commitment to move in that direction. The unmistakably Christocentric focus seen (in the desire to be conformed to the image of Christ) added yet another dimension to this spirituality. As the goal is not only described in concepts and adjectives but has a concrete example in the person of Christ, the believer is able to have a clear model to follow. Further encouragement is given to the believer as he or she realises that Christ has indeed lived that kind of life as a full human being, proving that what the beliver is striving for is not an impossible dream but is a possible and realisable reality.

Second, the goal-orientated spirituality has an equalising effect. Christian perfection as the goal of the Christian's life meant that both clergy and lay were addressed in the call to and the seeking of holiness in heart and life.

Third, it had a communal dimension in that the community of faith plays a vital role in one's pilgrimage towards that goal. It is to this that we turn in our next section.

5. Forming lives through the eucharist

5.1 *Intentional and active formation*
In Wesleyan eucharistic spirituality, Christ is the one who calls us, enabling us by his grace and through his Spirit to grow towards the goal: Christian perfection. The calling and the goal would form the character of the Methodists and also colour their perceptions of life.

Campbell identified three uses of Christian antiquity by theologians during the time of the Wesleys. There was the polemical use—to refute opponents, the conservative use—to defend customs and teachings of the established church, and the programmatic use—aimed towards creating a program for Christian antiquity to change the status quo (1991: 20–21). The Wesleys, especially John, held Christian antiquity in high regard all their lives (it must be said that after 1737 John subjected it to the norms of Scripture). In a talk given to the World Methodist Historical Society's Asian Conference in Singapore (1992), Campbell commented that John Wesley's interest in Christian antiquity and his attempt to popularise the reading of their writings through his publication of The *Christian Library* were because he wanted to use the vision of ancient Christianity to challenge the culture and the church of his time. John sought in that to do two things: to give a renewed vision to his church of what the Christian faith should be and to provide a program to help people follow that vision. In short, he had a programmatic use for antiquity.

I believe that the Wesleys' stringent observance of 'who can celebrate' at communion, the issue of 'usages' (like the *epiclesis* and the mixed chalice), and the call to have the restoration of a 'daily' sacrifice serve the same purpose. Dismissing them as 'high church' or even 'Manchester non-juror' quirks would deprive us of exploring deeply one possible reason: that the Wesleys saw, in the following and teaching of what they considered 'universal practices of the primitive church' which have apostolic origins, they could bring people back to this authentic Christianity of the church, a life of love towards God and neighbour: Christian perfection. Formation of their people towards that goal was intentional and active.

5.2 Communion as chief means of grace for growing towards Christian perfection

The Wesleys understood that the grace of God for the attainment of Christian perfection comes through many means (*Sermon* 16). Methodist practices like gathering into Societies, bands, classes (modelled like the ancient church's cate-chumenate, according to Campbell), observing the watchnight service, five o'clock preaching services etc helped the believer to grow towards the goal (Campbell 1992: 97–101). John told the Methodists that if they neglected the classes and bands, their soul's salvation would be in peril. Methodism, John said, would degenerate without the early five o'clock preaching services (*JWJ* 15/3/1784). Yet much as he valued these means, he felt that they were not enough. Methodist services, for example, lacked 'the four grand parts of public prayer: deprecation, petition, intercession, and thanksgiving' and he urged them to attend weekly church services (*JWW* 5) which should include holy communion.

John Wesley found 'much of the power of God in preaching, but far more at the Lord's Table' (*JWJ* 13/11/1760). One sign of revival to John ('wherever the power of the Lord spreads') is when 'the houses of God are filled; the table of the Lord is thronged on every side' (*JWW* 6). Even as he admitted that no soul will die without communion, the ordinations that John

Wesley carried out for America were primarily because the believers there were deprived of that sacrament. So important was communion to the Wesleys that John Wesley turned against the mystics of the passive school which he had read with great fervour in his younger days. We have seen in chapter two that the mystics were certainly not totally against the prudential means of grace. They were only against the instituted means (Tuttle 1989: 88–89) and that meant that they were throwing out the most important means to John: holy communion. John echoed Brevint in saying:

> Of these Blessings, Christ from above is pleased to bestow sometimes more, sometimes less, in the several ordinances of his Church, which as the Stars of Heaven, differ from each other in Glory. Fasting, Prayer, Hearing his Word, are all good Vessels, to draw Water form this Well of Salvation. But they are not all equal. The Holy Communion when well used, exceeds as much in Blessing, as it exceeds in danger of a Curse, when wickedly and irreverently taken . . . (Wesley 1745: 15; cf. Brevint 1673: 49).

Charles Wesley referred to communion as

> the great sacrifice of thanksgiving, the last office of love, a passover much to be remembered, an ordinance which God always magnifies and honours with His special presence (Bowmer 1951: 189).

Communion for the Wesleys was not only a means of grace but the *chief* means of grace. Other means are used in tandem with it. Outler claimed that for John Wesley the 'Lord's Supper is the paradigm of all the means of grace', the 'chief actual means of actual grace and, as such, literally indispensable in the Christian life' (quoted by Johnson 1987: 27).

Is the difference between it and the other means, a difference in degree or a difference in kind ie is it a special means of grace or is it a means of special grace? It is a difference in degree. In communion, all the senses of a person is involved—including the sense of taste. All instituted means of grace can be included as preparation or reinforcement of the sacrament: prayer and fasting (though not required as absolutely necessary as preparation for communion by the Wesleys), the hearing of the word and even Christian conference (through societies, bands, classes and holy conversations). The possibility of one being open to and for divine–human interaction at communion far exceeds the other means available.

For the Wesleys communion was the chief means of grace *for growing towards Christian perfection* and they sought to utilise the sacrament in a conscious and intentional way in their training program. We will now look at the means through which this was attempted and what this training sought to inculcate specifically in the lives of the early Methodists.

5.3 Structured and unstructured formation

Wesleyan eucharistic formation was both structured and unstructured. The general rules which all Methodists were bound by required them to practise constant communion. In this sense eucharistic formation was structured into the lifestyle of the Methodists right from the start.

The Wesleys had three main groupings for their people. The societies were for the newly spiritually awakened who needed to be encouraged and strengthened in their resolve to 'take up their cross' to follow Christ (JWW 24). All Methodists were members of the societies. The societies were divided into classes. Made up of smaller numbers of people, the classes met weekly. Their commitment to discipleship is evidenced by the three marks of the general rules, ie the avoidance of all known sin, doing all good within their power and the faithful attendance upon all the ordinances of God (*Sermon* 107). They submitted to the monitoring of their inner lives and outward practices. Their leaders kept records of the state of their members as being either 'awakened', 'doubtful', able to 'profess justification' or 'profess perfect love for God' (Watson 1985: 97). Members were advised, reproved, comforted and exhorted by their leader in order that 'their souls would prosper' (JWW 25:

Question 11). This disciplined engagement included a commitment to contribute financially (if one could afford it) towards poor relief. Where the classes were for those who sought new birth, the bands were more for those who sought sanctification. Band members practised mutual accountability and sought to be transparently honest and radically receptive to each other regarding the real state of their souls, confessing their sins to and receiving from each other prayerful and spiritual support. The general rules which governed the classes were given more stringent attention by the bands: they were to 'carefully' avoid evil, 'zealously' do good works, 'constantly' observe the ordinances of God (JWW 4). Those who needed more help and nurture after backsliding became part of the 'penitent Bands'. Many of these soon grew stronger in faith and joined another subgroup for the spiritually more mature ones: the 'select societies'. These are incited to love one another more and to watch more carefully over each other. The only special rules Wesley gave them were that of confidentiality (to be kept within the group), submission to their ministers in all indifferent things and sharing of all they can spare by putting these weekly toward a common stock (JWW 24). Not all Methodists were members of the bands.

While it can be said that the rules played a major part in inculcating eucharistic spirituality, it cannot be forgotton that the undergirding of those rules by leaders and group members (in the case of select societies) who functioned almost like spiritual directors and exemplars (as in the case of the Wesleys, through their published journals) was vital to the formation.[5] Eucharistic spirituality was therefore not only 'taught', it was also 'caught' (through seeing the examples of Methodist leaders in their journals). It was also actively monitored: individual Methodists reported to John and Charles the state of eucharistic

---

5.   The Wesleys were very serious about their responsibilities as spiritual directors. An example of this is in Charles's, *Journal* (11/6/1740). He spoke with Mrs Delamotte and Betty who refused his guidance: 'Do you, therefore, at this time, in the Presence of Jesus Christ, acquit, release, and discharge me from any further care, concern, or regard for your souls? Do you desire I would never more speak unto you in his name?'

observance in their communities (*AM* 1785: 491) and in their own lives (*AM* 1778: 276).

The place of discernment in formation is very important for many schools of spirituality (eg the Jesuit). Very often, the spiritual director or superior has the key role to play in discernment of the progress in the individual's spiritual journey. Wesleyan eucharistic spirituality gave the role of discernment primarily to the members of the classes and the bands. Although the leaders had a slightly bigger role to play (eg in the classes) in sifting and evaluating the spiritual status of their members, the active participation and contribution of the group members were significant. In the select societies, mutual accountability and hence mutual discernment were practised. Pure democracy was not the issue—for the Wesleys and their appointed leaders did exercise a rather strong pastoral and spiritual authority over all their members.

Regularity in the practice of receiving communion had an effect of deepening formation. The Wesleys expected their members to participate fully at the Table. Methodists were required actually to receive communion when they came for the eucharistic services. They were not allowed merely to observe the reception of communion by others. There is no understanding akin to that of the later medieval period, where 'heavenly merit' could be gained by the 'piety of presence' (simple attendance, observation of the liturgy and adoration of the elements). Popular teaching during that late medieval period was that adoration was a safer practice than actual reception of the sacrament, for the latter might bring upon the unworthy communicant severe divine judgment (Taft 1989: 430–432). By insisting on communicating attendance at communion, the Wesleys forced Methodists constantly to re-examine their lives, responding in repentance and radical trust in the generous grace of God—hence, consistently growing in holiness. The discipline of frequent reception made faithfulness in reception and faith in the God who acts through the sacrament, not individual emotions, the priority.

Less structured but no less intentional was the formation in eucharistic spirituality done through books: the published *Sermons* and *Journals* of the brothers, the *HLS*, articles on the eucharist in the *Christian Library*, Brevint's *Treatise*. Brevint's work, appended to the *HLS* and sold at all the Wesleys' preaching houses in town and country (Methodist 1869: 83), contained very moving, personal prayers which nurtured the relationship of intimacy between the believer and the Christ of the Table.

The Wesleys encouraged reading: John chided one of his preachers for neglecting the discipline of reading (*AM* 1780: 449). The works did need to be strictly eucharistic in nature to promote eucharistic spirituality. In 1733 the Wesleys published *A Collection of Forms for Prayer for every Day of the Week*. The prayer for Wednesday evening was an adaptation of the prayer for confession found in the eucharistic service of the *BCP*. Surely this unexpected mid-week reminder of the eucharist would surface associated thoughts and reflections about the sacrament and its implications for an individual's life.

One must not underestimate the place of testimonies—given by the Wesleys, their preachers and ordinary members about their encounters with Christ at the eucharist—in Methodist eucharistic formation. One can imagine the impact of a testimony like the one by Methodist Thomas Joyce who was convinced of the necessity of entire sanctification. In his account, he wrestled with God in prayer for it and in taking the sacrament he was 'exceedingly comforted and strengthened to wrestle still more earnestly' (*AM* 1781: 421).

If rules and regularity of participation, modelling and monitoring of eucharistic observance set the early Methodists firmly on the path of sacramental and spiritual formation, books and testimonies can be said to be some of the key means through which eucharistic spirituality was nurtured and fed.

Formation in Wesleyan eucharistic spirituality did not address merely the intellect. It sought to touch both head and heart, affection and imagination. A very important element in eucharistic formation was the use of the eucharistic hymns. One does wonder how a person can visualise the crucifixion and resurrection of Christ at the communion table. The mind wanders, the eye sees only what is on the table: bread, wine. The ear hears words and more words. The only way that the early Methodists could have been brought to focus on the crucifixion, would be if they were actually singing the *HLS* which would focus their thoughts and which would sculpture for them the verbal ikon, the 'Protestant crucifix' (Rattenbury 1948: 16). The hymns helped Methodists to focus on Christ and his cross. This is the secret of Wesleyan eucharistic spirituality: the singing of the hymns during the long communion services. The hymns fed Wesleyan eucharistic spirituality. Berger highlighted the power of doxological language used in hymns: she saw it as being more inclusive, more transparent and 'open ended', where theological language was 'argumentative, descriptive . . . ' and concerned with intellectual 'coherence' (p 22–24). Birthed in the womb of prayer by the church, hymns go beyond the 'purely rational and logical'; 'use figures and images which would be too daring for prose . . .' and 'celebrates paradox' (Wakefield 1995: 159). The power of the hymns is such that scholars have commented that the essential spirit of Methodism can be found more in Charles Wesley's hymns than in John's *Sermons*, *Notes* or *Rules for the Societies* (Flint 1957: 193). The decline of this practice of singing (in this case, the eucharistic hymns) left Methodists only with the orderliness of the service, its original spirit and focus missing.

Singing does make a difference. Pope Gregory was attributed with this saying: 'He who sings prays twice'. The singer of hymns not only prays but he or she is formed by the hymns in a very physical way through the singing. Although hearing is one sense affected by singing, the sense of touch—of feeling the words vibrating in one's throat—would be another. The words soon become a part of the person. Law had written this in his book, *A Serious Call to a Devout and Holy Life,* a book which was much loved by John:

> Whilst you only read it, you only like it, and that is all; but as soon as you sing it, then you enjoy it, you feel the delight of it; it has got hold of you, your passions keep pace with it, and you feel the same spirit within you that seems to be in the words (1965: 146).

If Christian perfection—perfect love of God and neighbour—was the goal of Wesleyan eucharistic spirituality, the singing of the eucharistic hymns would be able to impart both the desire as well as the on-going enthusiasm (eg John Wesley would not allow 'draggy' singing [JWW 26]) to move towards it. We must note here that it is not simply the singing of the hymns that made formation effective. John Wesley, for example, objected to the style of singing promoted in some places which called for different words to be sung by different persons at the same time (the 'counterpoint' style focusing on musical 'harmony' rather than simple 'melody'), which meant that the words could not be followed (*AM* 1779: 106–7). The words of the hymns are important.

The use of hymns (as opposed to psalms alone) and the style in which the hymns were written made them excellent formational tools. The Anglican Church of Wesley's days was singing ponderous psalms, either using the old version of Sternhold and Hopkins or the new version of Tate and Brady. There existed great suspicion that hymns were non-scriptural because the words were not strictly taken from the Bible. The only hymns allowed were well-vetted anthems sung by able choirs in cathedrals and churches. The Calvinists in Geneva allowed only metrical paraphrases of Scripture because they held music and arts suspect (Hodges 1966: 44). Dissenters in England, like the Congregationalists, however, preferred hymns because they felt not all the psalms were suitable for worship (Moorman 1983: 144–5). Isaac Watts was to be one of the most popular hymn-writers (Bouyer 1968: 194). Lutherans, too, enjoyed freely composed hymns (Cousins 1990b: xx), combining objective doctrinal hymnody with verses of affective and devotional nature (Hodges 1966: 44).

The hymns of the Wesleys were different in that they were intensely personal. In the case of the eucharistic hymns, there was a sense of joy about them. They were simple, yet they contained profound reflections of theological truths, linking the world of experience with the world of the academia. Using the language and imagery of the Bible, the hymns reinforced the preaching of the Wesleys, educated the masses for whom the written word was not the main medium of communication, forming their faith, understanding and theology. The fact that hymns can be easily memorised meant that they could be sung at home and at work, allowing their faith to break into the other areas of their lives, both testing their faith's authenticity in the face of life's harsh realities as well as witnessing to faith's relevance to life. Methodist Nancy Bissaker was reported to have read the Wesley hymns very often, describing them as 'a treasure of divine truth, a body of divinity, and a good commentary of Scripture' which 'prepares the mind for love of Scripture, and for following Christ' (*AM* 1785: 164). John Wesley pointed to John Fletcher's use of a sacramental hymn, quoting Fletcher as saying:

> I proposed to receive the Lord's Supper on the following Sunday. I therefore returned to my room, and looked out a sacramental hymn. I learned it by heart, and prayed it over many times, intending to repeat it at the table. Then I went to bed with rather more hope and peace than I had felt for some time (JWW 27).

Music was also important for forming eucharistic spirituality. What one cannot convey discursively, music with its varying rhythm, pitch, mood, harmony and dissonance does. That which cannot be expressed in merely rationalistic terms is presented in a way that preserves both the basic message and the mystery which surrounds it. It thus has the capacity to speak into the depths of the human soul. It has the capacity of triggering off many mental, emotional and spiritual associations. Charles Wesley was very aware of the power of music. He believed that music could be used for evangelism, for encouragement, for holy enjoyment. It was to be a handmaid, not a mistress, of liturgy and spiritual life. Charles and his friends once 'caught a physician by the ear' (*CWJ* 24/3/1746), commenting 'this is the true use of music'. Reading between the lines, one can surmise that a physician came to the faith when he heard music which Charles and his friends produced. When Charles met his discouraged brother one day (*CWJ* 13/5/1738), he forced him to sing a hymn to Christ 'as he had often forced me' and the depression lifted as they felt his presence. In 'The true use of Musick', Charles wrote:

> The true use of Musick.
> Listed into the Cause of Sin
> Why should a Good be Evil?
> Musick, alas! too long has been
> Prest to obey the Devil:
> . . . Who on the Part of God will rise,
> Innocent Sound recover
> Fly on the Prey, and take the Prize,
> Plunder the Carnal Love
> Musick in Virtue's Cause retain,
> Rescue the holy Pleasure?
>
> Jesus the Soul of Musick is; His is the Noblest Passion
> . . . Fill us with all the Life of Grace
> Carry us up to Heaven (Wesley 1749: No 189).

Charles was not averse to using secular tunes for his hymns. Kirk reported a tradition that Charles was interrupted during an open air service at a sea port by half-drunken sailors singing a bawdy song entitled *Nancy Dawson*. Mastering the tune, Charles turned up later and introduced a hymn which he had just written to the same tune (Kirk 1860: 44–49). Should the eucharistic hymns be sung to tunes as popular and as catching as *Nancy Dawson*, it is not surprising how the words would etch themselves in the memories of the singers, indelibly shaping their lives.

Although the stages of the spiritual journey were not indicated by the Wesleys, what John Wesley did provide was the distinguishing marks of those who have been perfected, namely, an awareness of death of sin within oneself and the experience of the renewal of love for God and for people. Joy, thankfulness and prayerfulness regardless of the situation one is in characterises the 'perfect'. It is therefore not surprising that the specific virtues aimed at and inculcated in eucharistic formation are: thankfulness and love—thankfulness for the amazing grace of God towards oneself and love towards him who first loved us, leading us to love others as we have been loved. The inculcation of specific virtues in the practice of spiritual disciplines was a practice observed by those who were serious about spiritual formation in the days of the Wesleys. Law, for instance, sought humility in the morning, universal love at mid-day, conformity to the will of God in the afternoon. He would then confess his sins in the evening (Law 1965: 12). Deacon taught the replacing of sinful habits by the conscious and grace-assisted implanting of contrary virtues (Deacon 1716: 395). The Oxford Methodists practised this as well. It is interesting that when the Oxford Methodists carried out their 'particular examination' of themselves every day, holding before themselves a list of questions based on a traditional list of virtues for each day (Meeks 1995: 56–7), thankfulness was the virtue aimed at on Saturday; the 'love of God' was the virtue on Sunday, and Monday was the 'love of one's neighbour'; Saturday was usually the day before taking the sacrament; Sunday was the day for the celebration of communions. Monday is the day after! Another possible source of the highlighting of one of these virtues might be from Herbert. In his *Gratefulnesse* (from the series of poems in *The Temple*), he wrote:

> Thou that hast give' so much to me,
> Give one thing more, a grateful heart (Herbert 1941: 123).

We have noted that Charles Wesley was deeply influenced by Herbert's *The Temple* poems. Could gratitude/thankfulness as a mark of Christian perfection be something he had imbibed from Herbert's writings? Whatever the sources were for the Wesleys, it is clear that there were certain spiritual virtues which eucharistic spirituality sought consciously to inculcate. These virtues in themselves—a life of thankfulness and love—are marks of Christian perfection. These virtues can also create in the person a generous and and spacious spirit which brings about further holiness in heart and life—ie Christian perfection.

We have seen that Wesleyan eucharistic formation was intentional and active. Formation was intentionally carried out through rules, the regular practice of communion reception, monitoring personnel (class leaders, lay members, spiritual directors like John and Charles Wesley), written inspirational resources, testimonies and hymns with specific short-term goals (implantation of certain specific virtues). For the Wesleys, however, formation did not depend solely upon these activities. In their perception of the primacy of grace, they saw the divine hand at work even as the Methodists strove towards Christian perfection through eucharistic formation (and other means). The Spirit of God was at work in the lives of the individuals in his role primarily as companion-sanctifier. He could be trusted to bring forth the desired fruits in his time.[6]

Using the Wesleys' therapeutic model of salvation, formation towards Christian perfection can be said to be a long-term spiritual therapy towards healing and wholeness defined as 'holiness in heart and life'. In many spiritual writings, stages along the road to holiness have distinct features which can be identified although the journey or pilgrimage might be described as more spiral in form than strictly linear. The usual strong emphasis on the 'purgation, illumination, union' movement, with detachment from sensory inputs and passions of the world, of one's imagination, even of one's spiritual experiences ('disinterested love' of Fenelon), seem to be conspicuously played down in the Wesleyan corpus. There was indeed the call in the *Sermons, Journals* and *HLS* to die to self, and take up one's cross to follow Christ. Methodists were to hold with open hands their material possessions. Absent from the eucharistic spirituality of the Wesleys was the world-abandoning nature of the mystics and their deep suspicion of the senses. There were records of depressive periods in their spiritual lives, even when they partook of the sacrament, but for the Wesleys there was no

---

6. One notes the reticence of Charles Wesley on many occasions to intervene when a soul was wrestling with God for a sense of assurance or for a blessing. He preferred to step aside in prayerful waiting, while the Spirit's timing and work were made manifest (*CWJ* 12/7/1738, 21/2/ 1739, 23/9/ 1739).

description of these as the 'dark night of the soul' or 'dark night of the senses'. We will look at the implications of this 'lack' in the next chapter.

6. Seeing life through the eucharist

Intentional formation uses methods and has short- and long-term goals. Formation as a whole, however, also involves the creating and colouring of one's perception of life. Often this aspect of formation is not pre-programmed but evolves with the formation. Where these results are seen to be in line with the formational goals, affirmation and reinforcement of them takes place. Formation in Wesleyan eucharistic spirituality seems to follow this pattern. Intentional eucharistic formation affected the way the early Methodists viewed life.

6.1 Seeing the self
John Wesley quoted Brevint:

> When Christian posterity, like the young Israelites who had not seen the killing of the first Passover . . . ask after the meaning of the bread broken, the wine poured out, and the partaking of both: The holy mystery . . . set (s) forth both the martyrdom and the sacrifice of this crucified Saviour, giving up His flesh, shedding His blood and pouring out His very soul, to atone for their sins (Wesley 1745: 5).

The eucharist then sets forth before Christians, as the Passover meal does before the 'Israelite', a physical, tangible reminder of who there are, whose they are, what they are called to be and what they are called to do. Other means of grace lack the full involvement of all the senses. The eucharistic observance and practice of the Wesleys could not but colour the way Christians see themselves, the divine, other people, the world and time. Identity formation takes place at the eucharist.

The one who comes to God is identified by the Wesleys as the one in need, who can perhaps offer only simple trust in the promises of God. This is the person who desires deeply what God offers although he or she may not have satisfied the 'preparation schools' or read their manuals. The person comes, hungry, lost, a sinner with other sinners, with dirty hands open, longing for and willing seriously to make a new start. Yet there is no place for self-hate nor grovelling. In the *Sunday Service*, John Wesley's 'revised and edited version' of the *BCP* for the Methodists in America, Wesley sought to underline this position of the Christian. The sinner goes *forward* to receive the eucharist. The ability to respond to the invitation to 'draw near' (instead passively sitting, awaiting for the elements to be distributed in the pews in the reformed fashion) is an affirmation of the sinner's graced and empowered state. Communion is received in humility and meekness, on one's knees (the preferred position of the Wesleys), for one is conscious of one's own sinfulness (White 1991: 132). The gravity of sin is not forgotten. The high cost of redemption seen in the atoning sacrifice is always before the ransomed sinner's eyes during the eucharist. Yet because the power of forgiveness from the cross is not simply received through a memory trip back to the Calvary of the past but is experienced now in the present through the eucharistic presence of Christ and is further reinforced both by the 'pleading of His sacrifice' and by the theme of Christ as constant intercessor, the sense of release and love is overwhelming.

The communicant comes as a valued 'darling' (*HLS* 45/1) who 'forgot (his) heavenly birth' (*HLS* 160/4). The communicant is the 'well beloved of heaven' (*HLS* 163/1), the ' flesh of his flesh' (*HLS* 114/6), a 'royal priest' (*HLS* 137/1) with dignity and value (*HLS* 39/3). Tripp in his book on Wesley's covenant service, noted that the eucharist and the renewal of covenant became firmly associated in practice (Tripp 1969: 126). John Wesley's 1780 covenant prayer begins:

> O Most dreadful God, for the passion of thy Son,
> I beseech thee accept of thy poor Prodigal now
> prostrating himself at thy door: I have fallen from
> thee by mine Iniquity, and am by nature a Son of
> Death, and a thousand–fold more the Child of

> Hell by my wicked practice; but of thine infinite
> grace thou hast promised mercy to me in Christ if
> I will but turn to thee with all my heart: therefore
> upon the call of thy Gospel, I am now come in,
> and throwing down my weapons, submit myself
> to thy mercy (Tripp 1969: 185).

It is significant that Wesley chose to include a prayer like this for the Methodist covenant-cum-communion service, for it uses the image of the prodigal son which encapsulates the Wesleyan understanding of the identity and position of the one who comes to the table as the valued sinner, returning home to his Father.

There is yet another identity which is presented. This identity is shaped by the sacrificial eucharistic language of the Wesleys. In response to the grace and love of God in Christ, the Christian becomes a living sacrifice (cf Romans 12: 1), living a crucified life (Galatians 2: 20) in union with Christ, sharing in the fellowship of his sufferings. The Christian's life is not his or her own. We have already seen in chapter 2 that there were those whose experience at the Table led them to renew their baptismal commitment to Christ and some made radical changes in their lives. One's sins, one's property, one's body parts and one's life itself, in the *now*, have been offered up to God. Eucharist is seen very strongly as 'offering'. This is a great contrast to the modern consumeristic understanding of the eucharist where the focus is on what one gets out of it rather than Whom one encounters or what one gives to him at the table. It is not surprising that the second-favourite term of John Wesley for communion is 'sacrament'. The word appears at least eighty-one times in Jackson's edition of Wesley's Works. The word has its roots in the soldiers' pledge of allegiance to their commanding officer. It is therefore a very appropriate term for a service where Christians are reminded of their commitment to give their all as their sacrifice to the one who gave his all. Another interesting fact we mentioned earlier underlines this theme: John Wesley favoured using the term 'Lord' instead of 'Jesus' (Brevint 1673: 5, 11, 81, 82; Wesley 1745:

4, 6, 24, 24). In Wesleyan eucharistic spirituality, Christ is not simply saviour of the sinner. He is the Lord of their lives.

While the two views of the self are not exactly new in Christian theology nor eucharistic spiritualities of other traditions (eg the *BCP*), yet they are special in the Wesleyan eucharistic tradition: they stand out as the two main emphases or themes about the self found in the Wesleyan eucharistic corpus.

Lake, the father of *Clinical Theology*, wrote that acceptance is a gift, not a reward. Life flows where one starts from graced acceptance, receives sustenance, stands in the status of a son rather than a slave, and from that direction moves into activity or achievement as an expression of 'ontological resources' within rather than doing it from 'ontological needs' (1986: 50–52). It can be said that Wesleyan eucharistic spirituality creates and flows with this graced self-identity which Lake spoke of with its images of restored prodigals loved into lives of total commitment to God.

6.2 *Seeing the divine*

To whom do Christians belong? To a just God, say the Wesleys. Perhaps our reaction of horror today to a bloody sacrifice needed for 'propitiation' or 'expiation', the slaying of a lamb, the setting apart of a scapegoat, betrays our lack of understanding of the gravity of sin. Rattenbury believed that the cross should shock people, for it shows forth the foul and tragic character of sin. Sin destroys the innocent one. The horror of human sin is displayed at Calvary as well as the love of God (Rattenbury 1948: 102). While the substitionary theories of the atonement favoured by the Wesleys do raise more questions than they answer, they also display in vivid language the depth of the divine commitment to love. The just God to whom one belongs, seen through the eucharist, is a vulnerable, risktaking, loving God whose love will not let us go, nor let us off either. In his hands are written our names (Rattenbury 1948: A3–3). The Christological link and focus of this perception are unmistakable.

We have already seen the major role the Wesleys gave to the Holy Spirit in their eucharistic spirituality. If one word could describe the combined ministries of the 'remembrancer divine', the lifegiver, the companion-sanctifier and the assurance-giver, it would be the word 'intimacy'. Eucharistic spirituality of the Wesleys placed the Spirit alongside the struggling believer, initiating, inspiring, encouraging, correcting and leading the person into deeper consecration of heart and life. The believer is not left bereft. The picture of the divine painted in the eucharistic spirituality of the Wesleys is that of an intimate God.

There is yet another picture of God which Wesleyan eucharistic spirituality brings to the fore. God is seen as the God who surprises. From the end of the seventeenth century, the misuse of reason and science slowly diminished the authority of tradition. In such a rationalistic age, even Charles Wesley in his early years had difficulty accepting the possibility of supernatural intervention. Justification by faith seemed impossible to him—not only because he felt that good works must have some value and place—but because he had real doubts about the possibility of immediate or instantaneous conversions (*CWJ* 3/6/1738). The actual 'breaking in' of the divine into his human time and space did not seem conceivable.

The Wesleys held certain presuppositions and had certain experiences which underline their eucharistic faith. The eucharist has often been called a 'holy mystery' by those in the Orthodox and Anglican traditions. Very often, theological discussions on the validity and nature of Christ's presence obscure the fact that something mysterious, surprising and which breaks out of neat theological formulations can actually happen at eucharistic celebrations. To the Wesleys, something actually happens at the eucharist as the present Christ encounters the communicant. John Wesley, on one occasion at least, referred to the sacrament as 'the mysteries of God' (*JWJ* 11/8/1737). During the eucharistic services, there were unusual situations which pointed to the dynamic 'breaking in' of the divine into the normal ritualised service. Although there were no reports of people falling down, accompanied by screamings and groanings (we noted in chapter 3 that John Wesley did not rule out the possibility of these, cf supernatural power inherent in the sacrament JWL 19),[7] we mentioned in chapter 2 that there were phenomena involving sound and sight, physical healings took place, lives were changed and people felt intensely the presence of Christ as they communicated. If two words were to be used to describe the attitude the early Methodists had when they came for communion, the words would be: openness and expectancy. Wesleyan eucharistic spirituality has an element of excitement. The God whom they encounter at the eucharist, is the one who surprises.

6.3 *Seeing other people*
The Orthodox liturgy of Malabar has these words:

---

7. In the course of their ministry the two brothers experienced unusual phenomena. These ranged from feeling 'the power of God' come into the room where they were gathered (*JWJ* 2/1/1739)—sometimes with the sensory effect like that of experiencing 'a mighty rushing wind' (*CWJ* 12/4/1741 in Kingswood), to people falling down, some crying in joy (*JWJ* 1/1/1738). Very often, there would be cries of agony, groanings, screams, tears (*JWJ* 4/3/1761, 20/5/1759, 24/5/1759, *CWJ* 27/6/1738, 12/3/1739, 15/4/1739, 8/4/1740, 5/5/1740), indicative of what Charles called 'birthpangs' (15/5/1740) or intense inner struggles taking place within the hearts of those who come for their meetings. There were reports of exorcisms (*CWJ* 11/12/1738, 5/10/1739, 2/9/1741, *JWJ* 28/8/1759), dreams of Christ (*CWJ* 21/4/1738, 24/5/1738), dreams of exorcism (*CWJ* 22/5/1738), visions (*CWJ* 7/6/1738, 20/9/1739, 3/10/1739, 14/5/1740, 14/5/1741) and unexplainable laughter (*JWJ* 9 May 1740). Although some of these manifestations were feigned by attention seekers (*CWJ* 5/8/1740, 13/10/1740, 4/6/1743) and used by the devil to cause those who were upset by them to stumble (*CWJ* 15/6/1741, *JWJ* 5/6/1772), the Wesleys especially the more discerning Charles, knew how to deal with them (*CWJ* 15/10/1756, 15/12/1738, 26/8/1739, 15/10/1739, 22/12/1739, 8/6/1743, 13/6/1743). They did not encourage the whipping up of emotions to create such happenings (*JWJ*: 27/8/1763). Charles would often leave people to wait for God to act after he had talked and prayed with them (*CWJ* 12/7/1738, 21/2/1739, 23/9/1739). He disliked these unusual manifestations including dreams and visions (*CWJ* 22/4/1739), although he did not dismiss them as unreal.

> Strengthen for service, Lord, the hands that holy
> things have taken;
> Let ears that now have heard thy songs to
> clamour never waken.
> Lord, may tongues which 'Holy' sang, keep from
> from all deceiving;
> The eyes which saw Thy love be bright, Thy
> blessed hope perceiving (*HP* 1983: 626).

Immersion in sanctity through handling holy things evokes the response of living holy lives.

The church is changed by the celebration of the sacrament.

> The eucharist must not only be regarded in terms
> of bringing Christ down to the earthly altar, but
> also of Christ raising the church up to the
> heavenly palace. There is a transfiguration of the
> Church at every eucharist, and a sacralizing of it.
> This sense of glorification is stronger in the
> Eastern than the Western Church (Cowley 1953:
> 97).

Roman Catholic priests are told at their ordinations: 'Imitate what you handle' (Wainwright 1997a: 94), ie their lives are to be shaped by and modelled after Christ's life as set before them in the eucharist, ie *imitatio Christi*. While Methodists do not have, like the Orthodox, a strong theology about the ethical implications of handling holy things nor the Roman Catholic priests' deep understanding of having to 'imitate what (they) handles', the social dimension of eucharistic spirituality does emerge.

Wesleyan eucharistic spirituality is relational. Wesleyan eucharistic spirituality did not develop any inclinations to be mystically 'absorbed into God' to such a degree that obligation to care for others is forgotten. There are no mere privatised eucharistic devotions, because John Wesley believed that religion is not solitary (*Sermon* 24). Works of piety like hearing and reading of Scripture, taking the sacrament, public and private prayer and fasting must be followed by works of mercy

(*Sermon* 98). Wesley took issue with the mystics for slighting both. His comment about them was that they did not have any 'conception of church communion' (*JWJ* 5/2/1761).

This social dimension is based firmly on the recognition that people are spiritual beings whose first need in life is God. The obligation laid upon the Christian is to strengthen the divine–human link. Hence we have the strong evangelical preaching of the Wesleys which accompanies the celebration of the sacrament, the invitations in the eucharistic liturgy and hymns, the nurture, caring and formation that goes on in the societies, classes and bands. One element which Wesleyan eucharistic spirituality highlights in this perception of people is in the area of prayer. Wesleyan eucharistic spirituality is a spirituality of intercession. The early Methodists prayed for people—for both the living and the dead—during the eucharist. Charles had recorded several times in his *Journal* about the coming of the 'spirit of intercession' during the eucharist. Although there are no spiritual benefits from a storehouse of grace to be acquired at the eucharist for the departed Christians by those still in this world, Charles did record once that there was 'strong intercession for departed friends' during their eucharistic celebration. Christ is the Intercessor. The church joins in his intercession. The prayers for the living were possibly that those prayed for would become 'poor in spirit' (*Sermon* 21) and thus be receptive towards whatever God sought to give them in his love. There was no record of the prayer content for the 'departed friends'.

Was Wesleyan eucharistic spirituality only for the privileged intellectuals, the comfortable rich, the detached spiritual hermit, reinforcing the conservatism of its society? Or was it subversive, undermining the values of society, replacing it with scriptural alternatives? Was the spirituality concerned with only what the Revd Brian Beck, then secretary of the British Methodist Conference, reflecting on the eucharistic hymns in a public lecture at the Methodist Church in Filton, Bristol in 1995, called 'micro' issues (ie individualistic concerns), lacking in teaching on the social implications ('macro' or societal issues), in following Christ?

While people are seen to be spiritual beings in need of God and hence in need of spiritual nurture and prayer support, Wesleyan eucharistic spirituality recognised also that people are also very physical entities with material and emotional needs. Sometimes, the socioeconomic situation in which people find themselves limits their access to the gospel and to the care of the church. The inhabitants of Pill and Kingswood for instance, were shunned by most respectable church-going people (*JWJ* 3/10/1755 cf JWW 23). Wesleyan eucharistic spirituality could be said to have a special concern for the poor, giving them special dignity, laying the foundations for viewing them with respect and commiting one's life to serving them and others in the Lord.

First, there was special concern for the poor during the eucharistic service: John Wesley's *Sunday Service* liturgy continued the tradition of taking a collection of alms for the poor (Westerfield-Tucker 1995: 58). Second, in contrast to the prevailing culture of their times, the Wesleyan eucharistic spirituality affirmed the dignity of all those suffering from the consequences of poverty. It was true that Richard Challoner (1671–1781), a Roman Catholic bishop and Vicar Apostolic of the London district, was known for his work among the poor during the time of the Wesleys (Butler 1992: 9ff). Rich Puritans helped the poor through endowments, trusts, hospitals, almshouses, loan funds, schools, etc. However, the prevailing attitude was that the poor were basically lazy and that only the 'worthy' poor who were willing to attend services and submit to certain disciplines (Monk 1992: 11–13, 20–22) were deserving of assistance. People concerned with spiritual formation—like the SPCK and Law (Law 1965: 12)—saw the poor as objects of charity and felt that the poor needed to be kept in their place in society.

In contrast, Wesleyan eucharistic theology and practice affirmed the value of each individual, regardless of whether they proved 'worthy' of help or not. The eucharist testified to Christ's death for *all*. We have noted earlier that the 'for all' theme echoes through many of the hymns. Two categories of needy people were addressed in the *HLS*: the first were those who were caught up in a situational bondage (cf *HLS* 9). They were those in pain, 'stranger to a moment's rest' (*HLS* 120/2), the 'worms' (*HLS* 161/1), the 'worthless rib', the 'feeble, famishing and faint' (*HLS* 82/1), the 'dust and ashes' (*HLS* 143/2). Perhaps many of the poor colliers of Kingswood to whom Charles gave the sacrament were of this group. It is significant that the first communion service that the Methodists celebrated outside the Church of England was for 80 colliers at Kingswood (*CWJ* 29/6/1740). The second group of 'the poor' were those who had been deliberately sinful and rebellious —those who would probably be considered 'unworthy of help'—the 'rebels' (*HLS* 121/2), the 'poor heathen' (*HLS* 138/2) with 'carnal heart and mind', having the Adamic nature 'like Cain with inbred sin', the 'all polluting strain' (*HLS* 32), these, the 'vilest and meanest of the fallen race' (*HLS* 155/2–3). Charles in his ministry to condemned prisoners, spending the night with them prior to their execution, giving them the sacrament just before he accompanied them to the gallows, saying goodbye to them with a brotherly kiss, affirmed the worth of these people. In his comment on the passage about communion found in 1 Corinthians 11: 22, John Wesley remarked after the verse, 'Have ye not houses to eat and drink your common meals in? Or do ye despise the church of God?': 'Of which the poor are both the larger and the better part. Do ye act thus in designed contempt of them?'

Third, the Wesleys laid a foundation of viewing the poor with respect, basing it on the fact that the eucharist is an eschatological meal which equalises ultimately all humankind. John Wesley in his *A Plain Account of the People Called Methodists* reported that he and other preachers eat with the poor, sharing the same food at the same table. He then adds, 'and we rejoice herein, as a comfortable earnest of our eating bread together in our Father's kingdom'. The use of the word 'earnest' in this context brings to mind the frequent use of that word in the *HLS* regarding the eschatological dimension of the sacrament. At the Table, the process of being made 'one body' in Christ has begun (cf *ENNT* I Corinthians 11: 17). One's economic status is not a barrier in this process.

Fourth, Wesleyan eucharistic spirituality laid on all who came to the Table a sense of responsibility to live Christ's life of loving service to all in need. Brown saw the sacramental moments as 'the normative moments that show us what ordinary life is meant to be and is usually not' and where the Lord's supper is meant to be the 'model for other meals'; that 'the way bread is shared' at communion is the way 'bread is meant to be shared on all other occasions' (Brown 1988: 94–5). While the Wesleys did not verbalise their position as clearly and as radically as Brown, they shared the same vision. In his *ENNT*, John reminded Christians at the table of their 'obligations to love' (his comments on 1 Corinthians 11: 24). To 'eat this bread unworthily' meant eating it not only in an 'irreverent manner without regarding Him who appointed it . . . ' but also without regarding 'the design of its appointment' (1 Corinthians II: 27), ie to love one's neighbour as oneself. As one partakes constantly of the sacrament, one's values and life are shaped: the 'mind of Christ' is formed in the person and one begins to 'walk as He walked' (cf. *HLS* 130, 135), imitating his loving attitude and acts towards the poor and towards society.

6.4 *Seeing the world*
Wesleyan eucharistic spirituality names the world as the arena for praise and discipleship. The Wesleys followed Brevint's subheadings very closely as they worked on their eucharistic hymns. There is, however, one new category which the Wesleys added. They called it: 'After the Sacrament'. In this category, they portrayed the followers of Christ shouting and singing with joy after their encounter with Christ at the Table. The 'groaning' of creation in brokenness (cf Romans 8: 22–25) is put aside. The 'stammerers' have now found voice to praise God. The human world is seen from the point of view of the redemption. Sin is sickness, redemption is the beginning of healing the brokenness of the world. Healing has begun in the lives of Christians. They who have received it pass it on in the healing of relationships as they make real their discipleship by forgiving those who have wronged them. Healing of the world also takes place through the Christians' willingness to stand for God's values in the world, even if that means paying the ultimate price of one's life—ie through martyrdom: the cup of Christ's love and sorrow are one (*HLS* 142/5–8).

The material world is seen as an instrument for divine use. As bread and wine can be sanctified and transformed by the *epiclesis* into vehicles of divine grace, so the common things of life can be intentionally set apart as and converted into instruments of God's love. The Wesleys were not averse to using secular tunes for their hymns. The physical senses of touch, sight, smell, taste and sound are blessed and utilised.

John Wesley wanted all the senses to participate in response to God. Quoting Brevint, he wrote:

> . . . surely, it is no common Regard we ought to have for these Venerable Representations which God himself hath set up in and for his Church. For these are far more than an Ordinary Figure. All Sorts of Signs and Monuments are more or less venerable, according to the Things which they represent. And these, besides their ordinary Use, bear as it were on their Face the glorious Character of their Divine Appointment, and the express Design that God hath to revive thereby, *and to expose to all our Senses, his Sufferings, as if they were present now* . . . (Wesley 1745: 5, 6).

Charles Wesley sang:

> The Tokens of thy Dying Love,
> O let us All receive,
> And feel the Quick'ning Spirit move,
> And *sensibly* believe (*HLS* 30/4).

One of the problems John Wesley had with transubstantiation was that it was against the senses (JWW 16, WW 15 Section IV). When looking at the life of Lopez, Wesley highlighted that although Lopez experienced the sus-pension of the exercise of his senses and understanding during his initial encounters with God ('large manifestations from God'), in later times he was left with the full exercise of these. In other words, while communion with God can be experienced without any apparent sensory impact, it can equally be experienced through the senses (JWL 30).

In the *HLS*, it is interesting to note the number of references made to each of the five senses. One would expect the work of Protestant writers to focus on hearing, not sight (Leenhardt 1994: 82–106). Saliers wrote that the ear had replaced the eye as the principal organ of faith from the second generation of the Reformation forward (Cousins 1990: xx). A deeper study of the *HLS* produced some surprises (see Appendix F). References to the sense of sight appeared at least seventy-two times, making it the top choice of the Wesleys. The sense of touch came second, with a minimum of fifty–nine references. Third came the sense of taste, mentioned about fifty-five times. Hearing came as a poor fourth—about sixteen times. The count for the sense of smell was low—a mere three times. Comparing my research with a 1969 study conducted by Morris of 63 texts of Charles Wesley verses (ie not exclusively from the *HLS*), I found that Morris and I came to almost the same conclusion regarding Charles's order of sense preference. We differed in one area: out of 623 references to the senses in the texts he studied, Morris found that 266 referred to sight, 126 to touch, fifty-two to sound, forty-two to taste and eight to smell (Morris 1969: Appendix B). Sound or hearing was third on Morris's list. Taste was fourth. It seems that in the *HLS*, the reverse is true. The sense of taste was referred to more than the sense of hearing. This does not seem surprising because the sacrament entailed actual eating of bread and drinking of the wine. However, if we consider that both touch and taste require tactile participation, we see the shift from the largely hearing-dominated preference of Protestant spirituality to a spirituality that is very visual and extremely tactile in its reception and expression.

This is significant for it marks a departure from the Anglican liturgical tradition so familiar to the Wesley brothers. In that tradition, the word is preached, read and repeated in the offices of morning and evening prayer and in the daily Communion service. The *Offices* in the *BCP* go through most of the Old Testament books once a year and the New Testament books three times a year, underlining the Protestant focus on word-orientated edification, education and formation. The eucharistic spirituality of the Wesleys seems to be more in line with the visually orientated monastic traditions of the early Middle Ages which expressed devotions to the wounds of Christ (Ward 1992: 25) and their style bears certain similarities to the 'application of the senses in meditation' of the *Spiritual Exercises of St Ignatius*.[8]

According to Ruffing, the senses of taste, touch and smell, given through imagery in mystical experiences, are the most intimate ones. Vision and audition, which do not require physical contact, have been favoured in the medieval philosophical traditions because they seem 'safer' (1995: 106). If Wesleyan eucharistic spirituality has two of the top three senses as touch and taste, one immediately sees the surprising level of familiarity or intimacy that the Wesleys expect the communicant to have with God at the eucharist. Although sight might be a more 'distant' sense, counsellors say that babies bond with their mothers through eye contact. Lake pointed out that acceptance to a child is transmitted most effectively through 'the umbilical cord of sight' (Lake 1986: 140). Annie Long and Joyce Huggett, both well-known Christian coun-

---

8. The style of prayer used by St Ignatius of Loyola is not really that new: St Bonaventure in *Lignum vitae* (Tree of Life), for example, had meditated on events in the life of Christ by visualising the scenes and becoming a participant in the action. 'Mysticism of the historical event', as it has been termed, is a way of experiencing the meaning and value of the event in a deeper way through participation (Cousins 1990: 382–6). What St Ignatius did was to develop, structure, deepen and popularise that prayer experience practised since the 13th century. Martz indicated that the *Spiritual Exercises* with their 'composition of place', analysis and colloquy, use of imagination and visualisation influenced the style of the 'metaphysical poets' like John Donne, George Herbert and William Crashaw (Martz 1954: 38, 53). Martz postulated that Herbert, who had abounded in private devotions, would have included the *Exercises* among them (Martz 1954: 38). Through their poems, the style of the *Exercises* influenced many high churchmen of the early seventeenth century and even Puritans like Baxter (Martz 1954: 38, 163–172). We know that Charles and John were both influenced by metaphysical poet Herbert (Hutchinson 159: 181–2; Morris 1969: 375–379). Could the imaginative/visualisation style of the Ignatian *Spiritual Exercises* have filtered down to the Wesleys' hymns through the metaphysical poets?

sellors, share his views (Huggett 1988: 181). Sight was the most favoured sense of the Wesleys in the eucharistic hymns. Perhaps the Wesleys expect—the believers to bond with Christ as they see him with their eyes of faith, beholding him on his cross at Calvary, crucified for them.

The Wesleys' appreciation for the physical, the material and the sensory as instruments of grace is apparent. It follows a more kataphatic tradition as opposed to an apophatic one. Kataphatic traditions use pictures, concepts, images to view and describe the divine. Apophatic traditions prefer the absence of these, describing the unknowable mystery of God using negations—ie saying what he is not rather than what he is. Indeed, a study by English (1997) held the thesis that Wesley became dissatisfied with the apophatic spirituality of Law and embraced the kataphatic tradition of pseudo-Macarius.

Interestingly, this positive affirmation of the senses contributed to the Wesleys' readiness to accept the validity of what could be termed the more 'unusual' and surprising work of God in their people like the ones mentioned in the last section. John Downes, then rector of St Michael's, Wood Street, London wrote an article entitled *Methodism Examined and Exposed*, accusing the Methodists of describing grace as perceptible to the heart as sensible objects are by senses. He believed that Scripture speaks of grace that is conveyed imperceptibly, visible only through the actions of the recipients. John Wesley replied to him, affirming that grace is perceptible to the senses and through its works of comforting, refreshing, purifying and shedding the love of God (JWL 17/11/1759). Hence John had no qualms accepting the validity of sensory and physical happenings (what someone called 'psychomotor activity'—visible, bodily evidence of the Spirit's presence) and there were many such which appeared during both Charles's and his ministry, although both brothers were very cautious about extremism. In 1759, for example, John commented after preaching at Everton:

> The danger was to regard extraordinary circum
> stances too much, such as outcries, convulsions,
> visions, trances; as if these were essential to the

inward work. Perhaps the danger is to regard them too little, to condemn them altogether; to imagine they had nothing of God in them. Whereas the truth is: God suddenly and strongly convinced many they were lost sinners, the natural consequences whereof were sudden outcries and bodily convulsions: to strengthen and encourage them that believed, and to make His work more apparent, He favoured several of them with divine dreams, often with trances and visions: in some of these instances, after a time, nature mixed with grace: Satan likewise mimicked this work of God, in order to discredit the whole. At first it was, doubtless, wholly from God. It is partly so at this day, and He will enable us to discern how far in every case the work is pure, and where it mixes or degenerates (*JWJ* 25/11/1759).

This spirituality of the senses could be the Wesleyan answer to the perpetual question posed to Protestants: 'Why bother with the eucharist when it is possible to receive the grace of God through other means?'[9] The physicality of the bread and

---

9. Both Zwingli and Calvin felt that there was something 'extra' that communion brought to the Christian. To Zwingli, sacraments are given for the instruction of the 'outward' man who learns through the senses (Stephens 1986: 182–3). Calvin saw the effectiveness of communion not as imparting a different gift but in the different manner of its giving. In the recruitment of the five senses, not hearing only, the message gets through to the person more clearly and effectively (Gerrish 1993: 162–3). Yet one must remember that in Wesleyan eucharistic spirituality, the sacramental 'plus' is undergirded by the greater weight the Wesleys gave to sensory input or impact (Zwingli and Calvin appeared to be more condescending about the human need for sensory inputs). The sacramental 'plus' is also given in Wesleyan eucharistic spirituality by the expected personal encounter with the dynamic and intimate presence of Christ at the Table which makes the sacrament the chief means of grace.

wine, the expected sensory and physical experience of the eucharistic encounter with Christ, make the eucharist a very special means of grace. The unconscious anti-gnostic element inbuilt in the eucharist affirms the wholeness of the human person and the goodness of creation. Here, as nowhere else, the person with *all* his or her human faculties is touched by the divine. The material world is affirmed and appreciated as a possible instrument of his love. Wainwright wrote: The beginning of the transformation of our sense is needed for our response to God's self–gift in revelation and redemption.

The response has three effects: it calls forth a 'return offering of ourselves to God', we are then able to be 'employed to mediate the gifts (of God) to others', and

> the gradual transformation of our senses prepares us for the final resurrection when we shall start to enjoy those things which even now, our eyes have not seen, our ears heard, nor our hearts conceived, but which God has in store for those who love him (1 Corinthians 2: 9) (Wainwright 1997a: 20–21).

Although the Wesleys might be quite affirmative of the world, they were also realistic about the provisional nature of all created things. One day, the world will come to an end (*HLS* 93, 98) and the need for the means of grace will be no more. There is a certain amount of detachment in Wesleyan eucharistic spirituality from material things because of their provisional nature and their relative value in the light of one's faith. It is possible, therefore, to own things and yet not be owned by them. One need not, as a disciple of Christ, divest oneself physically of all of one's possessions (*HLS* 145/5). Detachment is sufficient. In that sense Wesleyan eucharistic spirituality cannot be said to be merely world-affirming. While it is certainly not world-denying for its kataphatic approach, rejoicing in the use of the five senses and imagination, it can be best termed as world-transforming, like other evangelical spiritualities (Gillett 1993: 90–93). There is a joyousness in the Wesleyan approach which might not be as present in other evangelical spiritualities which are more solemn and penitential. This presupposes a stronger link between the Wesleyan eucharistic spirituality's understanding of nature and of grace, of incarnation and of redemption.

The same attitude of detachment does not seem to manifest itself with regard to non-human creatures. John Wesley had always shown an interest in the destiny of creatures. He believed that the future state of the world, with its non-human creatures, will lie in the hands of the God who loves it and who will transform it. Lee in his study of Wesley and the Eastern Fathers of the church (1991) believed that Wesley's belief in the restoration of the *imago dei* is linked to his overall vision of the restoration of the whole of creation to the reign of God. Todd recorded that John had worked on three papers for his Master of Arts degree at Oxford on 14 February 1727. One was on Julius Caesar, one was on the love of God and the third, a natural philosophy paper, was on *Animal Souls* (1958: 39). In his sermon on *The General Deliverance*, John wrote:

> The whole brute creation will then, undoubtedly,
> be restored not only to the vigour, strength, and
> swiftness which they had at their creation, but to
> a far higher degree of each than they ever enjoyed
> . . . Thus in that day, all the vanity to which they
> are helplessly subject will be abolished; they will
> suffer no more, either from within or without; the
> days of their groaning are ended (*Sermon* 60).

This view of John's was not fleshed out in his eucharistic spirituality. As we noted, the Wesleys do not share the church Fathers' sentiments that present in the eucharist is 'the whole creation and the world God loves' (Thurian 1966: 20). They do not have the 'offering of the fruits of creation to God' with the offertory procession and the accompanying theology of creation and industry. Wakefield believes that for the Wesleys the elements are already at the table at the beginning of the service, representing God's hospitality rather than the offering of the people. In this, he said, the Wesleys echoed the positions of both Brevint and the 1662 *BCP* (Wakefield 1966: 146).

6.5 Seeing time

To the Orthodox, the eucharist liturgy is the entrance to heaven (Wakefield 1995: 28). Eternity and 'the Now' intersect. There seem to be two views of time for the Wesleys. One is linear, moving purposefully from the time of creation, Old Testament events, the cross, towards a final consummation when the final feast will be celebrated. The focus is not so much on the origin of time but its process and its final destination. This time is not lonely time. It is time visited upon (cf John 1: 14), time made holy because God is a God of history. The present moment is where the benefits of Christ's death are pleaded for, where the Sacrificed is at the moment interceding for us, when the Spirit descends and where heaven meets us. As Oliver Clement, the Orthodox theologian puts it, 'Time is the God-given oppor- tunity to learn to love' (Wainwright 1980: 34). It is for the Wesleys the training ground to loving God and others in a richer and fuller way. The speed of time is not important, for it is time pregnant with expectation. It is true that John Wesley, in his later years, abandoned the observance of most holy days except All Saints Day. Yet he never lost his sense that time is sanctified each day by the eternal priest-cum-sacrifice who still intercedes for his people (*HLS* 117/2).

Time can be also, as Ole Borgen puts it, an 'eternal now' (Stacey 1988: 71). Eternity is just 'a veil' away. Remove the veil and one beholds the crucifixion of Christ—an unrepeatable event nearly two thousand years ago. The only word that comes close to describing this; is a 'time-warp'. This time is encoun- tered through sanctified imagination, faith and surprising divine interventions. The church triumphant is also present in this timeless holy space. They, 'our Elder Brethren' (*HLS* 162/2), existing beyond our time, join us and the angels in worship. We in turn lift them up before the throne of grace, as we do those who are with us in this life in the here-and-now.

Holding these two coexisting views of time, the Wesleys were able to avoid what Thurian describes as the Protestant pitfall of seeing Calvary as a mere past event to which one returns by faith, in one's intellect, and sometimes, with great sentimentality. Thurian pointed out that such a view often leads to separation of seeing the life of Christ as connected to his call to discipleship, reducing the Christian faith to activism and moralism. Calvary is seen, not as a sacramental repetition of the past event—as Protestants feared the Roman Catholics were doing in the mass—but as the very unrepeatable event, experienced in the *now*. This meant the removal of the danger of 'ritualism' or 'formalism', as Thurian puts it, in favour of a more dynamic, encounter–centred faith (II 1966: 102–3).

There is no contradiction between the two views of time. What they seem to affirm in unison to the individual believer is a very personal: You are not alone in time. I (Jesus) am here with you. This is obvious when one looks at the eucharistic hymns and Brevint's prayers. Wesleyan eucharistic spirituality views time as celebrating 'The Presence'. It is the presence of a person—Jesus. It is not 'vampire Christianity'—where all one looks for in Christ is, figuratively speaking, his blood and all its benefits. Jesus is there in the past-hidden in the types of the Old Testament. It is Jesus whom one finds in the elements. It is Jesus whom one meets in the world. It is Jesus to whom one is joined, inseparable—as parts of the body to its head. It is Jesus who is still interceding for his people as the high priest before the Father. The Holy Spirit opens the eyes of the believers to see this as reality. For the Wesleys, this very personal love relationship with Christ exists in time and in eternity.

7. A summary picture

In summary, Wesleyan eucharistic spirituality painted this picture: The prodigal returns to a just and loving Father, whose love will not let the prodigal go nor let the prodigal off either. Reconciled to the Father, the prodigal sees life as being no longer one's own. The person lives a life as sacrificed offering, in union with Christ's offering, entering into the world which is the place for praise and the area for a discipleship, committed to healing the brokenness there. Participating in the spiritual and physical healing of human lives, seeing and affirming the special dignity of marginalised people, valuing the material blessings of the world, celebrating with all one's human sensory and creative mental faculties, the person lives in the world, with a detachment born of understanding the provisional nature of material things. Life is lived before a 'cloud of witnesses' of the church triumphant, in the consciousness of the constant, intimate presence of one's Lord which will continue beyond the span one's human years. Life is lived with a sense of positive expectancy ('on tiptoe') for the God one knows is a God who surprises.

If Wesleyan eucharistic spirituality provides for the Christian this way to seeing life, what is the significance of this view? What difference does this way of seeing make for the individual? Our perceptions colour our attitudes and the way we live. The Wesleyan eucharistic spirituality's view of life creates a very secure person, grounded in the assurance that one is deeply and truly loved. There is a freedom of healthy detachment in one's life. There is no need to grab at things or people for security. Life has meaning. The meaning is not tied to a mere self-centred understanding of fulfilment. Instead, meaning comes as one gives one's life away to God and others in response to the love one has experienced. There is a great deal of joy there—for the world is a place of promise and life. Time is not an enemy but a space for God's surprising work and for love to mature. Eternity is tasted and the feast awaits beyond the door of death. The person walks thus in the world with a sense of spaciousness, utilising its gifts, enjoying them with the five senses as well as with imagination, always conscious of the fact that the one who loves him/her is always with him/her, never leaving him/her nor forsaking him/her.

8. Characteristics of Wesleyan eucharistic spirituality

First, Wesleyan eucharistic spirituality is strongly *Christological*. The focus is solely on Christ. Nothing is allowed to take His place as the focal point. It is a spirituality of immanence where intimacy, immediacy and expectancy are the key descriptions of the divine–human relationship. Second, the *primacy of grace* in the sacrament is clear: the efficacy of the sacrament does not depend solely on the communicant's worthiness or even the person's adequacy of faith. Grace enfolds the communicant from first to last. The atonement has been made. We plead for its effects even as the sacrificed one continues to intercede for us. His Spirit works in and through us as companion-sanctifier. To celebrate that grace is to experience it by responding to it with gratitude and in obedience. Third, Wesleyan eucharistic spirituality has Christian perfection as the goal of the Christian life firmly in view. The eucharist is the main formational instrument towards that goal. Formation and growth towards that goal are intentional and active. Fourth, growth towards that goal of *Christian perfection* is seen in a *therapeutic manner.* From the sickness of sin the believer grows towards healing and wholeness. Formation is seen as a forms of healing. Fifth, it is a *hymnic spirituality.* The *HLS* not only informs the Christian's faith: the hymns form the Christian's outlook in life. Hymns deepen the eucharistic experience. Sixth: it is a *community –supported spirituality.* Eucharist was celebrated in the midst of the church's corporate act of worship, accompanied always with the preaching of the word and, sometimes, testimonies of the believers. Mentoring and monitoring of one's spiritual life and discipline are done by those who function as leaders of groups. Lay people played an important role in eucharistic formation as did strong centralised leadership (ie exercised by both the Wesleys) which kept this formation alive. Seventh: Wesleyan eucharistic spirituality *provides a way of looking at God, at the self, at others, at the world and at time.* God is just and loving, capable of intimacy and surprises. The self is a returned and restored prodigal turned living sacrifice. People matter—first as spiritual beings, then also as physical beings whose dignity and worth does not depend on their worldly possessions or position. The world is the arena for praise and discipleship, all things can be instruments for divine use. The senses and the imagination are affirmed. There is a healthy sense of detachment from the gifts the world presents because of their provisional nature. Time seen both as linear and as 'eternal now' is blessed with the divine presence and is space for growth, for love, for life. Eighth: Wesleyan eucharistic spirituality is *a spirituality of joy.* The eucharistic hymns and the records of early Methodist eucharistic services are characterised by reverential joy in what God has and is doing in his people.

In the next and final chapter, we will explore why the Wesleyan eucharistic revival declined after the deaths of the

Wesleys, evaluate Wesleyan eucharistic spirituality and explore how relevant it is (or can be) to a specific ecclesial context in our world today.

5

The Future of Wesleyan Eucharistic Spirituality

1. decline of eucharistic observance and fervour

Even though the Wesleys' ideal was for Methodists to have daily communions, John was only able to take communion once in four to five days and Charles no less than twice a month (cf chapter 1). While they did instil in their people the importance of and desire for regular communions and there was indeed a eucharistic revival, the lack of celebrants limited the number of eucharistic services available to the Methodists. This situation worsened after the death of John Wesley. What were some of the reasons for the decline of eucharistic observance and fervour among the Methodists?

Firstly, there was disagreement as to who were acceptable celebrants for communion. At the point of Wesley's death, there were only two groups of people who could celebrate communion for the Methodists: the Church of England clergy who had been assisting him in this area (be they his friends or those hired for this purpose) and the small number of preachers whom he had ordained. Even so, the latter group (comparatively small in number) were not fully recognised by certain powerful Trustees who were able to block them from celebrating communion in some chapels when Wesley died.

While John Wesley lived, the 'who can celebrate?' issue was held firmly in check: he would not allow unordained preachers to celebrate even though some societies wanted it. His educated theological principles, sustained by his strong character, could not continue to prevail against the spiritual discernment and emotional sentiments of those in his societies who preferred their own unordained preachers as celebrants to the unfamiliar or 'less spiritual' hired ordained clerics. The Methodist Conference in the 1795 *Plan of Pacification* allowed all preachers (ordained or unordained) to celebrate under certain circumstances eg, where there were strong local demands for the preacher to do so (Rattenbury 1948: 135–6). There were many of those who would not accept the sacrament from the hands of the preachers. Some stopped coming for communion services of their societies. Others returned to the Church of England.

For those societies which would not accept preachers as celebrants, there were not many options open to them. They had infrequent communions.

Beyond these practical difficulties, the spiritual and cultural landscape changed, resulting in a change of attitude to the sacrament. Davies indicated that the 'supernaturalism' of Calvinism (and of the Wesleys regarding the experience at the sacrament) became 'less congenial to the spirit of the age' than was Zwinglianism with its more 'cerebral inclinations'. Reason was beginning to be valued above other human faculties including experience which had been highly valued by the Methodists at the Table. The spiritual and social impact of the non-sacramental Salvation Army and the Quakers led many to question if the sacrament was that crucial to living a truly spiritual life. The focus of the communion became more inclined towards the horizontal dimension: it became more a meal of fellowship and 'brotherhood'. Methodists also became increasingly cautious about the centrality of the eucharist in their tradition as they observed the rise of the sacra-mentally-inclined Oxford Movement where many were led to embrace the Roman Catholic faith (Davies 1996: 83–84).

The *HLS*, a key resource in feeding eucharistic piety, also declined in popularity and use. The *HLS*, which fed eucharistic fervour among the Methodists with ten editions by 1790, was not published again until 1875, and then by a group of Anglo-Catholics (Hoskins 1994: 73). A study of fourteen representative hymnbooks from the British and the United Methodist traditions[1] revealed the decreased use of eucharistic hymns in United Methodism since the start of the twentieth century. In

---

1. A charismatic non-denominational congregation once called 'Stone Mountain Church' in San Clemente, California, for example, is now St Michael's Church. Their pastor was later consecrated a bishop (by other bishops of the Anglican and branches of some Orthodox Churches) of a growing new denomination—the Charismatic Episcopal Church of North America (Thigpen 1992: 44). Churches like theirs have grown.

1786, fifteen eucharistic hymns were included in the official hymnal. In 1847 the number included in the new hymnal went up to twenty-nine. In 1849, it was decreased to twenty-three, in 1878 to fourteen, in 1889 to eighteen and in 1905 to two. There was one in 1935 and the 1966 hymnal had four. The 1989 one had only two (Wainwright 1995: xi–xii).

Wakefield suggested that the *Hymns* were largely ignored by the Methodists in the nineteenth century because of

> the Catholic revival which thrust Methodists into the Free Church camp, and their discovery by Anglo-Catholic controversialists, who gave them a Roman Catholic interpretation (Dudley 1995: 159).

Brian Beck, Secretary of the British Methodist Conference, in a sermon at Bristol cathedral on 18 June 1995 and in a lecture at Filton Methodist Church in October of the same year, mentioned some reasons for the declining use of the *Hymns*. There was a shift of theological and cultural paradigms over the years which made the language and theology of a substitutional sacrifice sound foreign. The change of musical taste of congregations was another reason and Charles Wesley's creative and colourful English did not prove very translatable into languages native to places where Methodism had taken root and flourished around the world.

New and more pressing agendas confronted emerging Methodist communities around the world. In the expanding frontier of North America, literacy was an ongoing challenge; spontaneity rather than formality was the order of the day. Unlike the situation where the Wesleys laboured, most people of the American frontier had little or no acquaintance with Church of England subculture and consequently had less respect and appreciation for the church's liturgical and eucharistic format. Services were held in homes, halls, tents, school houses and, later, simple chapels. Architecture in early American churches placed the pulpit, not the altar, in the central position. Conversion was the primary concern of the church; the sacrament was sidelined. In a world of evangelistic and revival meetings, the liturgically-orientated 'ritual' of communion did not seem to have a place.

The vastness of the North American terrain also meant that Methodist circuit riders had to cover large areas to minister to scattered settlers. Communion services were therefore few, limited to special services held usually four times a year when the presiding elder would be present at a quarterly conference (Littrell 1995: 27–28). There was no pressing reason for increasing the number of communion services nor the number of acceptable celebrants. There was no Methodist leader who shared the stature and eucharistic passion of the Wesleys to implement any changes.

From America, Methodism spread to many countries. An example would be the coming of Methodism to Singapore. It came in 1885 via American missionaries from India. The imported practice of having monthly communion remained as the current practice of Methodist churches in the country. Like American Methodism in its early frontier situation, evangelism is a priority of the Methodist Church in Singapore. Discipleship and nurture are seen to be key concerns of the church as well. In a place where services are usually packed and tight scheduling of service times is practised to accommodate the numbers, the length of the communion service which takes up the valuable pulpit time (utilised usually for evangelism or discipleship training) and preparation time (preparation and cleaning up of little cubes of bread and tiny shot-glass cups of grape juice) does not make the sacrament any more welcome by church leaders beyond its obligatory monthly round.

2. Signs of hope

Although some of the causes listed as responsible for the decline of eucharistic observance and spirituality are still present in global Methodism, there are hopeful signs that the situation has improved and will continue to do so. We have seen that the dire shortage of ordained ministers to celebrate communion was a reason for the decline of eucharistic observance in the Methodist Church in years past. This is not necessarily true for Methodism in many parts of the world today. Where ordained ministers are lacking, authorised lay-persons have been given 'letters of dispensation' by their bishops/conferences to conduct the sacrament and, in most cases, these persons are recognised and well accepted by their Methodist communities. Some will argue that the availability of these lay eucharistic ministers betrays a basic tenet of the Wesleys: that communion be celebrated only by ordained ministers. Yet we cannot dismiss the fact that the purpose behind the Wesley's insistence on clerical celebration, ie to highlight the sacrificial aspect of the sacrament, focusing it on divine initiative, grace and generosity rather than on human response (cf chapter 2) continues to be strongly affirmed.

The era of enlightenment with its enthronement of reason in the West has not made a great impact on the growing Methodist churches in the two-thirds world (eg Asia and Africa), many of which can be considered 'evangelical' and/or 'charismatic' in theological orientation and practice. These churches share their own culture's innate belief in the impingement of the supernatural upon daily life. Personal spiritual experiences are valued highly even in what appears to be Western–orientated and highly technological societies, eg in Singapore. The theology of substitutionary atonement which Brian Beck in Britain felt was difficult for church members to appreciate is not a problem for Methodists in many parts of the world. It is the vital part of the faith of most Methodists in these growing churches.

The effects of international Methodist ecumenical dialogue have resulted in an openness to the other traditions in a way that was not possible before. It has allowed for a cross-fertilisation of resources and ideas, eg Methodists learning from the Salvationists and Roman Catholics and vice versa. It has lessened the suspicions and barriers which had existed between the heirs of the reformation and the Roman Catholic Church. There is a gradual recovery of sacramental spirituality in many churches—even in the non-traditional ones around the world. There are reports that several newly inaugurated charismatic non-denominational churches are finding new appreciation for the liturgy, taking up the practice of weekly eucharists, using'. . . clerical vestments, litanies, incense, pro-cessions, fixed prayers and creeds . . . ' (Thigpen 1992: 43–44).[2] There are several reasons for this: growing discontentment with the 'need' to make every service 'unique' and the awareness that 'empty ritual' can refer to 'praise choruses' as it can to old hymns; the advantage of having liturgical forms which shift the attention from the skills/charisma of the minister/worship leader to the One who is worshipped; a desire for services which bring about deeper change rather than providing mere 'entertainment'. Thigpen writes:

> For . . . others, the primary motivation for change was a deep sense—often felt more than understood—that the Lord's Supper needed to be recognised as a source of spiritual life and health to be received every Sunday. Through study, they learned that from ancient times the Eucharist has been held by the church as the climax of the worship service, when worshippers encounter Jesus in a unique way; and they experienced the reality for themselves (1992: 45–46).

> The shift to more liturgical type of worship also meant that some aspects of life in the Spirit are best communicated and experienced through concrete, visual and acted symbols rather than through words (1992: 50).

It is not inconceivable that in the future the sacramental spirituality might touch Methodism through charismatically - orientated churches.

While the number of eucharistic hymns have declined in the hymnals of the American Methodists, the British Methodists have increased in their use of the eucharistic hymns since 1780.

---

2.   Full communion means that only baptised communicant members of one's one church may be admitted to the Table. Open communion is where baptised communicant members of other churches are admitted. Free communion refers to a situation where anyone regardless of baptismal and confirmation status can come if they can say 'yes' to the words of invitation.

In my study of fourteen representative hymnals from both the British and American Methodist communities, the British had seven eucharistic hymns in 1780. The number went up to twenty-one in 1831, twenty-one in 1875, down to seventeen in 1904, fourteen in 1933 and up to sixteen in 1983. From the study, we know that there *are* hymnic resources of the eucharistic type which can be used for formation in Wesleyan eucharistic spiritualilty. Seventeen such hymns have been available to Methodists of at least two generations (Appendix G). It must be admitted that American Methodism and Methodism influenced by them has a greater disadvantage because of its declining use of eucharistic hymns. More work has to be done for a conscious reclaiming of the Wesleyan eucharistic spirituality heritage.

Interest in the Wesleys' eucharistic hymns has gained momentum over the years with the work of the Order of St Luke and the Charles Wesley Society. The two groups reprinted a modernised version (1990) and a facsimile (1995) of the *Hymns* respectively. Admittedly it has some way to go in terms of making it available to more Methodists around the world and providing a translation of it for those whose language is not English.

American and British Methodism has given birth to many (if not most) of the Methodist communities around the globe. Their influence on their 'daughter churches' often remains through these churches' use/adaptation of their worship resources. While the *HLS* and Wesleyan eucharistic teaching might be unfamiliar to many in this generation of American and British Methodists (and to those in the 'daughter churches'), present already in the hymnals and in the current eucharistic liturgy of the United Methodist Church and of the British Methodist Church are a few emphases of Wesleyan eucharistic spirituality. Present and practised also is a version of Wesley's covenant service. We have seen in chapter 4, the link between the covenant service and eucharistic formation.

Three of the Wesleys' strongest themes in the *HLS* have been consistently upheld by the inclusion of these eucharistic hymns in the fourteen representative hymnals from the two traditions. This is significant because it assures us that implanted in the deepest psyche of the Methodists are the beliefs in the primacy of grace in eucharistic spirituality, the call to respond sacrificially to the Lord in the sacrament and the remembrance of the Lord in the eucharistic memorial (Appendix G).

Looking at the liturgy of the United Methodist Church, the primacy of grace is clear through the section on confession and pardon and in the words of institution. As both clergy and laity acknowledge their sinful state before God, *both* declare to each other God's forgiveness (*UMH* 1989: 8). At the *Invitation*, all are invited—the main condition is the openness to change and desire to live a new life. Although *The Service of Word and Table IV* in the *UMH*, and the 1936 edition of the British *Communion Service* based on the 1662 *BCP* and Wesley's *Sunday Service*, still have the condition that one must be 'in love and charity with one's neighbour' (*UMH* 1989: 26; 1975: B41ff), the more recent and frequently used forms, *The Service of Word and Table* I (*UMH* 1989: 7) and *The Sunday Service* liturgy of the *Methodist Service Book* (1975: B15), do not. The latter, for example, simply invites people to 'draw near with faith' to receive the body and blood of Christ which have been given 'for you', feeding on him in one's heart 'by faith with thanksgiving'. While some congregations have expressed concern that the words of invitation seemed to be too 'lax', fearing the abuse of the grace proffered at the Table, yet we discern that the words are in the spirit of the Wesleys who equally 'risked' this grace in their eucharistic ministry to the dregs of society.

The dynamism of the encounter with the Lord who initiates the work is clear through the strong affirmation of the work of the Holy Spirit: the *epiclesis* is included in both *Word and Table I and IV* rites. The former invokes the Spirit's descent on the elements to be for the communicants, 'the body and blood of Christ', and prays for the Spirit to come upon the people so that they may be for the world the 'body of Christ, redeemed by His blood' (*UMH* 1989: 10). The latter rite now includes a prayer that the Father will 'bless and sanctify' with the word and the Spirit the elements so that reception of them will make communicants 'participants of the Divine nature' (*UMH* 1989: 29). In the same vein, the British *Methodist Service Book* prayer is for the power of the Spirit to empower the communicants to 'share in the body and blood of Christ' (1975: B14). The 1936 order for communion did not have an *epiclesis*. These 'acts' of the Spirit upon the elements, upon the people and for the effects of the sacrament are found in *HLS* 150, 72, 7, 16, 72/3–4. John Wesley's omission of the *epiclesis* in his *Sunday Service* is now restored to Methodism via the influence of the *HLS*. A final note is that the rubric in the *Methodist Service Book* states that at the conclusion of the service, the remains of the elements 'should be disposed of reverently' (1975: B4). This reflects the Wesleyan eucharistic belief that the elements have received through the work of the Spirit a change in their significance.

The picture of the just, vulnerable, risk-taking God is very clearly described in the *Great Thanksgiving* section of *Word and Table I*. The value of human beings is affirmed in a stronger way in *Word and Table I* and the true state of humanity coming before God as helpless sinners is seen in the *Word and Table IV* or in the British order of service, both of which still maintain the 1662 *BCP's* prayer of humble access. Response to the grace of God in the form of self-offering is strong in all the eucharistic liturgies mentioned.

Although the primary means of spiritual formation in many Methodist churches might not be liturgical, the dictum *lex orandi est lex credendi* (the law of prayer is the law of belief) can hold true in that whatever effects the liturgy will have some effect on local Methodists.

It must be admitted that there are several elements of Wesleyan eucharistic spirituality conspicuously missing or under-developed in British and American Methodist liturgies, eg the strong Wesleyan emphasis on the presence of Christ, the joy of the sacrament, the goal of Christian perfection with communion as the chief means of grace and the eucharist as a healing sacrament. These could be deliberately included in future liturgies or highlighted through the use (or adaptation) of the resources in the *HLS*. Nevertheless, hopeful signs for the rediscovery and restoration of Wesleyan eucharistic spirituality are many. What remains is for global twenty-first century Methodism to begin reclaiming is heritage.

3. Is there a desire?

Even with the hopeful signs mentioned above, one could ask, 'Is there really a desire for the restoration of Wesleyan eucharistic spirituality?' The lack of desire for Wesleyan eucharistic spirituality could be the biggest barrier to its restoration in Methodist congregations.

One cannot desire what one has not known or experienced. If teaching on Wesleyan eucharistic theology and spirituality had been lacking and if what has been taught in its place (and mistaken for their theology) for years has been the Zwinglian eucharistic position (as it is in the case of Singapore), it would be difficult to stir up any excitement about its restoration. However, if what we have uncovered as Wesleyan eucharistic theology and spirituality are made known to Methodists—its potential in enriching their faith, its possible contributions to discipleship and nurture (and even evangelism)—the desire could be greatly stimulated.

Where the key emphases of the spirituality can be clearly spelt out, ways can be found to encourage frequent eucharistic celebrations, change of styles in eucharistic services and so forth. We have noted that evangelism, discipleship and nurture are top priorities for many emerging churches and Sunday services provide the time for these to be addressed. There would not be a great deal of enthusiasm for the eucharist to be celebrated every Sunday since that would mean that there would be less time available for teaching and outreach. One way of dealing with it would be to have eucharistic celebrations at cell or church prayer meetings on a regular basis. Since the Wesleyan emphasis is on its celebrative nature, it would fit in those settings rather well. Where congregations are more inclined to appreciate spontaneous rather than liturgical worship, new celebration forms can be found to present the Wesleyan emphases, now that the distinctives have been identified and outlined clearly.

Desire can be stimulated with the clear presentation of what the Wesleys taught and practised as eucharistic theology and spirituality.

4. Reintroducing eucharistic spirituality

For Wesleyan eucharistic spirituality to be reintroduced to present-day Methodism, the Wesleyan human resources which undergird that spirituality will have to be easily accessible. Three barriers to accessibility exist which might affect the promotion of Wesleyan eucharistic spirituality: first, the language of the original Wesleyan resources; second, their mode or format; third, the difference in communication styles.

4.1 The language

Much of the Wesleyan corpus is written in English. While English is the *lingua franca* of many countries and is used as an international language for business and political communication, yet its place is going to be challenged in the future by other languages such as Mandarin (STI 1997: 19 December). The English spoken by people in different parts of the world today differs greatly from English used in England. Certainly the gap is wider if we compare their English with eighteenth century English. One could easily suggest translating the Wesleyan corpus into modern English, to the English spoken in that country or into other languages. This would take time, money and human resources—all of which are severely limited in developing nations. Added to this is the fact that something is usually lost in translation. It must be noted that while copies of John Wesley's *Journals* and *Sermons* are quite readily available in places like America and England, for many Methodists around the globe, even these very basic texts of the Methodist heritage have yet to be translated into their native tongue.

4.2 The mode/format

The second issue is the question of transferability: the mode or the format of the resources would be in prose (in the case of *Sermons* and writings) with a lot of it in poetry (hymns). Can the latter, eg *HLS*, be translatable effectively not only in a different language but to a different thought form and style? Professor Gerald Hobbs of Vancouver School of Theology informed me that there are no translated Wesleyan hymns in the French Methodist hymnal. Eddie Fowler, a former missionary to Fiji, pointed out that Wesleyan hymns have been translated into Fijian but, as one conversant in Fijian and English, he felt that a lot was lost through the translation. The task, though not impossible, could prove to be quite a challenge.

4.3 Communication styles

It has been observed that in a society which emphasises the collective rather than the individual, people prefer less use of words. The long tradition of living as 'collectives' has ensured that group members learnt intuitively the shared values and assumptions and the importance of maintaining group harmony. Words are not needed as much to convey communally 'known' issues (Law 1993: 90). Non-verbal communication speaks louder than the verbal in such contexts. Picture-language or the use of images is the natural way of perceiving, articulating and communicating (Amirtham 1988: 83), rather than prose and poetry. For some cultures, eg the Asian, there is less concern for doctrine but more for practice and action (Lane 1997: 57). The body is often utilised for worship and for learning spiritual concepts (eg in African and Indian cultures). If Wesleyan eucharistic spirituality is to be effectively carried into the non-English-speaking world, it might have to utilise more action-orientated, body-involving, picture/image-lined styles of communication rather than words.

Even among those for whom English is the mother tongue, there could be another communication challenge. During the time of the Wesleys, the favoured means of communication was auditory (eg hearing sermons) and through the reading of books. In the 1930s to 1950s with the advent of the radio, there was the 'audio' culture. It was replaced in the 1960s and 1970s by the 'visual' culture of television. In the last twenty years, advances in computer technology have introduced tactile inputs. People are no longer satisfied with simply hearing or seeing, they receive instantaneous tactile stimulation from their computer games. Would they who have been exposed to a variety of sensory stimuli be satisfied with the communication style of the 18th century Wesleys?

4.4 Dealing with the question 'how?'

How can Wesleyan eucharistic spirituality be reintroduced to global Methodism? We have noted earlier that the *HLS,* the Methodist communion liturgy and the covenant service are possible resources for introducing Wesleyan eucharistic spirituality. The *HLS* in particular has played a major role in the eucharistic formation and nurture of the early Methodists. Can the *HLS* overcome the challenges posed by language, mode/ form and communication differences so that it can be accessible to global Methodism?

Perhaps the task ahead involves not translating the heritage word for word, poem for poem but conveying the main gist of the message, the 'spirit' of the Wesleyan teaching. One might argue that there are difficulties in identifying the 'gist of the message' from the contextual baggage from which the message came, since no message is created in a cultural vacuum. Yet one cannot simply dismiss what has been called the 'husk and kernel' model of contextualisation (Schreiter 1985: 8–9). While it cannot be denied that the Wesleys' context in history and place did influence their message, yet it is still possible to identify the central foci of their teaching by noting the emphasis they have given to certain themes and especially when those themes appear to contradict those favoured by their counterparts in the same era and place. We have done this exercise with regards to Wesleys' 'core' eucharistic teachings in the last four chapters. The summarised findings are in chapter 4, under 'Characteristics of Wesleyan eucharistic spirituality'.

The ramifications of this exploration into the linguistic and mode/format and communication challenges seem to imply that for Wesleyan eucharistic spirituality to be transmitted to global Methodists, a group of persons will have to be identified as prime communicators who will bridge the gap between the Wesleyan resources (eg *HLS,* communion liturgy, covenant service) and global Methodism. These communicators will have to identify the heart of the Wesleyan message in eucharistic spirituality transmitted to them and pass that on to the people in summarised, simple and creative forms suited to their culture, language, and location. The Charles Wesley Heritage Centre in Bristol (which has a vision of promoting Wesleyan spirituality to global Methodism) had that in mind when it organised a conference in 1998 entitled, 'Wesleyan Hymnic Spirituality and Mission'. The conference focused on the Wesleyan *HLS* and *Hymns for the Poor* and their relevance to mission (defined as 'evangelism, social action, spiritual formation and missionary outreach'). While the speakers are well-known and respected Wesleyan scholars in their varying fields of interest, there was a conscious effort to include prac- titioners, ie people in the grass-roots ministry of the Methodist Church such as pastors, missionaries, evangelists, social workers, musicians, composers, at the conference. These participants would be the prime communicators of Wesleyan heritage to their people in their contexts. Some came with freshly composed local music for a few hymns in the *HLS*. Others came with *HLS*-inspired hymnic creations. The latter had learnt from Charles Wesley's hymn-writing technique. Charles would use lines from other people's poems or songs and weave them into his hymns, developing (sometimes changing) the thoughts further as he went along. One example was the reference of a song to 'Fairest isle excelling' (a song extolling England). Charles took it and developed it as a hymn about Christ: 'Love Divine all loves excelling . . . ' (Webb 1997: 17). A modern equivalent of such a practice is seen in the following song:

> Jesus, lover of my soul
> All consuming fire is in Your gaze
> Jesus, I want You to know
> I will follow You all my days
>
> No one else in history is like You
> History itself belongs to You
> Alpha and Omega you have loved me
> And I will share eternity with You
>
> It's all about You, Jesus
> All this is for You
> For Your glory and Your fame
> It's not about me
> As if You should do things my way

You alone are God
And I surrender to Your ways.

(Paul Oakley, Kingsway Thankyou Music)

The first line parallels Charles Wesley's hymn of the same title. Even though Oakley's song departs from the 'Christ as refuge' theme of this Wesleyan hymn, it nonetheless displays two characteristic themes found in the Wesleys' Christological hymns: intimacy with Christ and Christ's centrality in the believer's life. Wesley's is couched in images and terms familiar to 18th century Methodists, eg 'let me to Thy bosom fly'. The modern song uses more subjective and direct language easily understood by people in the pews today, eg 'It's all about You, Jesus . . .'

This style of taking on a key Wesleyan theme and developing it in a way which speaks to one's culture, language and situation might be a way forward to the passing on of the Wesleyan heritage. It also allows for experimentation with ethnic or modern musical techniques.

It must be noted that in 2000 the 'Wesley Music for Millennium' project initiated by the John Wesley's chapel, Bristol, continued this effort to find twenty-first century tunes for Charles Wesley's hymns. They challenged musicians around the world to write contemporary tunes for some of Charles' hymns (including eucharistic ones). Publication of a booklet with the selected compositions was in 2001.

Where literacy is not high and fewer words are preferred, the technique used by the frontier preachers in America might be worth emulating. The preachers used to get the congregation to repeat a few lines of the chorus while they would sing the full verses. The chorus would contain the heart of the message and it would be remembered by the people because of the repetition.

Worship liturgy (eg the communion liturgy, the covenant service) played a major role in the spiritual formation of Western Christians. In other parts of the world, formation is more likely to come through intensive teaching courses with practical exercises. Wesleyan eucharistic spirituality can be conveyed in these contexts through action-orientated programs where people are actually practising what they have just been taught, eg if the therapeutic aspect of the spirituality is the theme, then a communion and healing service could be conducted. Lessons can utilise drama, dance, movement, the use of audio-visuals. Daily communion services can be regularly held during retreats, camps and whenever the pastor visits a small group/cell group of the congregation.

5. The weak link of Wesleyan eucharistic spirituality

Beyond the 'how' question (which deals with the transmission of the eucharistic heritage to the present generation of Methodists) is a more serious one of 'why?' Is Wesleyan eucharistic spirituality worth reclaiming? I believe so. We have seen in previous chapters the value of that heritage. In reclaiming that heritage, however, we need to know its weaknesses as well and guard against them.

The only and consistent criticism of Wesleyan eucharistic spirituality was that it did not deal sufficiently with the 'dark side' of life, eg destruction in their eschatology and conflict, struggle with dark forces and with oneself as one grows towards Christian perfection. The first is understandable if we see the Wesleys seeking to emphasise God's grace and love to an audience so used to judgment and condemnation. The second is unhelpful because

> . . . a spirituality of peace, love and joy needs the mettle of contest and struggle if it is not to become merely sentimental (Young 1999: 13 cf Chan 1998: 135).

Knowing the Wesleys' history, we can understand their fear of mysticism's love for the subconscious. Yet Wesleyan eucharistic spirituality cannot be accused of being 'sentimental', for it has adequate challenges to robust discipleship. What it missed out on is the depth of description and discussion on spiritual warfare which could have further enriched their spirituality and assisted their followers more practically in their inner struggles.

By spiritual warfare, I mean the deliberate and conscientious engagement of the human soul in certain exercises. The first is critically discerning one's best intentions, knowing well the ability of the human heart to deceive oneself. Critical discernment is necessary if one is to remove the 'dross' of human desire from the 'gold' of authentic and responsive discipleship. As we have seen in chapter 3, the Wesleys departed from their counterparts' intense practice of using 'preparation manuals'. While this was done to highlight the grace of God in the sacrament, it did deprive Methodists of engaging in a certain level of discriminating spiritual introspection. As we have noted in chapter 4, the Wesleys had no access to what we now know as depth psychology and nor did they know the extent of possible effects of the psyche on the human body (eg in producing infirmities). If infirmities are tolerated as part of one's lot in life, then they are to be endured bravely by the sufferer. However, if they are perceived to have roots in one's negative and possibly sinful emotions/attitudes, then repentance is called for.

Second, spiritual warfare can be understood as actively engaging in the refining process where one 'wars' against one's human desire ('the flesh') and the temptations of the world so that one can respond positively to a specific divine calling. Some Wesleyan eucharistic writings like *HLS* 149: 1 do give brief descriptions of the inner battle. However, depth of discussion is lacking on the topic in the Wesleyan eucharistic corpus. The disciple is not instructed sufficiently on *how* one can fight the enemy on all fronts through the sacrament of holy communion. One is simply told that spiritual strength is and will be given. Perhaps one of the results of this lack is reflected in the fact that John Wesley's main rationale for constant reception of communion—simple obedience to God's commands—failed to hold his followers in the long run. Obedience without receiving 'emotional payoffs', be it in the form of having the security of known and respected celebrants (having their preachers instead of hired Anglican priests of sometimes questionable character) or in holding on to the expectation of experiencing emotional 'highs' while faithfully persisting in taking communion as a spiritual discipline, was not adequate to sustain eucharistic commitment of the Methodists. The outcome would be different had the Methodists been taught and trained more effectively through eucharistic spirituality to resist their human desire for emotional input, replacing that desire with simple obedience.

Third, spiritual warfare can refer to the dynamics of external spiritual engagement with the devil, eg in what has been called in recent years 'power encounters' (eg deliverance ministries). *HLS* 41/2 did state the expectation of spiritual deliverance at the Table. Again the Wesleys did not further elaborate their understanding of this aspect of eucharistic spirituality. In contrast, other Christians have identified the eucharistic service as a place where we are setting before the powers of darkness, the victory of Christ and boldly claiming the fruits of his victory. Payne thus utilises the sacrament in the ministry of inner healing with the practice of confession before communion (1991: 145, 178); McAll has the sacrament deliberately celebrated to effect healing and deliverance in individuals (1982); and Petrie claims spiritually defiled lands through communion:

> When we celebrate Communion together on the land where sin has taken place, we are undertaking a prophetic act that bears witness in the spiritual realm. Whatever is blemished, whatever is defiled, is being brought before the Lord by His servants so that the cleansing blood of Christ becomes the final sacrifice required for the removal of sin in that area (cf Numbers 35: 33). (2000: 199 cf. 198, 200)

The meagerness of literature present in the Wesleyan eucharistic corpus on the specifics of engaging in spiritual struggle with the enemy within ('flesh') the enemy without ('world and the devil') is a serious setback. We would do well to supplement any teaching of the Wesleyan eucharistic spirituality with equal instruction on spiritual warfare if we seek to build stronger Christian disciples for front-line ministry.

6. What restoration of Wesleyan eucharistic spirituality would mean

The restoration of Wesleyan eucharistic spirituality to the churches from the Wesleyan tradition would mean several things. First, it would mean that Methodists would have something concrete and distinctive to offer to the ministry of spiritual formation from its own tradition. This would enrich the whole body of Christ. The-often-referred to tension between the 'world' and the 'church' is removed when Wesleyan eucharistic formation is introduced. We noted in chapter 4 the ways the spirituality allows the believer to view the world and life and drives the person to deeper commitment to love and serve others rather than withdraw into a cocoon of individual piety. Spiritual formation of such nature would result in effective witness in the world. The therapeutic approach to the spiritual life which exists in Wesleyan eucharistic spirituality provides a gentle, encouraging and yet challenging model for Christians. The picture it portrays is not of Christians as passive and never satisfied consumers or as frenzied, activity-orientated 'servants of God'. Christians are seen as broken yet valued people who are moving—sometimes rather slowly—along the path of rehabilitation towards wholeness (holiness). This humbling vision of a 'process-orientated' rather than a 'closure-orientated' spiritual formation affirms continuous growth and learning with a sense of vulnerable openess. It has a place for surprising changes and radical movements in the person's life. The Christocentric focus and dynamic personal encounters expected in the spirituality not only underlines the place of grace in the experience of the divine-human interaction, but it also reinforces the faith of the church that Christianity is primarily a living relationship which cannot be reduced to a mere list of creedal statements or an impressive array of well-meaning activities. Spiritual formation is about relating to and thus becoming like Jesus, the beloved of one's life. It is not primarily a program to improve one's life and character.

Wesleyan eucharistic spiritual formation calls forth from the one under formation the willingness to 'come under authority' of a spiritual leader. The discipline of submission and accountability is expected and developed. The present concern for egalitarianism and democracy has often left the role of the leader-mentor in the cold for fear of authoritarianism and abuse of power. The Wesleys and their class leaders exercised strong pastoral authority and oversight. John Wesley had no qualms about insisting on clerical celebration of the sacrament even though he utilised and empowered lay people in ways which were frowned upon during his time. The 'priesthood of all believers' never meant for him that absolute equality is to be exercised in every relationship of the church. There is a place and role for certain kinds of leadership, and spiritual formation certainly required strong leadership.

Another contribution to spiritual formation is the emphasis on faithfulness, not experience. Faithfulness in frequent and constant reception of communion is a response of obedience to Christ's command. While one expects an encounter with the Christ and that the encounter will involve one's senses, one does not keep the discipline for the experience's sake.

Wesleyan eucharistic spirituality is tied in with the concept of the 'converting ordinance'. We have seen in chapter 1 the linking of that phrase by some to justify the present 'free communion' (practised by some Methodists around the world). While we affirm that John Wesley did not mean his phrase to be interpreted as opening the table to anyone who would come, regardless of baptismal state, yet we can make an argument that Wesley could have inadvertently laid a foundation which can be built upon by their followers in a different generation and culture facing a new missiological challenge.

For the early Christian church, their eucharistic services were open only to the baptised. For the Wesleys, most of their congregation would have already been baptised even though their faith might be nominal. They did not have to deal with eucharistic celebrations where there was a large number of unbaptised Christians nor did they have to encounter in their pews big groups of those who were from other religions. What the children of the Wesleys face today in different parts of the world, are large groups of unbaptised Christians (unbaptised because they are under the legal age of twenty-one and cannot depart from their family's faith unless permission is granted, and permission is often denied) and non-Christians (seekers) present during their eucharistic and other worship services. Wesleyan eucharistic spirituality affirms that Christ is truly present at the Table to meet, encounter, touch and heal the person even in a dramatic way. Cannot the understanding of 'converting ordinance' be stretched so that the Table becomes a meeting point between the unbaptised Christian/open seeker from another faith with the living Christ? Can the Table become more than a 'family meal' for baptised Christians? Can it not become a place for conversion (when people respond to an evangelistic 'altar call' to receive Jesus) and a place for a Christian youth in a non-Christian household to receive strength to hold on to the faith? This might be a shocking idea to those who venerate the practice of twenty centuries of church tradition but I would suggest that it would be an issue that will not be silenced as the children of the Wesleys enter deeper into the new millennium. The linking of eucharist with evangelism could prove to be a powerful combination.[3]

---

3.   The Wesleys did link evangelism with eucharist but not in such close proximity. Bowmer noted that 'one of the glories of the Methodist revival' was that the Lord's supper was 'enlisted in the service of evangelistic zeal' and was a 'very powerful agent in the revival' (1951: 188). Most evangelical revivals had been 'predominantly non-sacramental in character' (Todd 1958: 33). What surprises people is that despite the success encountered by the Wesleys and their people in their preaching of the word, the sacrament would be lifted up above other means of grace by the Wesley brothers and the *HLS* was written from the time when Charles Wesley was deeply engaged in his preaching ministry.

6

Conclusion

There *is* a distinctive Wesleyan eucharistic spirituality. It has three key themes, revolving around the dynamic encounter with a personal Christ, the grace-filled life, and the therapeutic growth towards holiness and wholeness. The spirituality provides a way of looking at life and forming character to conform to the image of the Christ. This spirituality owes much to the wisdom of many historical Christian traditions, particularly that of the early church and the Anglican heritage. While there were several reasons for the decline of Wesleyan eucharistic spirituality after the death of the Wesleys, we have seen that this spirituality can be rediscovered, revived and communicated in new forms so as to touch, empower and transform the children of the Wesleys in this generation and in the generations to come. Through these inheritors of the Wesleyan eucharistic spirituality, the world will be blessed with 'peace, righteousness, and joy, and love' as

> Thy Kingdom come to every heart,
> And all Thou hast, and all Thou art (*HLS* 125/4).

Appendix A

APPENDIX A: Tabulation of Charles Wesley's eucharistic participation recorded in his *Journals*

YEAR	1736	1737	1738	1739	1740	1741	*	1743	1744	1745	1746	1747	1748	1749	1750	1751	*	1753	1754	*	1756
No. of times he participated or assisted at the Eucharist**	8	7	46+	18++	14	7		9	16	23++	12+	12	16++	16	8	9		1	3		5
No. of times he celebrated or assisted at the Eucharist**	5	4	16	10	8	7		5	12	6	4	3	5	2	3	2		No mention	No mention		3
No. of months recorded in his Journal (Jackson's edition)	10 (Mar-Dec)	12	12	11 (no Dec)	10 (Mar-Dec)	6		9 (silence from 18 Feb-16 May)	12	12	12	12	12	9 (till Sept)	12	8 (Jan-Aug)		Less than 1 month (29Nov-6 Dec)	1 month (8 Jul-11Aug)		About 2 months (17 Sept-5 Nov)

238

Key:

+not including some daily communions in February

++not counting the communions of the Octive he observed

years missing from his Journal –1742,1752,1755

**It is not always clear when he assisted at Communion. Hence there are two columns to cover the possible times he not only participated but assisted and when he celebrated or assisted. Each service is only counted once in one or the other of the two columns

Appendix B

John Wesley's sermons as ordered in Albert Outler, *The Works of John Wesley* (Nashville: Abingdon, 1986)

Number and Title
1. Salvation by Faith
2. The Almost Christian
3. Awake, Thou That Sleepest
4. Scriptural Christianity
5. Justification by Faith
6. The Righteousness of Faith
7. The Way to the Kingdom
8. The First-fruits of the Spirit
9. The Spirit of Bondage and of Adoption
10. The Witness of the Spirit, Discourse I
11. The Witness of the Spirit, Discourse II
12. The Witness of Our Own Spirit
13. Of Sin in Believers
14. The Repentance of Believers
15. The Great Assize
16. The Means of Grace
17. The Circumcision of the Heart
18. The Marks of the New birth
19. The Great Privilege of those that are Born of God
20. The Lord Our Righteousness
21. Upon our Lord's Sermon on the Mount I
22. Upon our Lord's Sermon on the Mount II
23 Upon our Lord's Sermon on the Mount III
24. Upon our Lord's Sermon on the Mount IV
25. Upon our Lord's Sermon on the Mount V
26. Upon our Lord's Sermon on the Mount VI
27. Upon our Lord's Sermon on the Mount VII
28. Upon our Lord's Sermon on the Mount VIII
29. Upon our Lord's Sermon on the Mount IX

30. Upon our Lord's Sermon on the Mount X
31. Upon our Lord's Sermon on the Mount XI
32. Upon our Lord's Sermon on the Mount XII
33. Upon our Lord's Sermon on the Mount XIII
34. The Original, Nature, Properties, and Use of the Law
35. The Law Established through Faith, Discourse I
36. The Law Established through Faith, Discourse II
37. The Nature of Enthusiasm
38. A Caution against Bigotry
39. Catholic Spirit
40. Christian Perfection
41. Wandering Thoughts
42. Satan's Devices
43. The Scripture Way of Salvation
44. Original Sin
45. The New Birth
46, The Wilderness State
47. Heaviness through Manifold temptations
48. Self-denial
49. The Cure of Evil-speaking
50. The Use of Money
51. The Good Steward
52. The Reformation of Manners
53. On the Death of George Whitefield
54. On Eternity
55. On the Trinity
56. God's Approbation of His Works
57. On the Fall of Man
58. On Predestination
59. God's Love to Fallen Man
60. The General Deliverance
61. The Mystery of Iniquity
62. The End of Christ's Coming
63. The General Spread of the Gospel
64. The New Creation
65. The Duty of Reproving our Neighbour
66. The Signs of the Times
67. On Divine Providence
68. The Wisdom of God's Counsels

Appendix C

The documents of the Wesleys

A. John Wesley's Writings (JWW)

1. A Short History of The People called Methodists
2. A Farther Appeal to Men of Reason and Religion, Part II
3. The Life of the Revd John Wesley
4. Directions given to the Band–Societies, 25 December 1744
5. Minutes of Several Conversations between the Revd Mr Wesley and Others from the year 1744 to the year 1789
6. A Farther Appeal to Men of Reason and Religion Part I
7. A Farther Appeal to Men of Reason and Religion Part III
8. An Answer to Mr Rowland Hill's Tract, entitled *Imposture detected*
9. Thoughts on the Consecration of Churches and Burial Grounds
10. An Extract of a Letter wrote by the Church of Hernhuth, to the President of Upper Lusatia, 24 January,1732 (as recorded by John Wesley in *JWJ* 12/8/1748)
11. An Extract of the *Constitution of the Church of the Moravian Brethren at Hernhuth*, laid before the Theological Order at Wirtemberg, in the year 1733 (as recorded by John Wesley in *JWJ* 12/8/1748)
12. A Roman Catechism and A Reply Section IV
13. A Letter to a Roman Catholic
14. List of works revised and abridged from various authors by the Revd John Wesley, MA
15. A Roman Catechism, Faithfully Drawn out of the Allowed Writings of the Church of Rome with a Reply Thereto
16. Popery Calmly Considered
17. A Short Account of the School in Kingswood
18. The Doctrine of Original Sin Part II
19. List of Works Revised and Abridged from various authors by the Revd. John Wesley, MA

20. List of Poetical Works published by The Revd Messrs John and Charles Wesley with the
Prefaces connected with them.
21. Thoughts on Jacob Behmen
22. Notices regarding Deceased Preachers
23. The Principles of a Methodist Farther Explained Occasioned by the Revd Mr Church's Second Letter to Mr Wesley, 17 June 1746
24. A Plain Account of the People called Methodist
25. Large Minutes
26. Directions for Singing
27. The Life and Death of the Revd John Fletcher
28. An Account of Disturbances in my Father's House
29. On the Scarcity of Provisions

B. John Wesley's Letters (JWL)

1. Letter to his Mother, 28 February 1732
2. Introductory Letter (to Mr Morgan), 18 October 1732
3. Letter to Dr. Coke, Mr Asbury, and Our Brethren in North America, 10 September 1784
4. Letters to his brother Samuel, 23 November 1736
5. Letter CCXVI to Mr Knox, 30 May 1765.
6. Letter to his brother Charles, 31 October 1753 .
7. A Letter to the Revd Dr Rutherforth, 28 March 1768.
8. To the Printer of the Dublin Chronicle, 2 June 1789
9. Letter from John Wesley to Wesley Hall, 27 December 1745
10. The Principles of a Methodist Farther Explained (Occas–ioned by the Revd Mr Church's Second Letter to Mr Wesley), 17 June 1746.
11. Letter to a Friend, 10 April 1761
12. A Letter to the Revd Mr Clarke, 3 July 1756
13. To the Editor of the London Chronicle, 19 February 1761
14. Letter to Dr Coke, Mr Asbury and Our Brethren in North America, 10 September 1784
15. Letter of John Wesley to his mother, 18 June 1725

16. An Answer to the Revd Mr Church's Remarks on the Revd Mr John Wesley's Last *Journal* in a Letter to that Gentleman, 2 February 1744–5
17. Letter to the Right Revd The Lord Bishop of London Occasioned by His Lordship's Late Charge to His Clergy, 11 June 1747
18. To Mr Nathanael Price, of Cardiff, 6 December 1739
19. To the Revd Dr Conyers Middleton, 4 January 1748–9.
20. To Mr. Merryweather of Yarm (Brentford), 24 January 1760.
21.Second Letter to the Author of *The Enthusiasm of Methodists and Papists Compared* (undated)
21. A Letter to the Author of *The Enthusiasm of Methodists and Papists compared*
(Canterbury, February 1749–1750)
22. Letters to a Member of the Society (CCLVI), 6 July 1770
23. Letters to Miss Bishop (DCCV) 12 June, 1773
24. Letters to Miss Loxdale (DCCCLXIX), Douglas, Isle of Man, 10 June 1781
25. Letters to the Revd William Law (XXXIV), 30 May 1738
26. Letter to Robert Carr Brackenbury, Esq, 15 September 1790
27. Letter to Richard Morgan Senior, 15 January 1734
28. A Letter to the Right Revd. The Lord Bishop of Gloucester: Occasioned by his Tract *On the Office and Operations of the Holy Spirit*, 16 November 1762
29. Letter to a Young Disciple, 31 August 1772
30. Letter to Mrs Crosby (CCCLIII), 13 June 1771
31. To Mr Joseph Benson, 7 November 1776

C. Charles Wesley's Letters (CWL)

1. Letters to Dr Chandler, 28 April 1785 cf Gill 1964: 196–197; cf Baker 1948: 196f
2. Letter of Charles Wesley to John Wesley, 5 May 1729
3. Letter of Charles to his wife 10 April, Easter Day (Year not given) Moorfields.

Appendix D

Arminian Magazine (AM)

1778

AM 1778: 276 Letter XXXVII From Mr. Thomas Willis to John
Wesley dated 13 November 1744

1779

AM 1779: 471-3 An Account of Mr Thomas Tennant
AM 1779: 301-2 Account of Mrs Sarah Ryan
AM 1779: 183 Account of Mr Thomas Rankin
AM 1779: 186-7 Account of Mr Thomas Rankin
AM 1779: 471-3 An Account of Mr Thomas Tennant
AM 1779: 241 A Short Account of Mr Alexander M'Nab:
in a Letter to the Revd Mr John Wesley
AM 1779: 87 An Account of Mr Thomas Olivers.
AM 1779: 106-7 Thoughts on the Power of Music, 9 June 1779

1780

AM 1780: 263 A Short Account of Mr John Haime
AM 1780: 103 Letter XCIX Of Public Worship
AM 1780: 449 Letter CXXVII From the Revd Mr Wesley to
Mr Trembath, dated 17 August 1760

1781

AM 1781: 663 Letter CCII From Ruth Hall to the Revd Mr
Wesley dated 12 May 1762

1784

AM 1784: 196 An Account of the life of Mrs Margaret Baxter

1785

AM 1785: 491 (Letter CCCLXXVII) From the Revd L
Coughlan to the Revd J Wesley, 4 November 1772
AM 1785: 164 A Memorial for Ms Nancy Bissaker: written in
the 7th year of her age, by the late Mr C Perronet

1788

AM 1788: 36 An original Letter of Mrs Wesley to her Son, the late Mr Samuel Wesley, when at Westminster School, written about the year 1706

AM 1788: 516 An account of Mr John Prickard

AM 1788: 103 Letter CCCCXLVI from Miss MB, 4 March 1777

1789

AM 1789: 470,472 A Short Account of Mr Jonathan Simpson, of Horsley upon Tyne. Written by his Widow.

AM 1789: 11 A Short Account of Mr George Shadford. Written by himself.

1790

AM 1790: 11 A Short Account of Mr. George Shadford. Written by himself

1791

AM 1791: 420 An account of Mrs Planche.

Appendix E

Charles Wesley's readings

A study of Charles Wesley's *Journals* (Jackson's two volume edition which includes a selection of his correspondence and poetry) provides the names of several authors and books which he has read. They are:

a.   Pascal (*CWJ* 16/10/1736, 16/9/1737).
b.   William Law (*CWJ* 17/10/1736; 18/10/1738, 9/4/1737, 2/5/1737, 17/9/1737, 10/10/1737, 3/7/1739, 10/8/1739,10/10/1739 (cf *CWJ* Vol 2 278).
c.   Scougal (*CWJ* 13/9/1737, 24/9/1737).
d.   William Taylor (*CWJ* 7/7/1738, 11/7/1738, 24/10/1738)
e.   Thomas a Kempis (*CWJ* 20/9/1744, 27/9/1744, undated letter: CWJ Vol 2, 278)
f.   Bishop Beveridge (*CWJ* 25/2/1739)
g.   Martin Luther (*CWJ* 17/5/1738, 6/6/1738, 11/6/1738)
h.   Life of Mr Halyburton (*CWJ* 28/3/1738, 25/4/1738, 15/5/1738).
i.   Other books mentioned:
Lord Clarendon's *History* (*CWJ* 27/10/1736), *Pietas Hallensis* (a re-reading on 7/11/1737), Bishop Potter on Church government (*CWJ* 25/4/1739), 'H's account of the iniquitous Synod of Dort: iniquitous even in the judgement of a predestinarian' (*CWJ* 5/1/1744), Rapin's *History* (1/9/1750), *Marcus Antoninus* (*CWJ* 18/3/1751) and *Fourth Night Thought* (Letter to Sally 8/4/1773 and in an undated letter, *CWJ* Vol 2, 278). Charles also mentioned another writing which he did not identify–6/10/1737: 'read *SS* to the two sisters and prayed with them for conversion'. He is familiar with Bunyan's *Pilgrim's Progress* (*CWJ* 8/3/1744) Charles is familiar with the Roman Catholic liturgy–possibility the mass liturgy (*CWJ* 20/9/1744) and is no doubt, well

acquainted with Anglican *Homilies, Articles of Religion* etc (*CWJ* 17/5/1738).

Charles' list of readings seem to pale in comparison to John's and most of what he recorded are probably read before 1739. It is probable that he did not record much of his readings (even his journals are few compared to John's). One evidence of this could be found in his letter to wife Sally (3 August from Lakenham. Year unknown, *CWJ* Vol 2, 194): 'I can almost promise you more of my company here, than you could have anywhere else, as I have several useful books to read over, and defer it till you come'. No record exists of the books.

Appendix F

The Wesleys' use of the five senses in the hymns on the Lord's supper

A. Sight
Sight is referred to in at least 72 verses (not counting verses with only allusions to sight).

1. At least 33 verses had the word 'see':
2/1, 2/4, 4/4, 6/1, 6/2, 8/2, 9/3, 18/2, 19, 21/2,21/3,21/7,
23/1,24/1, 28/3, 29/9, 38/5, 59/2, 59/3, 64/1, 77/2, 80/5,
83/1, 92/12, 93/1, 98/2, 105/1, 114/1, 115/2, 123/3, 129/1,
131/2, 140/2

2. Other words used were:
'eyes' (at least 9 times) 18/1, 21/2, 29/2, 59/3,83/1, 91/2,
98/3, 105/1, 131/2
'behold' (at least 5 times) 8/2,40/2, 93/1, 98/3, 140/2
'seen' 4/3
'showed' 3/3,116/3
'show' 4/1,15/1,116/5
'view' 5/3
'look' 2/7,6/2, 16/2, 63/2, 133/1,2
'spectators' 7/2
'appears' 3/2, 22/3, 38/5, 46/3, 53/3, 116/5
'see' (in future) 12/4
'gaze' 21/2
'sight' 21/7,102/1
'display' 158/4

B. Touch/Feel
This was the most elusive to categorise. Included in this section are physical movements which requires the sense of touch. When the following words were counted, the score was fifty-nine times:

1. 'feel/felt' (at least 15 times)
4/3,11/3, 16/2, 21/7, 22/2, 24/2, 26/1, 62/8, 71/2, 73/4, 74/3, 92/3, 94/4, 131/2, 131/3

2. Other words
'take' 3/1, 58/3, 62/8, 155/4
'cast' 137/3,137/4,137/6, 160/5, 141/6
'bound' 133/1, 135/3
'laid/lie/laid our trembling hands/sins' 135/3, 131/4, 131/2
' touch' 39/1
'stretch/fasten' 149/1
'harboured/wipes/lulls' 93/4
'weep' 6/1
'stand' 6/2, 13/3
'smite' 6/2
'shook the ground' 7/3
'bow' 11/3
'broke the bread' 16/4
'groan' 16/2
'fall' 21/2
'sing' 21/8
'fill' 77/3, 33/4
'stamp' 'seal' 33/4
'kiss' 131/3
'prostrate' 131/3
'break' 30/2
'wash me' 27/3,31/1,31/2,37/1
'cooling shadow' 31/1
'bruising' 143/4
'wounded' 143/5
"applied' (to wash) 74/2
'grovelling' 160/4
'fall' 144/3
'mouths are filled' 112/1

C. Taste

Understandably, this sense is referred to quite often, since the topic covered is the eucharist. It appears in at least 55 verses.

1. 'Eat' occurs in at least 16 verses:
1/2, 1/3, 3/1,4/1,4/2,11/3, 28/4, 59/3, 71/2, 73/5, 84/2, 92/10, 93/2, 97/2, 144/4, 153/1

2. 'drink' appears in at least 14 verses
9/2,30/8,33/2,61/3,54/5,58/3,58/6,71/2,73/5,77/3,108/2, 153/1, 158/1, 166/4

3. 'taste' is mentioned in at least 10 verses
9/2, 9/3, 53/2, 57/4, 58/3, 77/3, 101/1, 158/2, 158/3, 160/3

4. 'feed/fed' comes up in 9 verses
30/2, 71/2, 71/3, 82/2, 92/6, 93/1, 158/1, 162/3, 165/2

5. Other words:
'banquet' 84/1, 93/2
'mouths are filled' 112
'streams of sweetness' 160/2, 160/3
'supped' (166/5)

D. Hearing

About 16 verses bear words associated with sounds:
'hear/heard'4/3,4/4,7/3,104/1
'shall hear/(shall) listen'3/2, 93/3
'cry' 7/4
'call' 9/6, 68/2
'whispers' 123/4
(Christ) 'speak' 10/4,17/2, 20/3
'echoing' 26/1, 161/2
'louder than gathered waters' 162/2

E. Smell
Only three references:

'smell'3/3
'perfumed/sweet smelling' 147/1
'savour sweet/divine perfumes' 116/4

(There was one reference 'as incense'—85/2—but there was no indication whether it is the smell or the smoke which it evoked that was the focus. It seemed more of the latter).

Appendix G

The choice of *HLS* found in fourteen hymnals

1. The fourteen representative hymnbooks are: the 1780 *Collection of Hymns for the Use of the People Called Methodists*, the 1823 (British) edition of the *Collection*, the 1875 (British) edition, the (British) *Methodist Hymn Book* of 1904, the (British) *Methodist Hymn Book* of 1933, the (British) *Hymns and Psalms* of 1983. On the American side, the *Pocket Hymn Book* of 1786, the 1849 book of the Methodist Episcopal Church (MEC), the 1847 book of the Methodist Episcopal Church, South (MEC, S), the 1849 MEC book, the 1905 joint *Hymnal* of the MEC and MEC, S, the 1935 Hymnal, the 1966 *Hymnal of The Methodist Church* and the 1989 *Hymnal of the United Methodist Church*.

2. The hymnbooks are the ones mentioned by Geoffrey Wainwright in his *Introduction* to the facsimile of the first edition of the *HLS*—reprinted by The Charles Wesley Society (The 15th that he listed—the 1935 American edition, did not have any Eucharistic hymns. Hence, it is not included in our study). This study is based on the figures found in Wainwright's research (p. xi-xii). It must be noted that there seems to be two discrepancies in his findings:

    2.a On page xi—Hymn number 145 is mentioned twice (second and third paragraph), affecting the count of the hymns listed for the 1831 edition (For our study, Hymn 145 was not recounted the second time it appeared).

    2.b On page xii: Nos 18, 30,163 are unaccounted for in the list mentioned for the 1983 edition. The three numbers would need to be there if one had followed the descriptions of the two paragraphs. If they are included, it means that British Methodism has 19, not 16 texts of the eucharistic hymns in the 1983 hymnbook. (For our study, the 1904 British Hymnal was consulted. It was found to have the 3 hymns. Both the 1933 and the 1983 ones did not have them. Wainwright was right in concluding that the British Methodists now have 16 Eucharistic hymns in their present hymnal).

3. The most forty-one most frequently chosen Eucharistic hymns in the fourteen hymnbooks of the British and American Methodist churches are:

3.a Twelve times
Happy the Souls to Jesus joined (No 96)
Father, Son and Holy Ghost (No 155)—first verse only in the
    1905 edition
Let Him whom we now belong (No 157)

3.b Nine times
Come Thou everlasting Spirit (No 16)

3.c Eight times
Let all who truly bear (No 4)
Glory be to God on High (No 163)
Lamb of God whose bleeding love (No 20)

3.d Seven times
O Thou eternal Victim slain (No 5)
Lift up your eyes of faith and see (No 105)
Victim Divine, thy Grace we claim (No 116)
God by all redeeming Grace (No 139)
Jesu, at whose Supreme Command (No 30)

3.e Six times
Jesu, we thus obey (No 81)
What are these array'd in White (No 106)
O God of our Forefathers bear (No 125)
Father, into Thy Hands alone (No 145)

3.f Five times
God of unexampled Grace (No 21)
Author of our Salvation Thee (No 28)
Jesu, dear redeeming Lord (No 33)

O Thou whose Offering on the Tree (No 123)
Thou very Pascal Lamb (No 51)

3.g Four times
Son of God thy Blessing grant (No 49)
All Praise to God above (No 158)
Lift your Eyes of Faith and Look (No 18)

3.h Three times
Come all who truly bear (No 13)
O thou who this Mysterious Bread (No 29)
Author of Life Divine (No 40)
Come Holy Ghost Thy influence shed (No 72)
See where our great High Priest (No 129)

3.I Two times
Saviour, and can it be (No 43)
O The Depth of Love Divine (No 57)
Thee King of Saints we praise (No 97)
Sons of God, triumphant rife (No 164)

3.j Once only
Come Holy Ghost, set to Thy seal (No 7)
Rock of Israel, cleft for me (No 27)
How long, Thou Faithful God shall I (No 58)
Christ our Passover for us (No 84) verse 3-4 only
Let both Jews and Gentiles join (No 144)
Lord and God of heavenly powers (No 161)
How happy are thy Servants, Lord (No 165)
In that sad memorial night (No 1)

4. The list of seventeen Hymns found in the 1983 *Hymns and Psalms*, the 1966 *Hymnal* and the *United Methodist Hymnal* of 1989:
Happy the souls to Jesus joined (No 96) British 1983, American 1966
Father, Son and holy Ghost (No 155) British 1983
Let Him to whom we now belong (No 157) British 1983

Come Thou everlasting Spirit (No 16) British 1983
Lamb of God whose bleeding love (No 20) British 1983
Victim Divine thy Grace we claim (No 116) British 1983
God by all redeeming Grace (No 139) British 1983
God of unexampled Grace (No 21) British 1983
Jesu, we Thus obey (No 81) British 1983
O God of our Forefathers hear (No 125) British 1983
O Thou who this Mysterious Bread (No 29) British 1983,
    American 1989
Author of Life Divine(No 40) British 1983, American 1966
Saviour and can it be (No 43) British 1983
O The Depth of Love Divine (No 57) American 1966, 1989
Come Holy Ghost Thine influence shed (No 72) British 1983
See where our great High Priest (No 129) British 1983
How Happy are thy Servants Lord (No 165) American 1966

Observations:

1. Forty-one hymns from the *HLS* (out of the original 166 written) are found in the fourteen hymnals listed above. Several hymns have been constantly chosen for inclusion—Numbers 96,155 and 157 of the *HLS* (12 times each), Number 16 (chosen nine times) and some made only single appearances.

2. In the *HLS,* the preference of the Wesleys were in this order (noting the percentage of hymns each section was allocated. The percentages are listed in rounded numbers):

- Communion as it is a sign and a means of grace (39% of the 166 hymns)
- Concerning the sacrifice of our persons (18%)
- As it is a memorial of the sufferings and death of Christ (15%)
- The sacrament, a pledge of heaven (14%)
- As it implies a sacrifice (7%)
- After the sacrament (5%)

The section preferences of the forty-one eucharistic hymns found in the fourteen hymnals were in this order:

- sign and means of grace (32%)
- memorial of sufferings and death of Christ (24%)
- sacrifice of our persons (15%)
- after the sacrament (12%)
- pledge of heaven (10%)
- as it implies a sacrifice (7%)

This preference seems to be in line with the Wesley's in that they share the top three billings.

3. The section entitled 'after the sacrament' seemed to have increased in popularity and 'as it implies a sacrifice', lessened in importance. To have a closer look at this fact, we have to check out the differing British and American Methodist tastes. There was a total of twenty-eight hymns which were specifically chosen for the British Methodist hymnals we listed from (a few of these hymns were also chosen by the Americans as well). Of the twenty-eigth hymns, the hymn sections preferred were in this order:

- memorial of suffering and death of Christ (28%)
- sign and means of grace (28%)
- sacrifice of our persons (18%)
- pledge of heaven (11%)
- as it implies a sacrifice (11%)
- after the sacrament (4%)

Of the thirty-four hymns favoured by the American Methodist hymnals (a few of which have also been chosen by the British), their order of preference was this:

- sign and means of grace (29%)
- memorial of suffering and death of Christ (20%)
- sacrifice of our persons (18%)
- after the sacrament (15%)
- pledge of heaven (12%)
- as it implies a sacrifice (6%)

Again we see that the top three correspond with the original focus of the Wesleys. Now we also see more clearly that the section on 'After the sacrament' is preferred more by the Americans. Unlike the British, there was very little interest in the section on 'as it implies a sacrifice'.

From the 1960s, three Methodist hymnals were used by the two churches. The 1983 (British) *HP,* the (American) *Hymnal* of 1966 and the *UMH* of 1989. I have chosen the 1966 *Hymnal* as the the start of the 'present era' because at least two to three generations of Methodists present today would have grown up using those hymnals. There are only seventeen Wesleyan eucharistic hymns in the three hymnals combined. Of the seventeen eucharistic hymns which have been in British and American Methodist hymnals published since the 1960s, the section preference for the top three is quite the same as that of the Wesleys:

- as a sign and means of grace (35%)
- sacrifice of our persons (24%)
- memorial of the suffering and death of Christ (17%)
- as it implies a sacrifice (12%)
- pledge of heaven (6%)
- after the sacrament (6%)

The 'as it implies a sacrifice' has become more important than the 'pledge of heaven' section.

A closer look of it shows that again, the British and the Americans differ rather drastically in their choices. The British preference was this:

- as a sign and means of grace (33%)
- sacrifice of our persons (27%)
- memorial of suffering and death of Christ (20%)
- as it implies a sacrifice (13%)
- pledge of heaven (7%)

They left out the 'after the sacrament' section.

The American preference:
- as a sign and means of grace (60%)

- pledge of heaven (20%)
- after the sacrament (20%)

They left out sections on 'sacrifice of our persons', 'as it implies a sacrifice' and 'as it is a memorial of the sufferings and death of Christ'.

It is amazing that the twelve of the fourteen hymnals had the same top three sections as the Wesleys. The 'as a sign and means of grace' has always come up as the Number One choice. The 'sacrifice of persons' and 'suffering and death of Christ' sections share the second and third billing interchangeably (The exceptions are the 1780 one and the present *UMH*). The consistent preference for the 'after the sacrament' and their lack of interest in 'as it implies a sacrifice' section by the Americans is very clear. The sustained interest in latter section (it was in the fourth position in the past and in the last hymnal of 1983) of the British is noted.

In the 1780 *Collection* the seven eucharistic hymns were from these sections:

- sacrifice of our persons (57%)
- pledge of heaven (29%)
- as it implies a sacrifice (14%)

(The other sections were not represented)

In the 1739 *Hymns and Sacred Poems* published by the Wesleys, *HLS 9* ('suffering and death' section), *HLS* 85('means of grace' section) and *HLS* 160,161,163,164 ('after the Sacrament') were included. This could explain why Wesley left these sections out in 1780 *Collection*. *HLS* 161,163,164 are found in some of the fourteen hymnals though none of these hymns are in the recent hymnals of both countries.

Bibliography

Primary Sources:

Abbott, WA (editor)
    1966, *The Documents of Vatican II*. London: Geoffrey
        Chapman.

a Kempis, Thomas
    1977, *The Imitation of Christ*. Glasgow: Collins.

Andrewes, Lancelot
    1841, *Ninety Six Sermons*. Oxford: John Henry Parker.
        Volume II.

Arndt, John
    1751, 'True Christianity'. In *A Christian Library* edited by
        John Wesley. Bristol: Felix Farley. Volume I, 163–296,
        Volume II, 5–106.

Baker, Frank (editor)
    1962, *Representative Verse of Charles Wesley*. London: Epworth.
    1980, *The Works of John Wesley: Letters I* (1721–1739).
        Oxford: Clarendon Press.
    1982, *The Works of John Wesley: Letters II* (1740–1755).
        Oxford: Clarendon Press.

Beckerlegge, Oliver & Kimbrough, ST, Jr (editors)
    1988, *The Unpublished Poetry of Charles Wesley*.
        Nashville: Kingswood Press. Volume I & II.

Benham, Daniel (editor)
    1856, *Memoirs of James Hutton*. London: Hamilton
        Adams & Co.

Benson, Joseph
    1798, *The Life of the Revd Fletcher, Vicar of Mandeley*.
        Leeds: Baines & Fenwick.

Bettenson, Henry (editor)
    1963, *Documents of the Early Christian Church*. Oxford:
        Oxford University Press.

Beveridge, William
    1845, The Excellency and Usefulness of Common
        Prayer'. In *Library of Anglo Catholic Theology*. Oxford:
        John Henry Parker. Volume vi, 390–391.

Book of Common Prayer
> 1549, 'The First Prayer Book of King Edward VI'. In *The Ancient andModern Library of Theological Literature*. London: Griffith Farran Broune & Co.
> 1552, *The Book of Common Prayer* (microfilm edition).
> 1559, *The Book of Common Prayer*. Edited by John E Booty. Charlottesville: University of Virginia Press.
> 1662, *The Book of Common Prayer*. Oxford: Oxford University Press.

Brevint, Daniel
> 1673, *Christian Sacrament and Sacrifice*. At the Theatre in Oxford. Second Edition.

Bull, George
> 1842, *Harmonia Apostolica*. Oxford: John Henry Parker. Volume I : vi. 2

Calvin, John
> 1863–1900, '*Ioannis Calvini Opera*'. In the *Corpus Reformatorum*. Edited by G Baum, E Cunitz and E Reuss *et al.* Brunswick. 59 Volumes.
> 1926–59, *Opera Selecta*. Edited by P Barth and W Niesel, Munich. 5 Volumes.
> 1986, *The Institutes of Christian Religion*. London: Hodder and Stoughton Cave.
> 1753, 'Primitive Christianity or the Religion of Ancient Christians'. In *A Christian Library*. Edited by John Wesley. Bristol: E Farley. Volume 31: 53–198.

Connolly, R Hugh
> 1942, *The De Sacramentis, a Work of St Ambrose*. Bath: Downside Abbey. Volume I.

Cosin, John
> 1855, 'Notes on the Book of Common Prayer: On the Office of the Holy Communion'. In *Libary of Anglo Catholic Theology*. Oxford: John Henry & James Parker. Volume V: 345–6.

Cyprian
> 1844, 'Epistle 63: To Caecilius'. In *The Epistles of S Cyprian, Bishop of Carthage and Martyr, with the Council of Carthage on the Baptism of Heretics*. Oxford: John Henry Parker, 181–194.

Deacon, Thomas
> 1716, *Full, true and comprehensive view of Christianity*.
>> London: Printed for S Newton.
> 1734, A Complete Collection of Devotions, both Publick and
>> Private: Taken from the Apostolical Constitutions,
>> the Ancient Liturgies, and the Common Prayer Book
>> of the Church of England. London: printed for the
>> author.

De Sales, Francis
> 1988, *An Introduction to the Devout Life*. Edited by Peter
>> Toon. London: Hodder and Stoughton.

Duppa, Brian
> 1673, *Holy Rules and Helps to Devotion both in Prayer
>> and Practice*. Printed for J Collins.

Egmont, Earl of (John Percival)
> 1923, *Diary*. London: HMC. 3 Volumes.

Fenelon, Francois de Salignac de La Mothe
> 1973, *Let Go* (modern paraphrase of his letters)
>> Pennsylvania: Whitaker House.

Hooker, Richard
> 1836, *The Works of that learned and judicious Divine
>> Mr Richard Hooker*. Edited by John Keble.
>> Oxford: Oxford University Press. Volume II.
> 1940, *Laws of Ecclesiastical Polity*. London: JM Dent. Volume II.

Horneck, Anthony
> 1681, *The Happy Ascetik*. Printed by TN for Henry
>> Mortlock and Mark Pardoe Irenaus St.
> 1992, *St Ignatius against the Heresies*. Translated and
>> annotated by Dominic J Unger. New York: Paulist
>> Press.

Jackson, T (editor)
> 1849, *Journal and Poetry of the Revd C Wesley*. London: James
>> Nicols. Volumes I & II
> 1995, *The Works of John Wesley*. On Compact Disc. Franklin:
>> Providence House.

Jewel, John
> undated, *Writings of John Jewel*. London: Religious Tract
>> Society.
> 1847, 'A Treatise of the Sacraments'. In *The Works of John*

Jewel, Bishop of Salisbury. Edited by John Ayre. Cambridge: The University Press. 445–479, 1109–1124.

Johnson, John

1710, *The Propitiatory Oblation in the Holy Eucharist Truly Stated, and Defended, from Scripture, Antiquity*. Printed for John Morphew.

1714, *The Unbloody Sacrifice, and Altar, Unvail'd and Supported*. London: Printed for Robert Knaplock

1847, 'The Unbloody Sacrifice'. In *Library of Anglo Catholic Theology*. Oxford: John Henry Parker. Volume 1: 341–2.

Ken, Thomas

1679, *A Manual of Prayers for use of Scholars of Winchester College*. Printed for John Martyn.

Law, William

1965, *A Serious Call to a Devout and Holy Life*. Edited by JC Reid. London: William Collins and Sons Co. Ltd.

Leith, John (editor)

1973, *Creeds of the Churches*. Atlanta: John Knox

Lopez, Gregory

1755, 'The Life of Gregory Lopez'. In *A Christian Library*. Edited by John Wesley. Bristol: Felix Farley. Volume 50: 337–400.

Luther, Martin

1972, Babylonian Captivity of the Church. St Louis: Concordia

1848, The Table Talk or Famliar Discourse of Martin Luther. Translated by Wm Hazlitt. London: David Bogue.

Martyr, Justin

1912, *The First Apology of Justin Martyr addressed to the Emperor Antoninus Pius*. Edinburgh: J Grant. Chapter LXVMason, AJ (translator).

1921, *Fifty Spiritual Homilies of St Macarius the Egyptian*. New York: SPCK.

Middleton, Conyers

1729, *Letters from Rome*. London: Printed for W Innys.

1749, *A Free Inquiry into the Miraculous Powers which*

are Supposed to Have Subsisted in the Christian Church Through Several Successive Centuries. London: Printed for R Manby and HS Cox.

1752, 'Introductory Discourse'. In *Miscellaneous Tracts by Conyers Middleton.* London: Printed for Richard Manby and HS Cox.

Mosheim, John Lawrence

1826, *An Ecclesial History.* Translated by Archibald MacLaine. London: Thomas Tegg *et al.*

Nelson, Robert

1704, *A Companion for the Fasts and Festivals of the Church of England with Collects and Prayers for Each Solemnity* Printed by W Bowyer for Churchill.

1706, *The Great Duty of Frequenting the Christian Sacrifice.* London: Printed by W Bowyer, for A and J Churchill.

1812, *The Practice of True Devotion on Relation to the End, as Well as the Means of Religion; with an Office for the Holy Communion.* TB Wait & Co.

1909, *A Discourse of the Holy Eucharist.* London: Mackean. Volume I.

Patrick, Simon

1753, 'An Extract of the Christian Sacrifice'. In *A Christian Library.* Edited by John Wesley. Bristol: E Farley. Volume 32: 141–350.

Rattenbury, Earnest J

1948, *The Eucharistic Hymns of John and Charles Wesley.* Edited by Timothy J Couch, OSL, Ohio: Order of St Luke Publications. (1990 edition).

St Jure, Jean Baptiste

1795, *An Extract of the Life of Monsieur de Renty, a late Nobleman of France (1611–1648).* Printed by Henry Tuckniss.

Stevenson GJ

undated, *Memoirs of the Wesley Family.* London.

Sugden, EH (editor)

1983, *John Wesley's Fifty Three Sermons.* Nashville: Abingdon Press.

Taylor, Jeremy

1667, *The Worthy Communicant.* Printed by TR for J

Martyn, J Allestry, and T Discas

1844, 'The Rule and Exercise of Holy Living'. In *The Whole Works of the Right Rev Jeremy Taylor*. London: Henry G. Volume III: 158–9.

Telford, John (editor)

undated, *Wesley's Veterans: Lives of Early Methodist Preachers*. London: Robert Culley. Volume I & VI.

Tillotson, John

1728, *The Works of the Most Revd Dr John Tillotson*. London: Printed for J Round in Exchange Alley.

Tyerman, Luke

1866, *The Life and Times of the Rev Samuel Wesley, MA*. London: Simpkin, Marshall, and Co.

1883, *The Oxford Methodists*. London: Hodder and Stoughton Ward. Edited by W Reginald and Richard P Heitzenrater.

1988, *The Works of John Wesley: Journals and Diaries (1735–1738)*. Nashville: Abingdon Press. Volume 18.

1990, *The Works of John Wesley: Journals and Diaries II*. (1738–1743). Nashville: Abingdon Press. Volume 19.

Waterland Daniel

1737, *A Review of the Doctrine of the Eucharist as Laid Down in Scripture and Antiquity*. Cambridge: Printed for Corn. Crownfield and W Innys.

1738, 'The Christian Sacrifice Explained in a Charge Delivered in Part to the Middlesex Clergy at St Clement –Dames'. Edited by Innys and R Manby F Wendel.

1963 *Calvin's Sermon on Titus 1: 1–5*. London: Collins.

Wesley, John and Charles

1745, 'Hymns on the Lord's Supper'. In *The Eucharistic Hymns of John and Charles Wesley*. (American edition 1990). Edited by Timothy J Crouch, OSL Ohio: Order of St Luke Publications.

1745b, *Hymns for the Lord's Supper*. Bristol: Felix Farley. (A 1995 fascimile reprint. Edited by ST Kimbrough. New Jersey: CharlesWesley Society).

1872, *The Poetical Works of John and Charles Wesley*. Edited by G Osborn. London: Wesleyan Methodist Conference Office. Volumes 12 & 13.

1869, 'Hymns on the Redemption'. In *The Poetical Works of John and Charles Wesley.* London: Wesleyan Methodist Conference Office.

Wesley, Charles

1746, *Hymns for our Lord's Resurrection.* London: W Strahan (A 1992 fascimile reprint. Edited by ST Kimbrough, Jr. New Jersey: Charles Wesley Society).

1749, *Hymns and Sacred Poems*. Bristol: Felix Farley. Volume II.

1767, *Hymns on the Trinity.* Bristol: William Pine. (A 1998 fascimile reprint. Edited by ST Kimbrough, Jr. New Jersey: Charles Wesley Society).

1816, Sermons by the late Rev Charles Wesley, with a Memoir by the author. Edited by Sarah Gwyne Wesley. London: Balkdwin, Cradock and Joy.

1849, *The Journal of The Rev Charles Wesley MA.* Edited by Thomas Jackson. London: John Mason. Volumes I and II.

1983, *Collection of Hymns for the Use of the People Called Methodists.* Editors Fraz Hilderbrandt and Oliver A Beckelegge. Oxford: Clarendon Press.

1988, *The Unpublished Poetry of Charles Wesley.* Edited by ST Kimbrough, Jr, and Oliver Beckerlegge. Nashville: Abingdon Press. Volume I.

1990, *The Unpublished Poetry of Charles Wesley: Hymns and Poems on Holy Scripture.* Edited by ST Kimbrough, Jr, and Oliver Beckerlegge. Nashville: Abingdon Press. Volume II.

1992, *The Unpublished Poetry of Charles Wesley: For Church and World.* Edited by ST Kimbrough, Jr, and Oliver Beckerlegge. Nashville: Abingdon Press. Volume III.

1997, Songs for the Poor. Edited by ST Kimbrough, Jr New York: General Board of Global Ministries.

Wesley, John

1771, *Journals and Diaries: The Bicenntenial Edition of Wesley Works Poetical Works: Hymns and Sacred Poems.* Bristol: W Pine. Volume 18.

1754, *Explanatory Notes on the New Testament.* Grand Rapids: Baker Book House. (reprinted in 1983).

1980, *The Bicentennial Edition of the Works of John Wesley: Letters I.* Edited by Frank Baker. Oxford: Oxford

University Press. Volume 25.

1832, *A Collection of Hymns for the Use of the People called Methodists*. London: Mason. Volume 4

1983, *Explanatory Notes upon the New Testament*. Grand Rapids: Baker Book House. Volumes I & II

1983b, *John Wesley's Fifty–Three Sermons*. Edited by Edward H Sugden. Nashville: Abingdon Press.

1984, *The Works of John Wesley* (third Edition). Massachusetts: Hendrickson Publishers. Inc. Volumes 1–14.

1984b, *The Bicentennial Edition of the Works of John Wesley: Sermons I*. Edited by Albert Outler. Nashville: Abingdon Press. Volume 1.

1985, *The Bicentennial Edition of the Works of John Wesley: Sermons II*. Edited by Albert Outler. Nashville: Abingdon. Volume 2.

1986, *The Bicentennial Edition of the Works of John Wesley: Sermons III*. Edited by Albert Outler. Nashville: Abingdon Press. Volume 3.

1987, *The Bicentennial Edition of the Works of John Wesley: Sermons II*. Edited by Albert Outler. Nashville: Abingdon Press. Volume 4.

Wesley, John (editor)

1749–1755, *A Christian Library: Consisting of Extracts from and Abridgments of the Choicest Pieces of Practical Divinity which have been Published in the English Language*. Bristol: Felix Farley. 50 Volumes.

Secondary Sources

Addleshaw, GW & Etchells, Frederick

1948, *The Architectural Setting of Anglican Worship*. London: Faber and Faber Ltd, 54–177.

Albin, Thomas R

1985, *An Empirical Study of Early Methodist Spirituality. In Wesleyan Theology Today: A Bicentennial Theological Consultation*. Edited by Theodore Runyon. Nashville: United Methodist Publishing House.

Alexander, J

1995, *With Eloquence in Speech and Song: Anglican*

Reflections on the Eucharistic Hymns of John and Charles Wesley. Edited by ST Kimbrough, Jr Madison: Charles Wesley Society. Volume 2: 35–50.

Allison, CF

1966, *The Rise of Moralism: The Proclamation of the Gospel From Hooker to Baxter*. New York: Seabury Press.

Amirtham, Samuel & Pryor, Robin (editors)

1989, *Resources for Spiritual Formation in Theological Education*. Geneva: World Council of Churches.

Anderson Gerald H (editor)

1976, *Asian Voices in Christian Theology*. New York: Orbis Books.

Au, Wilkie, SJ

1990, *Toward a Holistic Christian Spirituality*. Bombay: St Paul.

Aumann, Jordon

1980, *Spiritual Theology*. London: Sheed and Ward.

1985, *Christian Spiriutality in the Catholic Tradition*. London: Sheed and Ward.

Baker, Frank

1948, *Charles Wesley as Revealed by his Letters*. London: Epworth.

1956, *Methodism and the Love Feast*. London: Epworth.

1962, *Representative Verse of Charles Wesley*. London: Epworth.

1963, *William Grimshaw 1708–1763*. London: Epworth.

1964, *Charles Wesley's Verse: An Introduction*. London: Epworth.

1970, John Wesley and the Church of England. Nashville: Abingdon Press.

1995, 'Approaching a Variorum Edition of the Hymns on the Lord's Supper'. In *Proceedings of the Charles Wesley Society*. Edited by ST Kimbrough, Jr. New Jersey : Charles Wesley Society. Volume 2: 7–16.

Balasuriya, Tissa OMI

1977 *The Eucharist and Human Liberation*. London: SCM Press.

Barrett, David B

1973, 'The Discipline of Africa in this Generation'. In *God, Man and Church Growth*. Edited by Alan R Tippett. Grand Rapids: Eerdmans. 397.

Bechte, Regina

1985, 'Convergences in Theology and Spirituality'. In *The*

Way. 23: 305–314.

Beintker, Horst

1968, 'Word and Sacrament in the Lutheran Theology of Today'. In *Word and Sacrament.* Edited by RR Williams. London: SPCK.

Berger, Theresa

1991, 'Charles Wesley and Roman Catholicism'. In *Charles Wesley: Poet and Theologian.* Edited by ST Kimbrough, Jr. Nashville: Kingswood: 205–222.

1995, *Theology in Hymns?: A Study of the Relationship of Doxology and Theology According to A Collection of Hymns for the Use of the People Called Methodists* (1740). Translated by Timothy E Kimbrough. Nashville: Kingswood.

Berkhof, Hendrikus

1979, *Christian Faith.* Translated by Sierd Woudstra. Grand Rapids: Eerdmans.

Bett, Henry

1913, *The Hymns of Methodism.* London: CH Kelly.

1937, *The Spirit of Methodism.* London: Epworth.

Bettenson, Henry (editor)

1963, *Documents of the Christian Church.* Oxford: Oxford University Press (Theological Collections 10).

Bondi, Roberta C

1986, 'The Role of the Holy Spirit from a United Methodist Perspective'. In *Greek Orthodox Theological Review.* Brookline MA: Greek Orthodox 31: 3–4.

1987, 'The Meeting of Oriental Orthodoxy and United Methodism'. In *Christ in East and West.* Edited by Paul Fries and Tiran Nersoyan. Macon: Mercer University. 171–184.

1989, Christianity and Cultural Diversity: The Spirituality of Syriac–Speaking Christians. In *Christian Spirituality.* Edited by Bernard McGinn & John Meyendorff. London: SCM Press. 152–161

Borgen, Ole E

1986, *John Wesley on the Sacraments: A Theological Study.* Grand Rapids: Francis Asbury.

Bossey, John

1976. *The English Catholic Community 1570–1850*. Oxford: Oxford University Press.

Bouteneff, Peter

1999, 'All Creation in United Thanksgiving: Gregory of Nyssa and the Wesleys on Salvation'. Unpublished paper presented at the Consultation on Orthodox and Wesleyan Spirituality sponsored by the General Board on Global Ministries (United Methodist Chruch) and St Vladimir's Orthodox Seminary in New York.

Bouyer, Louis

1968, *A History of Christian Spirituality*. London: Burns & Oates. Volume III.

Bowmer, John C

1951, *The Sacrament of the Lord's Supper in Early Methodism*. London: Dacre.

Bowmer, John C (editor)

1963, 'A Converting Ordinance and the Open Table'. In *The Proceedings of the Wesley Historical Society*, Leicester: Alfred ATaberer. Volume 34: 109–113.

1980 'Biblical Imagery and Religious Experience in the Hymns of the Wesleys'. In *Proceedings of the Wesley Historical Society*. Chester: Alfred ATaberer. Volume 42: 158.

Bradshaw, Paul

1995, *Two ways of Praying*. London: SPCK.

Brilioth, Yngve

1930, *Eucharistic Faith and Practice: Evangelical and Catholic*. London: SPCK.

Bromiley GW

1953, 'An Introduction'. In *On the Lord's Supper in Zwingli and Bullinger* (The Library of Christian Classics). London: SCM Press. Volume XXIV.

Brown, Robert McAfee

1988, *Spirituality and Liberation*. Philidelphia: Westminster.

Butler, David

1992, 'Good News to the London Poor: A Comparison of the Philanthropy of John Wesley and Richard Challoner (1691–1781), Vicar Apostolic of the London District'. Unpublished paper from the Oxford Institite for Methodist Studies.

1995, *Methodists and Papists*. London: DLT

Bynum, Caroline Walker

1987, *Holy Feast and Holy Fast*, London: University of California.

1991, *Fragmentation and Redemption*. New York: Xone.

Campbell, Dennis M

1988, *The Yoke of Obedience*. Nashville: Abingdon Press.

Campbell, Ted A

1979, *The Apostolate of United Methodism*. Nashville: Discipleship Resources.

1984, 'John Wesley's Conceptions and Uses of Christian Antiquity'. PhD dissertation. Dallas: Southern Methodist University.

1991, *John Wesley and Christian Antiquity*. Nashville: Kingswood.

1991b, *The Religion of the Heart*. South Carolina: University of South Carolina.

1993, 'John Wesley and the Asian Roots of Christianity'. Unpublished paper presented at the Asian Conference of the World Methodist Historical Society held in Singapore

1995/6, 'Sanctification in the Benedictine and Methodist Traditions'. In *The Asbury Theological Journal*. Wilmore: Asbury Theological Seminary. Volume 50/51: 57–70.

Cannon, William R

1946, *The Theology of John Wesley*. New York: Abingdon Press.

1971, 'Report on Conversations between the Secretariat for Promoting Christian Unity of the Roman Catholic Church and the World Methodist Council'. In *Proceedings of the 12th World Methodist Conference* (Denver, Colorado). Edited by Lee F Tuttle. Nashville: Abingdon Press. 37–68.

Cardwell, Edward

1884, *Documentary Annals of the Reformed Church of England being a Collection of Injunctions, Declarations, Orders, Articles of Iniquity etc*. Oxford: Oxford University Press.

Carter, David

1998, 'Pastoral Office and Sacrificing Priesthood: Towards Reconciliation in Concepts of Presbyteral/Episcopal Ministry'. In *MSF Bulletin*. Exeter: Methodist Sacramental Fellowship. No 127.

Casaldliga, Pedro and Virgil, Jose Maria
1994, Political Holiness: A Spirituality of Liberation. New York: Orbis Books.

Cell, George Croft
1935, *The Recovery of John Wesley*. New York: Henry Holt & Co.

Chan, Simon
1998, *Spiritual Theology: A Systematic Study of the Christian Life*. Illinois: Inter-Varsity Press.

Chilcote, Paul W
1993, *She Offered them Christ*. Nashville: Abingdon Press

Chong Chee Pang
1998, 'The Changing Christian Map'. In *Impact Magazine*. Singapore: Impact Christian Communications. December 1998: 5.

Church, Leslie
1948, *The Early Methodist People*. London: Epworth.

Clarke, Basil FL
1963, *The Building of the 18th Century Church*. London: SPCK.

Clarke, WK Lowther
1962, *Eighteenth Century Piety*. London: SPCK.

Clarke, WK Lowther (editor)
1964, *Liturgy and Worship: A Companion to the Prayer Books of the Anglican Communion*. London: SPCK.

Cocksworth, Christopher C
1993, *Evangelical Eucharistic Thought in the Church of England*. Cambridge: Cambridge University Press.

Cooke, BJ
1967, 'Epiclesis'. In *The New Catholic Encyclopedia*. Edited by GA Maloney. New York: McGraw Hill. Volume V: 465.

Cousins, Ewert H
1989, The Humanity and the Passion of Christ. In *Christian Spirituality: High Middle Ages and Reformation*. Edited by Jill Raitt. London: SCM Press. 223f, 375–391.
1990a, 'What is Christian Spirituality?' In *Modern Christian*

Spirituality: Methodological and Historical Essay. Edited by Bradley C Hanson. Atlanta: Scholars Press. 39–44.

1990b, 'Christian Spirituality: Post Reformation and Modern'. In *Christian Spirituality*. Edited by Louis Dupre & Don Saliers. London: SCM Press. Volume III.

Cowley, Patrick

1953, *The Eucharistic Church*. London: Faith.

Cross, Frank L (editor)

1974, 'Epiclesis'. In *The Oxford Dictionary of the Christian Church*. 2nd Edition. Edited by Frank L Cross. Oxford: Oxford University Press. 462–3.

Cunningham, Lawrence S

1995, '*Extra Arcam Noe*: Criteria for Christian Spirituality'. In *Christian Spirituality Bulletin*. Los Angeles: Loyola Marymount University.13.1 (Spring). 6–9.

Dabney, D Lyle

1998, 'Unfinished Business: Wesley and Schleiermacher on the Spirit'. Unpublished paper presented for the Reformed Theology and Wesleyan Studies Joint Session, American Academy of Religion.

Dalrymple, John

1970, *Theology and Spirituality*. Wisconsin: Clergy Book Service.

Davie, Donald

1993, *The Eighteenth Century Hymn in England*. Cambridge: Cambridge University Press.

Davies, Horton

1961, *Worship and Theology in England: From Watts and Wesley to Maurice 1690–1850*. Princeton: Princeton University Press.

1966, *Worship and Theology in England: From Watts to Wesley to Martineau1690–1900*. Grand Rapids: Eerdmanns. 83–84.

1970, *Worship and Theology in England: From Cranmer to Hooker 1534–1603*. Princeton: Princeton University Press.

Davies JG (editor)

1972, *A Dictionary of Liturgy and Worship*. London: SCM Press. 10–17.

Davies, Rupert E
  1976, *Methodism*. London: Epworth.
Davies, Rupert E, George, Raymond and Rupp, Gordon (editors)
  1965, *A History of the Methodist Church in Great Britain*.
    London: Epworth. Volume I.
De Ferrari, TM
  1967, 'Baptism'. In *The New Catholic Encyclopedia*. New York:
    McGraw Hill. Volume II: 65.
Dearing, Trevor
  1966, *Wesleyan and Tractarian Worship*. London: Epworth.
Deschner, John
  1960, *Wesley's Christology*. Dallas: Southern Methodist
    University.
Dix, Dom Gregory
  1945, *The Shape of the Liturgy*. London: Dacre.
Dolbey, George W
  1964, *The Architectural Expression of Methodism: The First
    100 Years*. London: Epworth. 12–133.
Doraisamy, TR (editor)
  1985, *Forever Beginning: One Hundred Years of Methodism in
    Singapore*. Singapore: Methodist Church in Singapore
  1991, *Methodism in Asia: A Bird's Eye View*. Singapore:
    Methodist Church in Singapore.
Downes Michael (editor)
  1993, *The New Dictionary of Spirituality*. Minnesota: The
    Liturgical Press.
Dudley, Martin (editor)
  1995, *Like a Two–edged Sword: The word of God in Liturgy
    and Ministry*. Norwich: Canterbury Press.
Duffy, Eamon
  1993, 'Wesley and the Counter Reformation'. In *Revival and
    Religion since 1700 (Essays for John Walsh)*. Edited by
    Jane Garnett and Colin Matthew. London:
    Hambleton Press.
Dugmore CW
  1942, *Eucharistic Doctrine in England from Hooker to Waterland*.
    London: SPCK.
Dupre Louis & Saliers, Don E
  1990, 'Christian Spirituality: Post Reformation and Moder'. In
    Christian Spirituality. Edited by Louis Dupre & Don

Saliers. London: SCM Press. Volume III.

Elkins, Heather Murray

    1995, 'Tangible Evangelism: The Healing Word'. In *Doxology*.
        Edited by David J Bort. Ohio: Order of St Luke
        Publications. Volume 14: 21–26.

Eng, Jerry Seow–Hng

    1995, 'The Contextualisation of the Eucharist in the Malaysian
        Church'. Unpublished MA (Religion) thesis.
        Tennessee: Emmanuel School of Religion.

English John C

    1995, 'The Path to Perfection in Pseudo Macarius and John
        Wesley'. Abstact of paper presented at the
        Melbourne Conference on 'Prayer and Spirituality in
        the Early Church'. American Academy of Religion.
        1–2.

Evan, Donald

    1995, 'Spirituality and Human Nature'. Quoted by Rob
        Repicky In *An Expansive Vision* of the *Christian
        Spirituality Bulletin*. (Spring 1995). Los Angeles:
        Society for the Study of Christian Spirituality.

Evdokimon, Paul

    1966, *The Struggle with God*. New York: Parker.

Faber, Heije

    1988, *Above the Treeline: Towards a Contermpory
        Spirituality*. London: SCM Press.

Farrell, Elizabeth

    1996, 'Aggressive Evangelism in an Asian Metropolis'. In
        Charisma Magazine. Illinois: Charisma and Christian
        Life. 54–57.

Flew, R Newton

    1960, *The Idea of Perfection in Christian Theology*. New York:
        Humanities.

Flint, Charles Wesley

    1957 *Charles Wesley and His Colleagues*. Washington DC: Public
        Affairs.

Forsaith, Peter S

    1994, *John Fletcher*. Peterborough: Foundery

Forsyth, PT

    1917 *The Church and the Sacraments*. London: Independent

Press.

Fox, Matthew
1976, *Whee, We, Wee all the Way Home: A Guide to the New Sensual Spirituality*. Wilmington: Consortium.

Frost, Francis
1995, 'The Veiled Unveiling of the Glory of God in the Eucahristic hymns of Charles Wesley: The Self–Emptying Glory of God'. In *Proceedings of the Charles Wesley Society*. Edited by ST Kimbrough, Jr. Madison: Charles Wesley Society. Volume 2: 87–99.
1997, 'The Three Loves: a Theology of the Wesley Brothers'. In *Epworth Review* (1995 Flamington Lectures) Peterborough: Methodist Publishing House. Volume 24: No 3, 86–116.

Gallaway, Craig B
1988, 'The Presence of Christ with the Worshipping Community: A Study in the Hymns of John and Charles Wesley'. Unpublished PhD Dissertation from Emory University, USA.

George, Raymond
1964, 'The Lord's Supper'. In *The Doctrine of the Church*. Edited by Dow Kirkpatrick. London: Epworth. 140–160.
1965, 'The People called Methodists: The Means of Grace'. In *A History of the Methodist Church in Great Britain*. Edited by Rupert Davies and Gordon Rupp. London: Epworth. Volume I: 257–274.
1976, 'The Sunday Service'. In *The Proceedings of the Wesley Historical Society*. Edited by John C Bowmer. Leicester: Alfred A Taberer. Volume 40: 4, 102–5.

Gernet, Jacques
1985, *China and the Christian Impact*. Cambridge: C.ambridge University Press.

Gerrish BA
1993, *Grace and Gratitude: The Eucharistic Theology of John Calvin*. Edinburgh: T&T Clark.

Gill, Frederick
1964, *Charles Wesley: The First Methodist*. London: Lutterworth.
1993, *Trust and Obey*. London: DLT.

Goldsmith, Malcolm

1994, *Knowing Me, Knowing God*. London: Triangle.
Goodloe, Robert W
1943, *The Sacraments in Methodism*. Nashville: Methodist
Publishing House.
Green, J Brazier
1945, *John Wesley and William Law*. London: Epworth.
Green Richard
1906, *The Works of John and Charles Wesley: A Bibliography*.
London: Methodist Publishing House.
Green, VHH
1961, *The Young Mr Wesley*. London: Edward Arnold
Publishers.
Gunther, Stephen W (editor)
1997, *Wesley and the Quadrilateral: Renewing the
Conversation*. Nashville: Abingdon Press.
Gutierrez, Gustavo
1984, *We Drink from Our Own Wells*. New York: Orbis Books.
Halevy, Elie
1987, *History of the English People in 1815*. London: Ark. Book
III.
Hanson, Bradley C (editor)
1990, 'Introduction and Spirituality as Spiritual Theology'. In
*Modern Christian Spirituality: Methodological and
Historical Essays*. Atlanta: Scholars Press. 1–12, 45–51.
Harding, Meyer and Vischer, Lukas
1984, *Growth in Agreement*. Geneva: WCC
Harmon, Nolan B
1974, 'John Wesley's Sunday Service and Its American
Revisions'. In *The Proceedings of the Wesley Historical
Society*. Leicester: Alfred A Taberer. Volume 5: 39,
140.
Harrison, DEW
1945, *The Book of Common Prayer*. London: Canterbury Press.
Heitzenrater, Richard P
1984, *The Elusive Mr Wesley*. Nashville: Abingdon Press.
Volumes I and II.
1985, *Diary of an Oxford Methodist: Benjamin Ingram 1733–34*.
Durham: Duke University Press.
1989, *Mirror and Memory*. Nashville: Abingdon

1995, 'The *Imitatio Christi* and the Great Commandment: Virtue and Obligation in Wesley's Ministry with the Poor'. In *The Portion of the Poor: Good News to the Poor in the Wesleyan Tradition*. Edited by M Douglas Meeks. Nashville: Kingswood. 56–9.

1995b, *Wesley and the People Called Methodists*. Nashville: Abingdon Press.

Hickman, Hoyt L

1984, *United Methodist Altars*. Nashville: Abingdon Press.

Hilderbrandt, Franz

1951, *From Luther to Wesley*. London: Lutterworth Press.

1967, *I offered Christ*. London: Epworth.

Hinton, Keith

1985, *Growing Churches Singapore Style*. Singapore: OMF.

Hobbs, Gerald and Webb, Pauline (editors)

1997, *All Loves Excelling*. Peterborough: Methodist Publishing House.

Hodges HA & Allchin, AM

1966, *A Rapture of Praise*. London: Hodder and Stoughton.

Hoke Donald (editor)

1975, *The Church in Asia*. Chicago: Moody.

Holifield, E Brooks

1974, *The Covenant Sealed: The Development of Puritan Sacramental Theology in Old and New England 1570–1720*. New Haven: Yale University Press.

Holmes, Urban T

1981, *A History of Christian Spirituality: An Analytical Introduction*. New York: Seabury Press.

Hoskins, Steven T

1994, 'The Eucharist and Eschatology in the Writings of the Wesleys'. In *Wesleyan Theological Journal*. Kansas City: Wesleyan Theological Society. Volume 29: No 1 and 2. 64–80.

Huggett, Joyce

1988, *Listening to Others*. London: Hodder and Stoughton.

Hughes, Gerald W SJ

1995, *God of Surprises*. London: DLT.

Huntington, Samuel P

1996, *The Clash of Civilisations and the Remaking of World Order*. New York: Simon and Schuster.

Hutchingson FE (editor)
> 1941, *The Work of George Herbert*. Oxford: Oxford University
>> Press.

Hwa Yung
> undated, 'The Search for an Authentic Asian Christian
>> Spirituality'. Unpublished paper. Kuala Lumpur.

Jackson, Michael and Butler, David
> 1988, *Catholics and Methodists*. Peterborough: Methodist
>> Publishing House.

Jackson, Thomas (editor)
> 1849, *Lives of Early Methodist Preachers*. London: Wesley
>> Conference Office. 6 Volumes.

Jacobs, Paul
> 1968, 'Word and Holy Communion in the Reformed
>> Tradition'. In *Word and Sacrament*. (SPCK Theological
>> Collections 10) Edited by RR Williams. London:
>> SPCK, 43–61.

Jeffrey, Thomas Reed
> 1960, *John Wesley's Religious Quest*. New York: Vantage.

Jennings, Theodore
> 1990, *Good News to the Poor: John Wesley's Evangelical
>> Economics*. Grand Rapids: Abingdon Press.

Johnson, Susanne
> 1987, 'John Wesley on the Duty of Constant Communion: The
>> Eucharist as a Means of Grace for Today'. In
>> *Wesleyan Consultation*. Nashville: Division of
>> Ordained Ministry, General Board of Higher
>> Education and Ministry. 25–36.

Jones Cheslyn, Wainwright Geoffrey, Yarnold Edward SJ (editors)
> 1978, *The Study of Liturgy*. Oxford: Oxford University Press.
> 1986, *The Study of Spirituality*. London: SPCK

Jones, Howard Watkin
> 1929, *The Holy Spirit from Arminius to Wesley*. London:
>> Epworth.

Jones, Richard G and Ivor H
> 1983, *Hymns and Psalms*. London: Methodist Publishing
>> House.

Jones, Scott J
> 1995, John Wesley's Concerption and Use of Scripture.

Nashville: Abingdon Press.

Jones, W Paul

1987, The Wesleyan Means of Grace. In *Wesleyan Spirituality in Contemporary Theological Education: Report of a Consultation*. Nashville: Division of Ordained Ministry, General Board of Higher Education and Ministry. 11–13.

1989, *Theological Worlds*. Nashville: Abingdon Press.

Kallstad, Thorvald Kallstad

1974, *John Wesley and the Bible: A Psychological Study*. Bjamam: Bjarnams Tryckeri.

Kane, J Herbert

1976, *Christian Missions in Biblical Perspective*. Grand Rapids: Baker House.

Kang Ho Soon (editor)

1985, *The Book of Discipline of the Methodist Church in Singapore*. Singapore: Methodist Book Room.

Kao Keng Tai, Dorothy Kao and Grace Tan

1996–7, *Singapore Every Home Crusade Directory 1996–7*. Singapore: Singapore Every Home Crusade.

Kavanagh, Aidan

1984, *On Liturgical Theology*. New York: Pueblo Publishing Company.

Khoo, L

1979, 'A Brief Study of the Charismatic Movement in Singapore'. An unpublished BTh Research Paper. Singapore: Trinity Theological College.

Kiersey, David and Bates, Marilyn

1984, *Please understand Me: Character and Temperment Types*. California: Prometheus Nemesis.

Kimbrough Jr ST

1987, *Lost in Wonder*. Nashville: The Upper Room.

Kimbrough, ST, Jr, (editor)

1990, *The Unpublished Poetry of Charles Wesley: Hymns and Poems on Holy Scripture*. Editor ST Kimbrough, Jr and Oliver A Beckerlegge. Nashville: Abingdon Press.

1992, *Charles Wesley, Poet and Theologian*. Edited by ST Kimbrough, Jr Nashville: Abingdon Press.

1995, *Hymns for the Lord's Supper by John and Charles Wesley*.

New Jersey: Charles Wesley Society (Fascimile
reprint of 1745 book John and Charles Wesley.
Bristol: Felix Farley)

1997, *Songs for the Poor*. New York: General Board of Global
Ministries.

King, Ursula

1991, 'The Spiritual, Personal and Political Religion in Global
Perspective'. Unpublished Inaugural Lecture.
University of Bristol.

1996, 'Christian Spirituality Today: Old and New Agendas in
Seeking Wholeness and Holiness'. (Lecture One)
Unpublished Brompton Lectures. University of
Oxford.

Kirk, John

1860, *Charles Wesley: The Poet of Methodism*. London: Hamilton,
Adams & Company.

Kirkpatrick, George Dunbar

1983, *The Eucharist in Bible and Liturgy* (the Moorhouse
Lectures 1975). Cambridge: Cambridge University
Press.

Kishkovsky, Leonid

1995, 'The Wesley's Hymns on the Lord's Supper and
Orthodoxy'. In *Proceedings of the Charles Wesley
Society*. Papers presented at the Sixth Annual
Meeting of the Charles of the Charles Wesley
Society, October 1995. Edited by ST Kimbrough, Jr.
Madison: Charles Wesley Society. Volume 2: 75–86.

Knight III, Henry H

1992, *John Wesley and the Means of Grace*. London: Scarecrow.

Kreider, Alan

1994, 'Worship and Evangelism'. In Pre–Christiandom: The
Liang Lecture. In *Vox Evangelica*. Cumbria:
Paternoster Press. Volume 24: 910ff.

Lake, Frank

1986, *Clinical Theology* (abridged version). London: DLT.

Land, Steven J

1990, Pentecostal Spirituality: Living in the Spirit. In *Christian
Spirituality: Post reformation and Modernism*. Edited by
Louis Depre and Don E Saliers. London: SCM Press.

Volume I/II: 479–499

Lane, Denis
    1995, *One World: Two Minds*. Littleton: OMF.
Langford, Thomas A
    1983, *Theology in the Wesleyan Tradition*. Nashville:
        Abingdon Press.
LaVerdiere, Eugene, SSS
    1993, Eucharistic Devotion. In *The New Dictionary of Catholic
        Spirituality* . Edited byMichael Downes. Minnesota:
        Liturgical Press.
Law Eric HF
    1993, *The Wolf Shall Dwell with the Lamb: A Spirituality for
        Leadership in a Multicultural Community*. St Louis:
        Chalice Press.
Lawson, AB
    1963 *John Wesley and the Christian Ministry*. London: SPCK.
Lawson, John
    1946, Notes on Wesley's 44 Sermons. London: Epworth
    1994, Charles Wesley: A Man of the Prayer Book. In *The
        Proceedings of the Charles Wesley Society*. Edited by ST
        Kimbrough. New Jersey: Publication Society.
        Volume l: 85–117.
Lean, Garth
    1964, *John Wesley: Anglican*. London: Blandford.
Lee, Hoo Jung
    1991, 'The Doctrine of New Creation in the Theology of John
        Wesley'. An unpublished PhD thesis for Emory
        University, USA. Chapter 5: 143–245.
Leech Kenneth
    1980, *True Prayer*. London: Sheldon Press.
Leehardt, Franz
    1964, *Two Biblical Faiths: Protestant and Catholic*. London: ET.
Lim Swee Hong
    1996, 'Chinese,Tamil and English Congregations: Sunday
        Worship of the Methodist Church in Singapore'. In
        The Sunday Service of the Methodists. Edited by Karen
        Westerfield–Tucker. Nashville: Abingdon Press.
        209–226.
Lindbeck George A
    1984, *The Nature of Doctrine: Religion and Theology in a Post*

Liberal Age. Philadelphia. Westminster Press.

Lindstrom, Harald

1946, *Wesley and Sanctification: A study in the doctrine of Salvation*. London: Epworth.

Littrel, Terril DOSL

1995, 'Holy Communion in the American Methodist Tradition'. In *Doxology*. Edited by David J Bort. Ohio: Order of St Luke Publications. Volume 12: 24–31.

Lloyd, Gareth

1994, 'Charles Wesley and the Methodist Religious Life 1750–1775. The Manuscript Resources'. In *The Proceedings of the Charles Wesley Society*. Edited by ST Kimbrough. New Jersey: Charles Wesley Society. Volume I: 33–45.

Luzbetak, Louis J, SVD,

1988, *The Church and Cultures: New Perspectives in Missiological Anthropology*. New York: Orbis Books.

Maas, Robin and Gabriel O' Donnell, OP

1990, *Spiritual Traditions for the Contemporary Church*. Nashville: Abingdon Press.

Macquarrie, John

1972, *Paths in Spirituality*. London: SCM Press.

Macquiban Tim A

1995, *The Pledge of Heaven: Eschatological Themes in the Eucharistic Hymns of the Wesleys*. To be Published.

Manning, Bernard L

1942, *The Hymns of Wesley and Watts*. London: Epworth.

Martz Louis, L

1954, Poetry of Meditation. London: Yale University Press.

Mason, Kenneth

1993, *George Herbert, Priest and Poet*. Oxford: SLG.

Maycock, AL

1938, *Nicholas Ferrar of Little Gidding*. London: SPCK.

McAll, Kenneth

1982, *Healing the Family Tree*. London: Sheldon Press.

McAdoo, Henry R

1988, *The Eucharistic Theology of Jeremy Taylor Today*. Norwich: Canterbury Press.

1991, *Anglican Heritage: Theology and Spirituality*. Norwich:

Canterbury Press.

1994 ,'A Theology of the Eucharist'. In *Theology*. Edited by
Ann Loades. London: SPCK. Volume XCVII:
245–256.

McAdoo, HR & Stevenson, Kenneth
1995 *The Mystery of the Eucharist in the Anglican Tradition*.
Norwich: Canterbury Press.

McCue James F
1987, Liturgy and Eucharist: West. In *Christian Spirituality:
High Middle Ages and Reformation*. Edited by Jill Raitt.
London: Routedge and Kegan Paul. 427–438.

McGoldrick, Patrick
1983/4, 'The Holy Spirit and the Eucharist'. In *Irish Theological
Quarterly*. Kildare: St Patrick's College. Volume 50/1:
48–66.

McGinn, Bernard
1989, The English Mystics. In *Christian Spirituality: High
Middle Ages and Reformation*. Edited by Jill Riatt.
London: SCM Press. Volume III: 94–107.

McKenna, John H
1975, 'Eucharistic Epiclesis: Myopia or Microcosm?' In
Theological Studies. Baltimore: Theological Studies
Inc. Volume 36/2: 265–284.

McKenna Megan
1997, *Rites of Justice*. New York: Orbis Books.

McPartlan, Paul
1995, *Sacrament of Salvation: An Introduction to Eucharistic
Ecclesiology*. Edinburgh: T&T Clark.

Meeks, M Douglas (editor)
1985, *The Future of the Methodist Theological Traditions*.
Nashville: Abingdon Press.

1990, *What Should Methodists Teach? Wesleyan Tradition and
Modern Diversity*. Nashville: Abingdon Press.

1995, *The Portion of the Poor: Good News to the Poor in the
Wesleyan Tradition*. Nashville: Kingswood

Meistad, Tore
1999, 'The Missiology of Charles Wesley and its links to the
Eastern Church'. Unpublished paper presented at
the Consultation on Orthodox and Wesleyan
Spirituality sponsored by the General Board on

Global Ministries (United Methodist Church) and St
Vladimir's Orthodox Seminary in New York.

Methodist, An Old

1869, *John Wesley in Company with High Churchmen.*
London: Church Press.

Methodist Conference Office

1975, *The Methodist Service Book*. Herfordshire: Garden City

Meyendorff, John

1990, Theosis in the Eastern Christian Tradition. In *Christian
Spirituality: Reformation and Modern*. Edited by Louis
Dupre & Don Saliers. London: SCM Press. Volume
III: 470–476.

Monk, Robert C

1966, *John Wesley: His Puritan Heritage*. London: Epworth.

1992, 'Puritan Poor and Wesleyan Poor'. Unpublished paper
presented at the Oxford Institute for Methodist
Studies, England.

Montagu, Ashley

1971, *Touching: The Human Significance of the Skin*. New
York: Columbia University Press.

Moorman, John RH

1983, *The Anglican Spiritual Tradition*. London: DLT.

Morris, Gilbert Leslie

1969, 'Imagery in the Hymns of Charles Wesley'. An
unpublished PhD dissertation for the University of
Arkansas.

Murphy, Debra Dean

1994, 'Bread, Wine, and the 'Pledge of Heaven': A (Wesleyan)
Feminist Perspective on Eucharist and Eschatology'.
In *Quarterly Review*. Nashville: United Methodist
Publishing House, United Board of Higher
Education. Volume 14: 401–412.

Music Committee, WFCMC

1997, Hymns of United Worship (official Hymnal of the
World Federation of Chinese Methodist Churches)
Hong Kong: Chinese Christian Literature Council.

Myers Isabel Briggs and Peter B Myers

1980 *Gifts Differing*. Palo Alton: Consulting Psychologist Inc.

Nelson, J Robert

1996a, 'Methodist Eucharistic Usage: From Constant Communion to Benign Neglect to Sacramental Recovery'. In *Journal of Ecumenical Studies*. Volume 13/2: 88–93.

1996b, Methodist Response to Gerald S Sloyan's 'Roman Catholic Eucharistic Reforms'. In *Journal of Ecumenical Studies*. Philadelphia: Temple University. Volume 13/2: 101–103.

Newport, Kenneth GC

1996, 'Charles Wesley and the End of the World'. In *The Proceedings of the Charles Wesley Society*. Edited by ST Kimbrough. Princeton: Charles Wesley Society. Volume 3: 33–61.

Newton, John A

1964, 'Methodism and the Puritans'. (18th Lecture for the Friends of Dr Williams Library). London: Dr Williams Trust.

1996, 'The Eucharist in Methodism'. In *MSF Bulletin*. Exeter: Methodist Sacramental Fellowship. No 125. 6–16.

Newton, John and Soper, Donald

1988, 'What I Owe to the Wesleys'. Papers Read at the MSF Public Meeting during the Methodist Conference in London. London: MSF.

Nolan, Harmon B

1974, 'John Wesley's Sunday Service and its American Revisions'. In *The Wesley Historical Society Proceedings*. Edited by John C Bowmer. Leicester: Alfred A Taberer. Volume 39: 5.140.

Ong Jin Hui, Tong Chee Kiong, Tan Ern Ser

1997, *Understanding Singapore Society*. Singapore: Times Academic Press.

Outler, Albert C

1964, *John Wesley*. New York: Oxford University Press.

1966, 'Studies in Vatican II' (Perkins Senior Colloguy: Unpublished bound copy) Dallas: Perkins School of Theology, SMU.

1967, Methodist Observer at Vatican II. New York: Newman.

1975, *Theology in the Wesleyan Spirit*. Nashville: Discipleship Resources.

1991, *Doctrine and Theology in the United Methodist Church*.

Edited by Thomas Langford. Nashville: Kingswood.

Overton, John Henry
    1903, *The Nonjurors, their Lives, Principles and Writings*. New
        York: Whitaker.

Padgett, Alan G (editor)
    1992, *The Mission of the Church in Methodist Perspective*. New
        York: Edwin Mellen.

Pannenberg, W
    1983, *Christian Spirituality and Sacramental Community*.
        London: DLT.

Parris, John R
    1963, *John Wesley's Doctrine of the Sacraments*. London:
        Epworth.

Payne, Leanne
    1991, *Restoring the Christian Soul*. Grand Rapids: Baker Books

Pellowe, Susan (editor)
    1994, *A Wesley Family Book of Days*. Illinois: Renard
        Productions.

Petrie, Alistair
    2000, *Releasing Heaven on Earth*. Grand Rapids: Chosen.

Piette, Maximin
    1937, *John Wesley in the EVolumeution of Protestantism*. London:
        Sheed and Ward.

Podmore, Colin
    1998, *The Moravian Church in England, 1728–1760*. Oxford:
        Clarendon Press.

Porter, Roy
    1990, *English Society in the Eighteenth Century*. London:
        Penguin.

Puhl, Louis J, SJ
    1951, *The Spiritual Exercises of St Ignatius*. Chicago: Loyola
        University Press.

Rack, Henry D
    1969, *Twentieth Century Spirituality*. London: Epworth.
    1989, *Reasonable Enthusiast: John Wesley and the Rise of
        Methodism*. London: Epworth.
    1997, 'Early Methodist Experience: Some Prototypical

Account'. In *Occasional Paper 4* (second series). Oxford: Religious Experience Research Centre, Westminster College.

Rattenbury J Earnest

1938, 'Worship and the Sacraments'. In *The Expository Times*. Edinburgh: T&T Clark (June issue).

1941, *The Evangelical Doctrines of Charles Wesley's Hymns*. London: Epworth.

1948, The Eucharistic Hymns of John and Charles Wesley. (American Edition 1990) Edited by Timothy J Couch, OSL. Ohio: Order of St Luke Publications.

Repicky, Robert A

1995, 'Expansive Vision'. In *Christian Spirituality Bulletin*. Los Angeles: Society for the Study of Christian Spirituality. Volume 3: No 1.

Rigg James H

1905, *The Living Wesley* (third Edition). London: Charles H Kelly.

Robson and Lonsdale

undated, *Can Spirituality be Taught?* London: ACATE.

Rowe, Kenneth E

1992, *United Methodist Studies: Basic Bibliographies*. (Third Edition). Nashville: Abingdon Press

Ruffing, Janet L

1995, 'You Fill up My Senses'. In *The Way*. London: The Way Publications. 101–110.

Runyon, Theodore (editor)

1985, *Wesleyan Theology Today: A Bicentennial Theological Consultation*. Nashville: United Methodist Publishing House.

Rynne, Xavier

1964–5, *Letters from Vatican City*. New York: Farrer Staus and Giroux. 4 Volumeumes.

Saliers Don E and Louis Dupre

1989, 'Introduction'. In *Christian Spirituality*. New York, Crossroad Publishing Company. Volume III: xx–xxv

Sanders Paul S

1966, 'Wesley's Eucharistic Faith and Practice'. In *Anglican Theological Review*. Evanston: (reprinted as a pamphlet.)

Sanneh, Lamin
  1989, *Translating the Message: The Missionary Impact on Culture*.
      New York: Orbis Books. Volume 3: No 48 (April
      issue).
Schneiders, Sandra, IHM
  1985, 'Scripture and Spirituality'. In *Christian Spirituality:
      Origins to the Twelfth Century*. Edited by Bernard
      McGinn & John Meyendorff. London: SCM Press.
      Volume I: 1–22.
  1990, 'Spirituality in the Academy'. In *Modern Christian
      Spirituality: Methodological and Historical Essays*.
      Edited by Bradley C Hanson. Atlanta: Scholars Press.
      5–37.
Scholes, Percy A
  1970, *The Oxford Companion to Music*. (Tenth Edition). Edited
      by John Owen Ward. London: Oxford University
      Press. 497–507, 624–634.
Schreiter, Robert J
  1985, *Constructing Local Theologies*. London: SPCK.
Schumacher, John SJ
  1974, 'The Third World and the Twentieth Century Church'.
      In *Mission Trends*. Edited by Gerald H Anderson and
      Thomas F Stransky, CSP. Grand Rapids: Eerdmans.
      5–6 and 213.
Selleck J Brian
  1983, The Book of Common Prayer in the Theology of John
      Wesley. Unpublished PhD dissertation. New York:
      Drew University Press.
Sheldrake, Philip, SJ
  1992, *Spirituality and History*. New York: Crossroad.
Sheldrake, Philip, SJ (editor)
  1991, *The Way of Ignatius Loyola: Contemporary Approaches
      to the Spiritual Exercises*. London: SPCK.
Sng, Bobby EK
  1979, 'Christian Churches in Singapore'. In *Impetus*.
      Singapore: Graduates Christian Fellowship.
      (December) 6.
Snyder, Howard A
  1980, *The Radical Wesley and Patterns for Church Renewal*.

Illinois: Inter–Varsity Press.

Sobrino, Jon, SJ
1985, *Spirituality of Liberation: Towards Political Holiness*.
New York: Orbis Books.

Sperry–White, Grant
1996, 'Eucharist and Eschatology: An Unanswered Question
for United Methodists'. In *Sacramental Life*. Ohio:
Order St Luke Publications. Volume IX: No. 4. 23–29.

Stacey, John (editor)
1988, *John Wesley: Contemporary Perspectives*. London:
Epworth.

Staples, Rob L
1991, *Outward Sign of Inward Grace: The Place of Sacraments in
Wesleyan Spirituality*. Kansas City: Beacon Hill.

Stein, Jock
1994, *Spirituality Today*. Edinburgh: Rutherford House.

Stephens WP
1986, *The Theology of Huldrych Zwingli*. Oxford: Clarendon
Press

Stevenson, Kenneth
1984, 'Anaphoral Offering: Some Observations on Eastern
Eucharistic Prayers'. Quoted by Rowan Williams in
Eucharistic Sacrifice: The Roots of a Metaphor.
Nottingham: Grove.
1994, *Covenant of Grace Renewed*. London: DLT.

Stibbs, AM
1961, *Sacrament, Sacrifice and the Eucharist*. London: Tyndale
Press.

Stookey, Laurence Hull
1993, *Eucharist, Christ's Feast with the Church*. Nashville:
Abingdon Press.

Sykes, Norman
1953, *The English Religious Tradition*. London: SCM Press.
1962, *Church and State in England in the 18th Century*. London:
Archon.

Sykes, Stephen and Booty, John
1988, *The Study of Anglicanism*. London: SPCK.

Taft, Robert
1989, 'Liturgy and Eucharist: East'. In *Christian Spirituality*.

Edited by Jill Raitt. London: SCM Press. Volume II: 415–437.

Thigpen, Paul

1992, 'Ancient Altars, Pentecostal Fire: Why Some Charismatic Churches are Returning to Liturgical Forms of Worship'. In *Ministries Today*. November & December issues. 43–51.

Thurian, Max

1959a, *The Eucharistic Memorial*. Virginia: John Knox Press. Part I

1961a, *The Eucharistic Memorial*. Virginia: John Knox Press. Part II

1966b, *The Mystery of the Eucharist: An Ecumenical Approach*. Oxford: Mowbray.

Thurian, Max and Wainwright, Geoffrey (editors.)

1983, *Baptism and Eucharist: Ecumencial Convergence in Celebration*. Geneva: WCC.

Todd, John M

1958, *John Wesley and the Catholic Church*. London: Hodder and Stoughton.

Towlson, Clifford W

1957, *Moravian and Methodist*. London: Epworth.

Townsend, Stuart (editor)

1991, *Songs of Fellowship*. Eastbourne: Kingsway Music.

Trickett, David

1990, Early Wesleyan Witness. In *Modern Christian Spirituality: Methodological and Historical Essays*. Edited by Bradley C Hanson: Atlanta: Scholars Press. 161–181.

Tripp, David

1969, *The Renewal of Covenant in the Methodist Tradition*. London: Epworth.

1972, 'The Covenant Service'. In *The Westminster Dictionary of Worship*. Edited by JG Davies. Philadelphia: Westminster Press.

Tuttle, Robert G, Jr

1969, 'The Influence of Roman Catholic Mystics on John Wesley'. An unpublished PhD dissertation. Bristol University.

1978, *John Wesley: His Life and Theology*. Grand Rapids:

Zondervan Press.

1989, *Mysticism in the Wesleyan Tradition*. Grand Rapids: Zondervan Press.

Tyson John R

1983, 'Charles Wesley's Theology of the Cross: An Examination of the Theology and Method of Charles Wesley as seen in his doctrine of the Atonement'. A PhD dissertation submitted to Drew University.

Vickers, John A

1990, *Charles Wesley*. Peterborough: Foundery.

Wakefield, Gordon S

1957, *Puritan Devotion*. London: Epworth.

1966, *Methodist Devotion: The Spiritual Life in the Methodist Tradition 1791–1945*. London: Epworth.

1995, The Wesley Hymns on the Lord's Supper (1745) in History and Eucharistic Theology. In *Like a Two Edged Sword*. Edited by Martin Dudley. Norwich: Canterbury Press. 139–160.

Wakefield, Gordon S (editor)

1983, A Dictionary of Christian Spirituality. London: SCM Press.

Wainwright, Geoffrey

1980, *Doxology*. New York: Oxford University Press.

1981, *Eucharist and Eschatology*. New York: Oxford University Press.

1983, *The Ecumenical Moment: Crisis and Opportunity for the Church*. Grand Rapids: Eerdmans.

1987, *Wesley and Calvin*. Melbourne: Uniting Church Press.

1994, 'Our Elder Brethren Join'. In *The Proceedings of the Charles Wesley Society*. Edited by ST Kimbrough, Jr. New Jersey: Charles Wesley Society. Volume I: 5–32.

1995, 'Introduction'. In *Hymns on the Lord's Supper* (fascimile Reprint of John and Charles Wesley's book). Edited by ST Kimbrough, Jr. New Jersey: Charles Wesley Society.

1995b, *Methodists in Dialog*. Nashville: Kingswood.

1995/6, '*Ora Et labora*: Benedictines and Wesleyans at Prayer and at Work'. In *The Asbury Theological Journal*. Wilmore: Asbury Theological Seminary. Volume 50/51: 95–114.

1997a, *For Our Salvation*. Grand Rapids: Eerdmans.

1997b, *Worship with One Accord: Where Liturgy and Ecumenism Embrace*. Nashville: Abingdon Press.

Wallace, Ronald S

1953, *Calvin's Doctrine of Word and Sacrament*. Edinburgh: Oliver and Boyd.

Ward, Benedicta, SLG

1992, *Signs and Wonders*. Hampshire: Variorum.

Watkin–Jones, Howard

1929, *The Holy Spirit from Arminius to Wesley*. London: Epworth.

Watson, David Lowes

1985, *The Early Methodist Class Meeting*. Nashville: Discipleship Resources.

1995, *Forming Christian Disciples*. Nashville: Discipleship Resources.

1995b, *Class Leaders*. Nashville: Discipleship Resources.

1996, *Covenant Discipleship*. Nashville: Discipleship Resources.

Watson, JR

1995, 'Hymns on the Lord's Supper, 1745, and Some Literary and Liturgical Sources'. In *Proceedings of the Charles Wesley Society*. Edited by ST Kimbrough, Jr. Madison: Charles Wesley Society. Volume 2: 17–34.

1997a, *The English Hymn: A Critical and Historical Study*. Oxford: Clarendon Press.

1997b, 'George Herbert and the English Hymn'. In *Theology*. London: SPCK. March–April issue. 101–108.

Westerfield–Tucker, Karen

1995, Liturgical Expressions of Care for the Poor: A Case Study for the Ecumenical Church'. In *Worship*. Collegeville: Liturgical. Volume 69: 51–64.

Whaling, Frank (editor)

1981, *John and Charles Wesley: Selected Writings and Hymns*. New York: Paulist Press.

White, James F

1983, *Sacraments as God's Self Giving*. Nashville: Abingdon Press.

1991, *The Development of the 1972 United Methodist Eucharistic Rite–John Wesley's Prayer Book: The Sunday Service of*

the Methodist Church in North America: Notes and
Commentary.* Cleveland: Order of St Luke
Publications.

White, Susan J

1994, *Christian Worship and Technological Change.* Nashville:
Abingdon Press. 80–129.

Whiteley JH

1938, *Wesley's England: A Survey of the 18th Century Social and
Cultural Conditions.* London: Epworth

Williams, Colin

1960, *John Wesley's Theology Today.* Nashville: Abingdon Press.

William, Rowan

1982, *The Eucharistic Sacrifice: The Roots of a Metaphor.*
Nottingham: Grove.

Wilson D Dunn

1968, 'The influence of Mysticism on John Wesley'.
Unpublished PhD thesis. Leeds University.

1969, *Many Waters Cannot Quench.* London: Epworth

Wimber, John

1985, *Power Evangelism: Signs and Wonders Today.* London:
Hodder and Stoughton.

Wood, D'Arcy

1976, 'The Sacraments: Methodism and the Ecumenical
Situation Today'. Unpublished paper presented at
the 13th World Methodist Conference in Dublin,
Ireland (August).

Wood A Skevington

1867, *The Burning Heart: John Wesley Evangelist.* Exeter:
Paternoster Press.

Young, Carlton (editor)

1989, *United Methodist Hymnal.* Nashville: United Methodist
Publishing House.

Young, Frances

1995, 'Inner Struggle: Some Parallels between the Spirit of
John Wesley and the Greek Fathers'. Unpublished
paper presented at the Consultation on Orthodox
and Wesleyan Spirituality sponsored by the General
Board on Global Ministries (united Methodist
Chruch) and St Vladimir's Orthodox Seminary in
New York.

Yrigoyen, Charles Jr
 1996, *John Wesley: Holiness of Heart and Life*. New York:
  Women's Division, General Board of Global
  Ministries.

Other Resources: From the Internet
(It must be noted that there has been constant upgrading of
information (news, discussion pages and articles) on some websites.
The articles listed here might no longer exist in the current website
address.)

Primary Sources:
1. *Didache*
Website:
http://www.antioch.com.sg/th/twp/bookbyte/hermas/didache.
html

2. Apostolic Constitutions
Website: http://www.newadvent.org/fathers/0715.htm http:
// www.ivanlewis.com/constitutions.html

3. Institutes of the Christian Religion
Website: http://www.ccel.org/c/calvin/institutes/institutes.html

4. Other Calvin resources
Website:
http://www.ccel.org/c/calvin/comment2/http://www.ccel.org/c/c
alvin/calcom/calcom.html

5. *Theologia Germanica*
Website: http://www.ccel.org/t/theo_ger/theologia.htm

Articles:
1. Burton–Edwards, Taylor Internet electronic mail discussion on
Worship and Evangelism on 13th March 1997 and 20th November 1996 on
the Order of St Luke Cyber Chapter.

2. Geert Hofstede quoted by Prof Stella Ting–Toomey in *Cross Cultural
Negotiation: An Analytical Overview* presented on 15 April 1992

(summary by Beverly Matsu and Stella Ting–Toomey in David See–Chai Lam Centre for International Communication, Paific Region Forum on Business and Management Communication. Simon Frazer University at Harbour Centre.) Website: http://www.cic.sfu.ca

3. Vu Kim Chinh, SJ Book Review. On Hans Kung and Julia Ching's *Christentum und Chinesische Religion*. Vietnamese Missionaries in Taiwan homepage.
Website: www.catholic.org.tw/vntaiwan/theology/christen.htm

4. 'One Minute Singapore: Singapore Facts and Figures
Website: http://www.sg/infomap/1min

News Releases:
Straits Times Interactive (STI) Website:
http://straitstimesasia1.com.sg

   1998
   April 16th 'Don't impose values on other nations, US urged..'
   April 15th 'Cultural sided the Asian Crisis'
   March 29th 'Asian values' idea: is it out?'
    Feb 13th 'Chinese Culture for English Educated...'

   1997
   December 19th 'In Fifty Years . . . English will be less important'

Magazines, Newspaper and News releases:
1. 'Asian Insights on Spirituality and Spiritual Formation' Ecumenical Press Service (88. 09. 35). newssheet. Geneva: World Council of Churches.

2. 'Christianity's Global Growth. Growth Rate of Christianity in Asia'(January 1998)

3. 'Around the World'(news section) Singapore: Methodist Message

Index

Printed in the USA
CPSIA information can be obtained
at www.ICGtesting.com
JSHW020853241223
54126JS00003B/139

9 781920 691318